Assessing Government Transparency in China (2021)

He Tian · Yanbin Lv
Editors

Assessing Government Transparency in China (2021)

中国社会科学出版社
CHINA SOCIAL SCIENCES PRESS

Springer

Editors
He Tian
Institute of Law
Chinese Academy of Social Sciences
Beijing, China

Yanbin Lv
Institute of Law
Chinese Academy of Social Sciences
Beijing, China

Translated by
Xiaoqing Bi
Institute of Law
Chinese Academy of Social Sciences
Beijing, China

ISBN 978-981-99-9733-6 ISBN 978-981-99-9734-3 (eBook)
https://doi.org/10.1007/978-981-99-9734-3

Jointly published with China Social Sciences Press
The print edition is not for sale in China Mainland. Customers from China Mainland please order the print book from: China Social Sciences Press.

This Springer imprint is published by the registered company Springer Nature Singapore Pte Ltd.
The registered company address is: 152 Beach Road, #21-01/04 Gateway East, Singapore 189721, Singapore

Paper in this product is recyclable.

Contents

Openness of Government Affairs in China: Developments in 2020 and Prospects in 2021

Innovation Project Team on Rule of Law Index, Institute of Law, Chinese Academy of Social Sciences

In 2020, the Center for Studies of National Rule of Law Index of the Chinese Academy of Social Sciences and the Innovation Project Team on the Rule of Law Index of the Institute of Law, Chinese Academy of Social Sciences (hereinafter referred to as the "Project Team") continued to carry out the third-party assessment of the open government work of governments at various levels in China. This report is the summarization and analysis of the results of the assessment.

1 Targets, Indices and Methodology of Assessment

The assessment in 2020 covered 49 departments under the State Council having external administrative authorities after the state institutional reform, 31 provincial-level governments, 49 governments of larger cities, and 120 county (city, or district)-level governments. With respect to the county-level assessment targets in this year's assessment, the Project Team eliminated the bottom 25 of the 125 county (city, or district)-level governments in the assessment in 2020, and took the top ten from

---

Leaders of the Project Team: He Tian, director of the Center for Studies of National Rule of Law Index of Chinese Academy of Social Sciences, a research fellow at the Institute of Law, and a distinguished professor at the Law School of the University of Chinese Academy of Social Sciences, and Yanbin Lv, research fellow and head of the Department of Survey and Studies of National Situation of the Rule of Law, Institute of Law, Chinese Academy of Social Sciences, and head the Teaching and Research Section of Administrative Law of the Law School of the University of Chinese Academy of Social Sciences. Other members of the project team: Xiaomei Wang, Yiming Wang, Wenbo Che, Yingying Feng, Yanpeng Liu, Xiaomin Mi, Changming Hu, Mei Hong and Yanjie Li.

Innovation Project Team on Rule of Law Index, Institute of Law, Chinese Academy of Social Sciences (✉)
Institute of Law, Chinese Academy of Social Sciences, Beijing, China
e-mail: 13693186775@163.com

H. Tian and Y. Lv (eds.), *Assessing Government Transparency in China (2021)*,
https://doi.org/10.1007/978-981-99-9734-3_1

the top 100 counties in China and the top ten from the top 100 districts in China,[1] respectively, in the previous year, as well as two district governments that volunteered for the assessment, namely that of Jinshan District of Shanghai and that Tianxin District of Changsha, as new assessment targets. Those that belonged to the top 100 counties or top 100 districts but had been eliminated according to assessment results of the previous year or were already in the reserved list of assessment targets were selected in turn. Ultimately, a total of 120 counties (cities, districts) had been selected.

In the assessment in 2020, the Project Team basically continued to use the index system used in the 2019 assessment. The level-one indices included openness of decision-making, the openness of administration and service, the openness of implementation and its results, the construction of open government platforms, and the disclosure of information upon application. Only the examination of "openness of law enforcement statistics" was added to the index of "implementation and its results", which was used for the assessment of provincial-level governments, governments of larger cities and county-level (city, or district) governments.[2]

The cutoff date of the assessment was December 31, 2020. The assessment of information disclosure upon application was carried out only on county (city, or district)-level governments. The Project Team carried out the assessment by applying for the disclosure of information about "the actual amount of investment in the dilapidated building renovation projects in the county (city, or district) in 2019". The assessment period for this index was from June 6 to October 23, 2020. The applications were submitted online or by mail. Online applications were submitted through platforms of information disclosure upon application on government portal websites. Where there was no such platform, the application was sent by e-mail to the e-mail addresses published in the government information disclosure guides. If the above methods were invalid, the application was submitted by registered letter.

2 Overall Assessment Results

In 2020, which was a crucial year for the preparation of the 14th Five-Year Plan, the Central Committee of the Communist Party of China (CPC) issued the Implementation Outline for Building a Law-based Society (2020–2025). This document, issued on December 7, 2020, is of great significance for constructing a law-based society and modernizing the state governance system and capacity. The year 2020 was also the first year of the implementation of the Guiding Opinions on Comprehensively Advancing the Standardization of the Openness of Grass-roots Government

[1] The data of 100 top counties and 100 top districts in China come from "Research Results on Indices of High-Quality Development of Small and Medium-sized Cities in China Released", *People's Daily*, October 8, 2019, p.8.

[2] For the description of assessment indices, please refer to the "Report on Indices of Transparency of Chinese Government (2019) - From the Perspective of Information Disclosure on Government Websites", in Tian He and Lv Yanbin (eds.)), *Report on the Development of Rule of Law in China No.18 (2020)*, Social Sciences Academic Press(China), 2020, pp. 175–176.

Affairs, the Notice on Matters Relating to the Standardization of Government Information Disclosure Platforms and the Notice on Matters Relating to Annual Reports on Government Information Disclosure Work, as well as the second year of the implementation of the Regulations on the Disclosure of Government Information (Revised in 2019) (hereinafter referred to as the "Revised Regulations"). In accordance with the requirements of these policy documents, governments at all levels and departments under them advanced in an all-round way the whole-process openness of decision-making, implementation, administration, service and results, comprehensively promoted the standardization of the openness of government affairs, expanded public participation, enabled the public to fully and deeply participate in all aspects of state governance, and gave full play to the three-in-one and complementary role of information release, policy interpretation and response to public concerns. The assessment shows that China achieved remarkable results in open government work throughout the country in 2020.

1. Significant results achieved in the openness of government affairs

(1) The "standardization" of openness of grassroots government affairs had been accelerated

According to the *Guiding Opinions of the General Office of the State Council on Comprehensively Advancing the Standardization of the Openness of Grass-roots Government Affairs*, issued on January 8, 2020, China will basically establish a unified national standard system for the openness of grass-roots government affairs by 2023, covering the whole process of the operation of administrative powers and government services at the grass-roots level. Focusing on the standardization work, local governments carried out a review of the lists of matters of voluntary information disclosure, established the disclosure standards, intensified platform construction, improved the information disclosure system and process, strengthened policy interpretation and response to public concerns, and explored the construction of special areas, demonstration areas and demonstration sites for the openness of government affairs, thus creating a good situation of comprehensively promoting standardization.

(2) The disclosure of decision-making information had been advanced steadily

Since the implementation of the *Interim Regulations on Major Administrative Decision-Making Procedures*, many bright spots had emerged in the pre-disclosure of major administrative decision-making in various areas. Many assessment targets formulated and published the catalog of major decision-making items this year. In 2020, 18 governments of larger cities disclosed the catalog of major decision-making items, an increase of 50.00% over the previous year; 151 assessment targets published the drafts of major decisions in 2020, among which 56 released the interpretations or explanations of the drafts together with the drafts. Most of the assessment targets opened various channels, such as e-mail, letter, online platform and fax, to solicit opinions on draft decisions, so as to facilitate the participation of the public.

The disclosure of normative documents became more standardized. Among the 200 local governments covered by the assessment, 199 made centralized and unified disclosure of the normative documents of their subordinate departments. Among the 249 assessment targets, 136 labeled the validity of normative documents, an increase of 34 over the previous year, and 196 disclosed information about the review of normative documents in the previous three years, among which 124 released the information in 2020.

The forms of policy interpretation were diversified and the quality of interpretation was improved. More than 98.00% of the assessment targets had set up special columns for policy interpretation on their portal websites, with most of the columns positioned accurately. The policy interpretations released by 182 assessment targets focused on the background and core contents of policy documents. Some local governments, such as those of Hangzhou City and Yuyao City in Zhejiang Province and Zhengzhou City in Henan Province, also provided the names of interpreters and other relevant information. The forms of interpretation became more diversified, with 191 assessment targets adopting such forms as graphic interpretation, video interpretation and H5 interpretation in addition to text interpretation.

(3) Disclosure of information about power allocation adjustment was timely

Most local governments were able to publish updated power lists in a timely manner after the institutional reform. The spot inspection of some departments involved in institutional reform, such as those involving medical security, veterans affairs administration, health, emergency management and ecological environment, showed that 111 assessment targets adjusted the power lists of all the departments covered by the spot inspection, and 72 assessment targets adjusted the power lists of some departments covered by the spot inspection. Compared with that in 2019, the adjustment of the power lists of departments covered by institutional reform had been greatly improved.

(4) The disclosure of administrative law enforcement information became more standardized

Firstly, the situation of building unified platforms for the disclosure of administrative law enforcement information was good, with nearly half of the local governments having built the platform in 2020, a substantial increase from 2019. Secondly, the "double-random inspection system" (the system of random selection of both inspectors and inspection targets and prompt release of inspection results) was further standardized, with 138 assessment targets having set up a special column on "double-random inspection"–an increase of 42 over the previous year–and 137 local governments having published the list of items of random inspection of their departments. Thirdly, the disclosure of information about administrative penalty results was satisfactory: the market regulation departments of 188 local governments disclosed the information about administrative penalty results in 2020, with an overall disclosure rate of 94.00%.

(5) The level of disclosure of government service information was further raised

Firstly, the disclosure rate of the catalog of government service items further increased: the disclosure rate of departments under the State Council increased by 3.54% points over the previous year, reaching 91.30%, and those of governments at the provincial, municipal and county levels continued to maintain at 100%. Secondly, the disclosure of service guides by provincial-level governments became more standardized. In the service guides of provincial-level governments covered by spot inspection, the disclosure rates of the elements such as application-handling basis, conditions of application, the time limit for handling applications, application-handling process, fee-charging standard, contact information and consultation channels all reached 100%, no vague catch-all materials were found in the list of application materials published by most provinces, and blank forms and sample forms were provided in their service guides. Thirdly, integrated and one-stop disclosure of service items for market subjects and individuals in the "whole life cycle" was satisfactory: 185 local governments realized integrated disclosure of service items for market subjects (enterprises) in the "whole life cycle" and 162 realized integrated disclosure of service items for individuals in the "whole life cycle". Fourthly, the disclosure rates of certification items that truly need to be retained increased significantly. In 2020, the disclosure rates of "certification items that truly need to be retained" among four types of assessment targets, namely departments under the State Council, provincial-level governments, governments of larger cities, and county (city, or district)-level governments, were 50.00, 61.29, 69.39, and 31.67%, respectively, an increase of 10.87, 29.03, and 30.61 percentage points, respectively, over 2019.

(6) The situation of the release of the annual report on the construction of a law-based government by most assessment targets was satisfactory

In 2020, which was the closing year of the *Implementation Outline for the Construction of a Law-based Government (2015–2020)*, compiling and publishing the annual report on the construction of a law-based government was an important means to supervise and assess the work of construction of a law-based government. First of all, the situation of the release of the report had been improving year by year. All provincial-level governments realized the full-text release of the annual report on the construction of a law-based government in the previous year for two consecutive years, and 34 departments under the State Council and 47 municipal-level governments released the report, both numbers were higher than in 2019. Secondly, most assessment targets published the annual report on time. 17 departments under the State Council, 25 provincial-level governments, 37 governments of larger cities, and 73 county (city, or district)-level governments released their annual reports on the previous year before April 1, 2020, an increase of 12, 21, 9 and 37, respectively, over the previous year. Finally, the level of standardization of some elements in the annual report was high. For example, among the reports released by departments under the State Council, 97.06% disclosed data on the adoption, revision and abolition of government rules and 91.18% disclosed information about public participation in the publicity of law; among provincial-level governments, the disclosure rates of information about the situation of deepening of the reform of the administrative approval system, the strengthening of the reform of law enforcement system, the adoption, revision and abolition of local legislation, dispute resolution, improvement of law enforcement procedures, and improvement of major administrative decision-making mechanisms reached 100.00, 100.00, 96.77, 96.77, 93.55, and 90.32%, respectively; and among governments of larger cities, the disclosure rates of information about local legislative reform, the deepening of the reform of administrative approval system, the strengthening of the reform of law enforcement system, the improvement of law enforcement procedures, disputes resolution, and the improvement of major administrative decision-making mechanisms reached 95.92, 95.92, 95.92, 95.92, 91.84 and 91.84%, respectively.

(7) The situation of disclosure of audit information by provincial-level governments was good

27 provincial-level governments disclosed their annual audit plan in 2020. Among them, 23 explicitly mentioned the audit arrangements for the prevention and control of the Covid-19 pandemic situation and other relevant work in the plan; 27 published audit reports on the implementation of the budget and on other financial revenues and expenditures at their corresponding level in 2019; 26 disclosed the follow-up audit results of the implementation of major policies and measures in 2019, many of them published the results on a quarterly basis. Some assessment targets also used illustrations in professional audit reports, which were novel and rich in form and convenient for the public to understand. For example, the Audit Report on the Implementation of Municipal-level Budget and Other Financial Revenues and Expenditures in 2019, prepared by the Government of Tianjin Municipality, used such illustrations as mind map, statistical table and cartoon image to make the report vivid, concise and easy to understand.

(8) The transparency of government debts increased steadily

First of all, the disclosure of information about the final accounts of the ceilings and the balances of local government debts was good. Among all the assessment targets, 116 disclosed the final accounts of debt ceilings in their own regions, 49 disclosed the final accounts of debt ceilings at their corresponding levels, and 42 disclosed the final accounts of debt ceilings in their affiliated regions in 2019, accounting for 58.00, 61.25 and 52.50%, respectively, of the total; and 128 disclosed the final accounts of debt balances in their own regions, 57 disclosed the final accounts of debt balances at their corresponding level, and 44 disclosed the final accounts of debt balances in their affiliated regions in 2019, accounting for 64.00, 71.25 and 55.00%, respectively, of the total. In addition, 11 provincial-level governments disclosed information about the final accounts of the ceilings and the balances of local government debts of their affiliated regions detailed down to all counties and districts under their jurisdictions, so as to facilitate concentrated consultation by the public. Secondly, the situation of disclosure, together with final accounts, of the final accounts of repayment of the principals and payment of interest on government debts by local governments in their own region and at the corresponding level at the end of the previous year was good. Among the assessment targets, 133 disclosed the final accounts of repayment of principals of local government debts and payment of interest thereof in their respective regions in 2019 and 133 disclosed the final accounts of payment of interest on local government debts in their respective regions in 2019, both accounting for 66.50% of the total; and 67 disclosed the final accounts of repayment of government debts at their corresponding level in 2019 and 69 assessment targets disclosed the final accounts of payment of interest on local governments debts at their corresponding level in 2019, accounting for 33.50 and 34.50%, respectively, of the total.[3]

(9) The disclosure of compulsory education information was improved significantly

93 county (city, or district)-level governments published local enrollment documents (such as enrollment implementation plans) for compulsory education in 2020, accounting for 77.50% of the total and increased by 4.7 percentage points over the previous year. Among them, 67.50% disclosed the telephone hotlines for inquiries about compulsory education enrollment policies, 80.00% disclosed the enrollment scopes of primary schools, 84.17% disclosed the enrollment scopes of junior high schools, 81.67% disclosed the admission requirements for ordinary students, and 81.67% disclosed school admission requirements for children living with their migrant working parents, an increase of 9.10, 24.80, 32.17, 9.67 and 11.27%, respectively, over the previous year.

(10) The platform construction was more standardized

Firstly, the construction of website columns became more standardized. Most assessment targets had set up special columns on their portal websites to disclose such information as institutional functions, persons in charge, policy documents, policy interpretation and response to public concerns, current work, interactive communication, etc. in accordance with the requirements of the *Guidelines for the Development of Government Websites*, and the information disclosure in these columns was standardized, and no overlap of contents in these columns was found. Secondly, the situation of the construction of the search function was good, with the portal websites of all but one assessment target having the search function. Thirdly, the opening rate of the government gazette platform was relatively high: all 31 provincial-level governments and 49 governments of larger cities and 66 county (city, or district)-level governments, or 55.00% of the total, released government gazettes at the corresponding level. Fourthly, the opening rate of new government media was relatively high: 44 departments under the State Council, or 9.80% of the total, and all 200 local governments covered by the assessment opened new government media.

[3] County (city, or district)-level units are the grass-roots units of statistical accounting of government debts. In this year's assessment, the Project Team no longer distinguished the accounting data of county (city, district) governments at their corresponding level and those of their affiliated regions. A total of 200 assessment targets at the provincial, municipal and county (city, or district) levels were covered by the assessment of the disclosure of relevant statistical data at their corresponding levels, while only 80 assessment targets, including 31 provincial-level governments and 49 governments of larger cities, were covered by the assessment of disclosure of relevant statistical data at their corresponding levels and those of their affiliated regions.

2. Problems still to be solved in the work of openness of government affairs

(1) There was still much room for improvement in the openness of decision-making

Firstly, the level of pre-disclosure of major decision-making needed to be improved. Some assessment targets did not specify the time limit for soliciting opinions or set a too-short time limit for soliciting opinions. Two assessment targets did not disclose the time limit for soliciting opinions and 86 assessment targets set the time period for soliciting opinions of less than 30 days without giving an explanation. Secondly, the disclosure of information about the review and recordation of normative documents needed to be strengthened. 53 assessment targets did not disclose information about the review of normative documents in the recent three years, 83 assessment targets did not label the validity of normative documents, and 152 assessment targets did not release information about the recordation and review of normative documents in 2020. Third, the quality of policy interpretation needed to be improved. Among the assessment targets, 26 did not establish a linkage between policy interpretations and the policies they interpreted, 129 did not release their policy interpretations in time, namely within 3 working days after the original policies were released, and 182 did not release the interpretations by their principal persons in charge.

(2) The power list information was not updated in time

Spot inspection and assessment show that the power lists of some local governments were not updated in time. Forty-three departments under the State Council had not released the list of powers in recent two years, and some assessment targets had only released a list of administrative licensing items. Meanwhile, a spot inspection of the power item of "group preventive vaccination" of governments at various levels shows that only the governments of Jiangxi Province, Hubei Province and Anshan City of Liaoning Province made corresponding adjustments to their power lists after the promulgation of the Vaccine Administration Law in June 2019. The power lists issued by 62 assessment targets did not include the power items relating to "group preventive vaccination", and the legal basis of the corresponding items in the power lists of 124 assessment targets was still the already abolished *Regulations on the Administration of Circulation and Vaccination of Vaccines.* A spot inspection on the power of human resources and social security departments of county (city, or district)-level governments to "pay in advance the wages of migrant workers in arrears and then to recover them from the employers that have defaulted on the wages afterward" shows that none of the county-level assessment targets made adjustments to the power list according to the *Regulations on Ensuring Wage Payment to Migrant Workers*, which came into force on May 1, 2020.

(3) There were still blind spots in the disclosure of government service items

There was still much room for improvement in the disclosure of information about government services by various local governments. At the city and county levels, a spot inspection was made on the service item of "registration as local non-agricultural permanent residents of elderly retirees who live with their adult children as dependents" shows that 29 governments of larger cities and 27 county (city, or district)-level governments did not disclose the corresponding service guide. Among the assessment targets that published the service guide, 13, such as the Government Haikou City of Hainan Province, did not disclose the conditions for the acceptance of applications. The quality of disclosure of the list of certification items that truly need to be retained was not high. The 23 departments under the State Council that published the list of certification items only published the exposure drafts of the lists, but not the final version of the lists. In the lists released by five provincial-level governments, 11 governments of larger cities and 19 county (city, or district)-level governments, some key elements, such as justifications for establishment, requesting entities, and issuing entities, were not disclosed. The lists published by some local governments were not updated in time. For example, the governments of Xizang Autonomous Region, Jilin Province, Shijiazhuang City of Hebei Province, Baotou City of Inner Mongolia Autonomous Region, Luoyang City of Henan Province, and Shishi City of Fujian Province published only the list of certification items in 2018 or even only that in 2017. Some others, such as the governments of Guangzhou City and Zhuhai City of Guangdong Province, Dongcheng District of Beijing Municipality, Wuhou District of Chengdu City of Sichuan Province, Bobai County of Guangxi Zhuang Autonomous Region, Hengyang County of Hunan Province, and Tianxin District of Changsha City of Human Province, released the lists of certification items of only some departments under them.

(4) The disclosure of law enforcement information still needed to be standardized and strengthened

Firstly, unified platforms for the disclosure of administrative law enforcement information still needed to be improved. 89 local governments had not set up an administrative law enforcement information disclosure platform, accounting for 44.50% of the total. The administrative law enforcement columns on the websites of some assessment targets were not standardized and detailed, the information released in these columns lacked diversity, the administrative law enforcement information was not fully disclosed as required by relevant documents, and some assessment targets released only information about their daily law enforcement work. Secondly, there was still room for improvement in the disclosure of information about "double random inspection". Among the 21 departments under the State Council that had disclosed their own lists of double random inspection items, ten disclosed lists with incomplete content, accounting for 47.62% of the total; among the 126 local governments that had published the list of random spot inspection items of their ecology and environment department, 54, or 42.86% of the total, disclosed lists with incomplete content. Among the departments under the State Council and the ecological environment departments of provincial-level governments, 85.29 and 87.10%, respectively, did not disclose the results of random spot inspection items and related investigation and punishment of violations in 2020. Thirdly, the disclosure of information about administrative penalties was unsatisfactory. Among the 37 departments under the State Council covered by the assessment, 26 (or 70.27% of the total) did not disclose the punishment results in 2020. Some local market regulation departments disclosed little information about administrative penalties in 2020. For example, the market regulation departments in Qinghai Province released only three pieces of administrative penalty information in 2020. Some local market regulation departments still had such problems as not releasing administrative penalty results in a timely manner, releasing incomplete administrative penalty results, and leaking personal information. Fourthly, the disclosure of statistical annual reports of administrative law enforcement was not satisfactory. Only 60 assessment targets published the annual report of statistical data on administrative law enforcement in 2019. The annual reports of some assessment targets contained only text descriptions, but no tables of statistical data on administrative law enforcement.

(5) The work of the annual report on the construction of a law-based government still needed to be strengthened

Firstly, the release of the annual report by county (city, or district)-level governments needed to be improved. In 2020, among the 120 county (city, or district)-level governments, 37 did not publish the annual report on the construction of a law-based government in 2019. Secondly, the problem of not releasing annual reports in a timely manner was quite prominent. Thirty-one assessment targets failed to release the annual report on the construction of a law-based government in 2019 in time, and some assessment targets even delayed the release until the second half of the year. Thirdly, the annual reports of some assessment targets were incomplete in content. Among the 34 departments under the State Council, the matters with low disclosure rate included: information about the appearance of the persons in charge of administrative organs in court to respond to a lawsuit in 2019 (5.88%); dada of accepted and closed cases of administrative reconsideration (23.53%); data of administrative litigation (23.53%); public participation in major administrative decision-making (38.24%); the construction of the normative document management mechanism (41.18%); the legality review of major administrative decisions (50.00%); problems in the construction of a law-based government in the previous year (52.94%); and the implementation of the responsibility system of a law-based government (58.82%). Among the 31 provincial-level governments, only 16, or 51.61% of the total, disclosed information about the construction of the normative document management mechanism in 2019; only eight, or 25.81% of the total, disclosed information about the appearance of the persons in charge of administrative organs in court to respond to a lawsuit. Among the 49 governments of larger cities, only 23, or 46.94% of the total, disclosed information about the construction of the normative document management mechanism in 2019; only 25, or 51.02% of the total, disclosed information about the appearance of the persons in charge of administrative organs in court to respond to a lawsuit. Among the 105 county (city, or district)-level governments that released the report, only 44, or 41.90% of the total, disclosed administrative litigation data in 2019; only 45, or 42.86% of the total, disclosed information about the appearance of the persons in charge of administrative organs in court to respond to a lawsuit in 2019. In addition, there were other problems, such as inconsistency in the title, publishing channels and publishing institutions of the report, in the work of various local governments.

(6) The disclosure of audit information of local governments below the provincial level needed to be improved

The disclosure of audit information by governments of larger cities and county (city, or district)-level governments was not satisfactory. Firstly, the disclosure of government audit plans was poor, with 31 governments of larger cities and 76 county (city, or district)-level governments, or 63.27 and 63.33% of the total respectively, not disclosing the audit plans for 2020. Secondly, the rate of disclosure by governments of reports on audit results of budget implementation and other financial revenues and expenditures at the corresponding level was not high, with 27 governments of larger cities and 102 county (city, or district)-level governments, or 55.10 and 85.00% of the total respectively, not disclosing the reports. Thirdly, the disclosure of reports on follow-up audits of the implementation of major policies and measures was not satisfactory, with 29 governments of larger cities and 103 county (city, or district)-level governments, or 59.18 and 85.83% of the total respectively, not disclosing the report.

(7) The disclosure of the results of the handling of suggestions from deputies to peoples' congresses and proposals from CPPCC members was not satisfactory

Firstly, the rate of disclosure of replies by the departments under the State Council and the county (city, or district)-level governments to suggestions from deputies to people's congresses and proposals from CPPCC members was low: 28.57% of the departments under the State Council and 45.00% of the 120 counties (cities, or districts)-level governments disclosed their replies to the proposals from deputies to people' s congresses in 2020 and 24.49% of the departments under the State Council and 46.67% of the 120 counties (cities, or districts)-level governments disclosed their replies to the proposals from CPPCC members in 2020. Secondly, the information disclosed by some local governments about their replies to suggestions from deputies to people's congresses and proposals from CPPCC members was incomplete. Some disclosed only their replies to the suggestions from deputies to people's congresses or only their replies to the proposals from CPPCC members, while some only disclosed the results of their handling of the suggestions and proposals from deputies to the people's congress at the next higher level and members of CPPCC at the next higher level.

(8) The disclosure of local government debt information still needed to be strengthened

Firstly, the disclosure of information about the arrangements for the use of funds raised from local government bonds needed to be improved. Only 13 provincial-level governments, 13 governments of larger cities and 47 county (city, or district)-level governments disclosed the information about the final accounts of the arrangement for the use of funds raised from local government bonds at the corresponding level, and only one of them disclosed the information detailed down to specific fund-using projects. Only ten provincial-level governments and 13 governments of larger cities disclosed information about the final accounts of the arrangements for the use of funds raised by government bonds at the corresponding level. In addition, some assessment targets did not distinguish between projects using the funds raised from the new bonds at the corresponding level and projects using the funds raised from the new bonds in their affiliated regions. Secondly, the statistics of government debt information released by some assessment targets were not standardized. Some assessment targets did not disclose the final accounts of debt repayment and interest payment; some provincial-level governments disclosed only the general information about the amount of government debt income and the amount of government debts, without providing detailed statistical data of bond issuance; and some others disclosed only the general information about final accounts of repayment of the principals of and payment of interest on government debts, without providing detailed statistical information thereof.

(9) The disclosure of information about compulsory education at the grassroots level was still inadequate

Firstly, the disclosure of information about planned numbers of enrollment was poor: 82 county (city, or district)-level governments did not disclose the planned numbers of enrollment of (public) primary schools in 2020 and 77 county (city, or district)-level governments did not disclose the planned numbers of enrollment of (public) junior high schools in 2020. Some other local governments disclosed only the total number of students or classes in the enrollment plan, without giving detailed numbers. Secondly, most assessment targets did not disclose the enrollment results of schools of compulsory education: 105 county (city, or district)-level governments did not disclose the enrollment results of primary schools and 106 county (city, or district)-level governments did not disclose the enrollment results of junior high schools. Thirdly, the disclosure rate of school enrollment guides was low. In the assessment, the Project Team randomly selected one public school in each of the 120 county (city, district)-level assessment targets to examine whether the school enrollment guide was disclosed. The assessment shows that only nine of the selected schools published the school enrollment guide, accounting for only 7.50% of the total. Fourthly, the overall level of disclosure of compulsory education information by some assessment targets was low. For example, the governments of Dongning City of Heilongjiang Province, Qianguo County of Jilin Province, and Wafangdian City and Haicheng City of Liaoning Province did not disclose enrollment documents (or annual enrollment work plan), telephone hotlines for inquiries, enrollment scope (the division of school districts), planned enrollment numbers, admission requirements for ordinary students and for children living with their migrant working parents, enrollment results and other information about compulsory education in 2020.

(10) The construction of platforms of openness of government affairs still needed to be improved

Firstly, there were still columns with overlapping contents on the websites of some assessment targets, mainly announcements columns and policy interpretation columns. Secondly, the websites of some assessment targets still did not provide a search function or the search function they provided was imperfect: the portal websites of 41 assessment targets, or 16.47% of the total, did not have a precise (advanced) search function and the websites of 128 assessment targets, or 51.41% of the total, were not connected with government services to realize "search as a service". Thirdly, the availability rate of interactive platforms on the websites of most assessment targets was relatively low, and the problems of not processing letters from the public in a timely manner and low public participation were common among some assessment targets. Fourthly, some assessment targets still had not yet opened new government media. They included five departments under the State Council, two governments of larger cities and 12 county (city, or district)-level governments, accounting for 10.20%, 4.08% and 10.00% of the total, respectively. Fifthly, the content of new government media of some assessment targets was not updated in time: five departments under the State Council, or 10.20% of the total, five governments of larger cities, or 10.20% of the total, and 20 county (city, or district)-level governments, or 16.67% of the total, updated their new media less than once a week. Moreover, some assessment targets failed to synchronize the release of information in government new media with the release of information on government websites.

(11) There were still shortboards in the work of information disclosure upon application of some local governments

The guides to government information disclosure published by some local governments were not updated or accurate. The guides of three assessment targets did not specify the time limit for giving replies to applications, those of 27 assessment targets described information that needs to be "processed and analyzed" as "information to be withheld", instead of "information that may be withheld" as provided for in the revised Regulations, those of 24 assessment targets described "procedural information and internal information" as "information to be withheld", instead of "information that may be withheld" as provided for in the revised Regulations, those of 41 did not specify the time limit for the notification of supplementation and correction of application, and those of 40 assessment targets did not update the provisions on complaints and reports of violations. In addition, the guides of 14 assessment targets did not contain such basic elements as office hours and contact telephone numbers. Some assessment targets failed to reply, to reply within the legally prescribed time period, or to give standardized replies to applications for government information disclosure. Nine county (city, or district)-level governments failed to reply within the legally prescribed time period, and 11 failed to give a reply. Some assessment targets failed to give the replies in a standardized form: the replies given by eleven assessment targets were only stamped with an official seal without specifying the name of the replying organ, 42 used unofficial work mailboxes in giving replies, and four only replied by telephone. Some others failed to give a reply with standardized content: 11 assessment targets that refused to disclose the information applied for did not explain the legal basis for the non-disclosure in their replies; 27 did not list the names of reconsideration agencies or courts with jurisdiction over related cases, eight gave incorrect information about remedy channels, and 37 did not give information about remedy channels.

3 Results of Assessment in Various Fields

1. Pre-disclosure of major decision-making

The index of pre-disclosure of major decision-making mainly examined the situation of disclosure of catalogs of major decision-making items, the setup of special columns on pre-disclosure of major decision-making and the release in a concentrated way of the information in such columns, and the disclosure of information about the solicitation of public opinions on major decision-making items and feedback on solicited public opinions in 2019 by 49 departments under the State Council, 31 provincial-level governments, 49 governments of larger cities and 120 county-level governments on their own portal websites or on the websites of the legal departments under them. In addition, according to Article 3 of the *Interim Regulations on Major Administrative Decision-Making Procedures*, which officially came into force on September 1, 2019, major administrative decision-making items mainly include major public policies and measures relating to public services, market regulation, social management, environmental protection, etc.; important plans for economic and social development; major public policies and measures for the development, utilization and protection of important natural and cultural resources; major public construction projects implemented in their respective administrative areas and other major issues that have a significant impact on economic and social development or involve major public interests or the vital interests of the public. Apparently, the definition of major decision-making items in this year's assessment was stricter than that in previous years.

(1) Bright spots found in the assessment

i. The voluntary disclosure of catalogs of major administrative decision-making items had been improved

The assessment shows that two provincial-level governments, 18 governments of larger cities (50.00% more than in 2019), and 39 county (city, or district)-level governments published the catalog of major administrative decision-making items in 2020 on their portal websites. Among them, the governments of Wuhan City of Hubei Province, Zhengzhou City of Henan Province, Haizhu District of Guangzhou City of Guangdong Province, Boluo County of Huizhou City of Guangdong Province, Luohu District of Shenzhen City of Guangdong Province, Gongshu District of Hangzhou City of Zhejiang Province, Yinzhou District of Ningbo City of Zhejiang Province and Xiaoshan District of Hangzhou City of Zhejiang Province published catalogs with complete elements, including decision-making items, undertaking departments, decision-making time and whether or not a hearing will be held; the government of Gongshu District of Hangzhou City of Zhejiang Province further distinguished the complete decision-making procedure from the general decision-making procedure in the catalog and listed the implementation plans in detail; and the governments of Zhuhai City of Guangdong Province, Zibo City of Shandong Province, and Yiwu City and Jinhua City of Zhejiang Province had set up the special column on the catalog of pre-disclosure of major decision-making items on their portal websites.

ii. The level of disclosure of information about the drafting of major decisions in 2020 was high

Article 15 of the *Interim Regulations on Major Administrative Decision-Making Procedures* stipulates that, where opinions on decision-making items are solicited from the public, the decision-making entity shall publish the draft decision and its explanation and other materials through the government website, new media of government affairs, newspapers and periodicals, radio, television, and other means accessible to the public, and specify the methods and period for offering opinions. For the policies of concern to the public or issues with a high degree of professional or technical requirement, the decision-making entity may publish drafting explanations along with the drafts, so as to help the public to understand the ins and outs of the drafts and increase public participation and feedback. The assessment shows that only a few provincial-level governments and governments of larger cities published drafts of major decisions. Therefore, the Project Team relaxed the requirements for the issuing institutions of draft decisions in this year's assessment, so that the statistical results include the draft decisions published by departments under provincial-level governments and municipal governments. The assessment shows that 34 departments under the State Council, 17 provincial-level governments, 41 governments of larger cities and 49 county (city, or district)-level governments published major draft decisions in 2020, which increased by 3.00, 13.30 and 21.20%, respectively, from 2019. Among them, 23 departments under the State Council, six provincial-level governments, 19 governments of larger cities and eight county (city, or district)-level governments published explanations of draft major decisions along with the drafts.

iii. Most local governments had opened diversified channels for soliciting opinions

The assessment shows that 34 departments under the State Council, 17 provincial-level governments, 41 governments of larger cities and 47 county (city, or district)-level governments had opened channels for soliciting opinions on major draft decisions, and the channels opened by most assessment targets were diversified, including e-mail, letter, online platform and fax, which were conducive to public participation.

iv. The disclosure of information about the adoption of opinions on draft decisions by some assessment targets was satisfactory

The assessment shows that eight departments under the State Council disclosed the overall situation of the solicitation of opinions on draft decisions, and six of them disclosed information about the adoption of opinions, an increase of 100% from 2019; ten provincial-level governments disclosed information about the overall situation of the solicitation of opinions, and six of them disclosed information about the adoption of solicited opinions, an increase of 100% from 2019; 31 governments of larger cities disclosed information about the overall situation of solicitation of opinions, and 16 of them disclosed information about the adoption of solicited opinions; 35 county (city, or district)-level governments disclosed information about the overall situation of solicitation of opinions, and seven of them disclosed information about the adoption of solicited opinions. For example, the Ministry of Commerce published the full texts of feedback on solicited opinions, which were classified by their nature. The State Administration of Market Supervision disclosed the number of solicited opinions, summarized and refined the main contents of the opinions, specifically introduced the adopted opinions and gave the reasons for not adopting some of the opinions.

v. Most local governments had set up special columns on their portal websites to disclose information about the pre-disclosure of major decision-making

The assessment shows that 35 departments under the State Council (an increase of 9.40% from 2019), 20 provincial-level governments, 40 governments of larger cities (an increase of 5.30% from 2019) and 57 county (city, or district)-level governments had set up such special columns as "pre-disclosure of policy-making", "pre-disclosure of decision-making", "solicitation of opinions", "public opinion surveys", and "online hearings" on their portal websites to release in a concentrated way drafts of major decisions and solicit public opinions on them. The special columns set up by some assessment targets on their portal websites were very convenient for public use, releasing in a concentrated manner information about pre-disclosure of major decision-making, such as draft decisions, feedback on the adoption of opinions, etc. Among them, six departments under the State Council, ten provincial-level governments, 31 governments of larger cities and 48 county (city, or district)-level governments released information about the pre-disclosure of major decision-making. For example, the Government of Hubei Province had set up an eye-catching red "feedback" quick jump button at the end of each draft decision on which opinions were solicited so that the public could directly view the feedback on public opinions. The governments of Guizhou Province and Wuhan City directly attached the results of opinion solicitation and lists of opinions solicited to the full texts of the drafts. The Government Yuexiu District of Guangzhou City of Guangdong Province set up two sub-columns, "Solicitation of Opinions" and "Feedback Results", under the "Pre-disclosure of Major Decision-making" column on its portal website. The Government of Jinjiang City of Quanzhou City of Fujian Province disclosed information about the solicitation of opinions, draft decisions, feedback and analysis of results of the solicitation of opinions all on the same webpage.

vi. Most assessment targets indicated the status of solicitation on the draft decisions released in the public opinion solicitation column on their portal websites

The assessment shows that 17 departments under the State Council, 11 provincial-level governments, 26 governments of larger cities and 32 county (city, or district)-level governments indicated the status of solicitation on the draft decisions released in the column of opinion solicitation. Some directly indicated the solicitation status or deadline for public opinion solicitation in draft decisions. For example, the Ministry of Civil Affairs and the governments of Guangdong Province, Qingdao City of Shandong Province, Kunming City of Yunnan Province, Huangpu District of Shanghai Municipality, and Zhangjiagang City of Jiangsu Province indicated "opinion solicitation completed" or "opinion solicitation in progress" at the end of each exposure draft of decision; and the Ministry of Housing and Urban–Rural Development noted the deadline for opinion solicitation at the end of each exposure draft of decision.

(2) Problems identified in the assessment

i. The catalogs of major administrative decision-making items issued by some assessment targets were incomplete

The catalog of major decision-making items includes such information as the list of decision-making items, the undertaking department, the decision-making time and whether a hearing would be held on a decision-making item. The assessment shows that two provincial-level governments produced and published the catalog of major administrative decision-making items in 2020, but the lists were incomplete in elements. Among the 18 governments of larger cities that produced and published the catalog of major administrative decision-making items in 2020, 16, or 88.89% of the total, published the catalog with incomplete elements. Among the 39 county (city, or district)-level governments that produced and published the catalog of major administrative decision-making items in 2020, 32, or 82.05% of the total, published the catalog with incomplete elements. The elements missing in their lists included decision-making time and hearing information.

ii. Most assessment targets did not disclose information about the interpretation of draft decisions

While soliciting opinions on draft decisions, decision-making organs should publish interpretations of draft decisions on government websites, news media or We-Media platforms, so as to enhance the public's understanding of the policies and facilitate their future implementation. The assessment shows that, among the 34 departments under the State Council that published draft decisions, 27, or 79.41% of the total, did not publish the interpretations of the drafts. Among the 17 provincial-level governments that published draft decisions, 14, or 82.35% of the total, did not publish the interpretations of the drafts. Among the 41 governments of larger cities that published the draft decision, 30, or 73.17% of the total, did not publish the interpretations of the drafts. Among the 49 county (city, or district)-level governments that published draft decisions, 48, or 97.96% of the total, did not publish the interpretations of the drafts.

iii. Some assessment targets did not specify the time limit or set an unreasonably short time limit for public opinion solicitation

Article 15 of the *Interim Regulations on Major Administrative Decision-Making Procedures* stipulates that the period for the public solicitation of opinions is generally not less than 30 days; if it is necessary to shorten the period due to urgent circumstances or any other reason, it shall be explained when opinions are solicited from the public. The assessment shows that, among the assessment targets that had solicited opinions on major draft decisions in 2020, two county (city, or district)-level governments did not specify the deadline for soliciting opinions. 18 departments under the State Council , ten provincial-level governments, 23 governments of larger cities and

36 county (city, or district)-level governments set a time limit of less than 30 working days for public opinion solicitation without giving an explanation.

iv. The quality of disclosure of information about the overall situation of feedback on solicited opinions needed to be improved

The information about the overall situation of solicitation of opinions on draft decisions includes the number of opinions solicited and the main viewpoints expressed in these opinions. Disclosure of information about the overall situation of solicited opinions by some assessment targets was unsatisfactory because of the lack of sufficient description of the overall situation. The assessment shows that 27 departments under the State Council, seven provincial-level governments, ten governments of larger cities and 14 county (city, or district)-level governments did not disclose information about the overall situation of solicitation of opinions on draft decisions.

v. The information disclosure in the special column on the pre-disclosure of major decision-making of the websites of most assessment targets was chaotic

The purpose of setting up a special column on the pre-disclosure of decision-making on government portal websites is to facilitate public access to recently released draft policies and the submission of opinions on them. However, the assessment shows that information disclosure in this column on the portal websites of most assessment targets was chaotic. For example, although some departments under the State Council had set up a column on the solicitation of opinions, no information about the pre-disclosure of decision-making in 2020 was released in this column. The opinion solicitation column on the portal websites of some provincial-level governments contained only information about opinion solicitation by the departments under them and those under cities divided into districts, while others put information about the solicitation of opinions on legislation, solicitation of opinions on decision-making, questionnaire investigation, and announcements on solicitation of opinions on event planning altogether in one column in a chaotic way.

2. Disclosure of results of the handling of suggestions from deputies to people's congresses and proposals from CPPCC members

The assessment of disclosure of results of the handling of suggestions from deputies to people's congresses and proposals from CPPCC members (hereinafter referred to as "suggestions and proposals") in 2020 covered 49 departments under the State Council, 31 provincial-level governments, 49 governments of larger cities and 120 county (city, or district)-level governments. The assessment indices of the disclosure of the results of handling of suggestions and proposals in 2020 mainly examined whether a special column had been set up on government portal websites to disclose in a concentrated manner the results of handling of suggestions and proposals, whether the replies to suggestions and proposals in 2020 had been disclosed in full text, and whether information about the general circumstance of the handling of the suggestions and proposals in 2020 had been disclosed.

(1) Bright spots found in the assessment

i. Most assessment targets had set up a special column on the handling of suggestions and proposals on their portal websites

The assessment shows that 93.88% of the 49 departments under the State Council, 100.00% of the 31 provincial-level governments, 91.84% of the 49 governments of larger cities and 85.83% of the 120 county (city, or district)-level governments had set up a special column on their portal websites to disclose the results of the handling of suggestions and proposals. Some of them had divided the column into sub-columns according to the content of the disclosed information so as to make inquiry more convenient. For example, the replies to suggestions and proposals from 2006 to 2020 in the special column on the website of the Ministry of Finance were further classified by year; the Government of Changsha County of Changsha City of Hunan Province subdivided the column into two sub-columns: "handling of suggestions from deputies to provincial- and municipal-level people's congresses and members of provincial- and municipal-level CPPCC" and "handling of suggestions from deputies to county-level people's congresses and members of county-level CPPCC"; and the special column on the website of the Government of Baotou City of Inner Mongolia Autonomous Region was subdivided into replies to suggestions and proposals given by various departments under the municipal government.

ii. The disclosure rate of the results of the handling of suggestions and proposals by governments at or above the municipal level was high and the replies were disclosed in full text

The disclosure rate of the results of handling of suggestions from deputies to people's congresses and the disclosure rate of the results of handling of proposals from CPPCC members by provincial-level governments were both 93.55%, ranking first among various categories of assessment targets; the disclosure rate of the results of the handling of suggestions from deputies to people's congresses and that of the results of handling of proposals from CPPCC members by governments of larger cities were 83.67 and 81.63%, respectively. Compared with other assessment targets, provincial-level governments and governments of larger cities showed higher efficiency in handling and responding to suggestions and proposals. Meanwhile, the disclosure of information about the handling of and replies to suggestions and proposals by provincial-level governments and governments of larger cities were more professional and standardized, with the contents of all their replies, including specific solutions or adjustments and plans made by government departments in light of the suggestions and proposals, disclosed in full text.

(2) Problems identified in the assessment

i. The disclosure of the results of the handling of suggestions and proposals by some assessment targets was not comprehensive

The assessment shows that, although some assessment targets had set up a special column on the handling of suggestions and proposals on their portal websites, the information in the columns was only updated to 2019. Under normal circumstances, the people's congresses and the CPPCC hold their sessions in the first quarter of the year. However, some assessment targets still had not disclosed their replies to suggestions and proposals by the end of December, the cutoff date of the assessment. Other assessment targets only disclosed their replies to suggestions from deputies to the people's congresses at the next higher level and proposals from members of CPPCC at the next higher level, but not replies to suggestions from deputies to the people's congresses at their corresponding level and proposals from members of CPPCC at their corresponding level.

ii. The rates of disclosure of the results of the handling of suggestions and proposals by the departments under the State Council and county (city, or district)-level governments still needed to be raised

Among the 49 departments under the State Council, 67.35% disclosed the full texts of their replies to suggestions from deputies to people's congresses in 2020 and 63.27% disclosed the full texts of their replies to proposals from members of CPPCC in 2020. Among the 120 county (city, or district)-level governments, 67.50% disclosed the full texts of their replies to suggestions from deputies to people's congresses in 2020 and 60.83% disclosed the full texts of their replies to proposals from members of CPPCC in 2020; and 5.83% disclosed only the summaries, but not the full texts, of their replies.

iii. The disclosure of information about the overall situation of handling of suggestions and proposals was not satisfactory

The assessment shows that the level of disclosure of information about the overall situation of handling of suggestions and proposals was low: by the end of December 2020, 44 of the 49 departments under the State Council, 26 of the 31 provincial-level governments, 45 of 49 governments of larger cities and 100 of the 120 county (city, or district)-level governments still had not disclosed information about the overall situation of their handling of suggestions from deputies to people's congresses in 2020; and 44 of the 49 departments under the State Council, 28 of the 31 provincial-level governments, 45 of 49 governments of larger cities and 100 of the 120 county (city, or district)-level governments still had not disclosed information about the overall situation of their handling of proposals from members of CPPCC in 2020.

Among the few assessment targets that had disclosed information about the overall situation of handling suggestions and proposals, many had the problems of incomplete and non-standardized information disclosure. For example, some district governments only disclosed information about the overall situation of handling of suggestions and proposals by the district housing management department; some disclosed information about the overall situation of handling suggestions from deputies to people's congresses and proposals from CPPCC members at the district level in the column of "the overall situation of handling suggestions from deputies to people's congresses and proposals from CPPCC members at the municipal level" on their websites.

3. Disclosure of powers lists

The Implementation Outline for the Construction of a Law-based Government (2015–2020), issued by the CPC Central Committee and the State Council, requires governments at various levels to vigorously implement the system of power list, responsibility list and negative list and the system of dynamic management of the lists. They should, on the basis of comprehensive review, adjustment, examination and confirmation, and process optimization, disclose such information as government functions, legal basis, implementation subjects, duties and competencies, management processes, and supervision methods in the form of power list, and clarify the items, subjects and methods of responsibility corresponding to each administrative power. The *Guiding Opinions of the Legislative Affairs Office of the State Commission Office of Public Sectors Reform on Deepening the Implementation and Perfecting the System of Lists of Powers and Responsibilities of Local Government Departments at Various Levels* require local government departments at various levels to implement the system of power lists, which is an important reform task set by the CPC Central Committee and the State Council, an effective means to consolidate and expand the results of the reform aimed at "simplifying administrative procedures, decentralizing powers, combining decentralization with appropriate control, and optimizing services", as well as an important basic system to promote the modernization of the state governance system and capacity. As such, it must be fully implemented, gradually improved and continuously deepened.

In 2020, the Project Team continued to assess the disclosure and dynamic adjustment of government power lists by government departments at various levels, mainly by examining whether the 49 departments under the State Council published the power lists on their portal websites; whether a set of unified, concise and easy-to-implement national regulatory rules and standards had been promulgated; whether the 31 provincial-level governments, 49 governments of larger cities and 120 county (city, or district)-level governments published the power lists on their portal websites, and whether the contents of power lists had been adjusted in light of new government functions (whether the latest power lists of governments at various levels contained lists of powers of the newly established medical security bureaus and the veterans affairs bureaus; and whether the names and power items of the health commissions, the emergency management bureaus and the ecology and environment bureaus had been adjusted in the latest version of the lists of powers of governments at various levels); whether the contents of power lists had been adjusted and updated in time in accordance with relevant policy documents (whether the competent medical and health departments of governments at various levels timely updated their power items relating to "group preventive vaccination" in the power list in accordance with relevant provisions of the newly adopted *Vaccine Administration Law*); and whether the governments of 120 counties (cities, districts) timely updated power items in their power lists in accordance with Article 63 of the *Regulations on Ensuring Wage Payment to Migrant Workers*, which provides that "If an employer is unable to pay the wages of rural migrant workers in arrears for a time, or flees while defaulting on migrant workers' wages, the local people's government at or above the county level may use emergency working capital to pay in advance some of the wages or basic living expenses of migrant workers in arrears by the employer. The emergency working capital that has been paid in advance shall be recovered from the employers that have defaulted on the wages of migrant workers in accordance with law."

(1) Bright spots found in the assessment

i. The disclosure of power lists by governments at various levels was satisfactory

The assessment shows that 30 provincial-level governments, or 96.77% of the total, 46 governments of larger cities, or 93.88% of the total, and 112 county (city, or district)-level governments, or 93.33% of the total, disclosed the power lists in the previous two years directly on their websites or by providing links to the power lists in the government service platforms. Among them, some published power lists on both government portal websites and government service platforms to facilitate access by the public through multiple channels.

ii. Most assessment targets disclosed their power lists in a concentrated manner

With the exception of the Government of Shanxi Province, the special column on the portal website of which cannot be accessed during the assessment period, all the assessment targets, including provincial-level governments, governments of larger cities and county (city, or district)-level governments, had set up a special column on their portal websites to disclose information about government power lists. Some of them, including the governments of Beijing Municipality, Anshan City of Liaoning Province, Luoyang City of Henan Province, and Gongshu District of Hangzhou City of Zhejiang Province, had set up columns related to the power list on both their own portal websites and government service platforms to disclose their power list in a concentrated manner. In addition, some assessment targets, such as the governments of Qinghai Province, Shanghai Municipality and Jiangyin City of Jiangsu Province, had set up keyword search boxes in the power list column of government service platforms to support the search for power items through keywords with such qualifications as a certain department or a certain type of administrative power, so as to help the public to find relevant information accurately and quickly.

iii. The disclosure of regulatory rules and standards by departments under the State Councils was satisfactory

The *Notice by the General Office of the State Council on Issuing the Key Tasks in Promoting the Transparency of Government Affairs in 2020* requires governments at various levels to implement the arrangements made by the CPC Central Committee and the State Council for deepening the reforms aimed at "simplifying administrative procedures, decentralizing powers, combining decentralization with appropriate control, and optimizing services" and optimizing the business environment, and fully disclose market regulatory rules and standards to all market players, so as to ensure the fairness of market regulation through the certainty of regulatory rules and standards. The assessment shows that, among the 49 departments under the State Council, 37 disclosed unified, concise and easy-to-apply regulatory rules and standards and provided clear document basis in the lists of administrative and approval powers, administrative penalty powers and other power items, ten of which also published relevant regulatory documents separately. For example, the State Grain and Material Reserve Bureau published the *Measures for the Administration of the Qualifications of Being Entrusted with the Storage of Central Grain Reserves*; the National Development and Reform Commission promulgated the *Notice on Strengthening the Regulation of Natural Gas Transmission and Distribution Prices* and the *Interim Measures for the Recordation and Regulation of Oil and Gas Development Projects*; and the State Intellectual Property Office published the *Work Plan for Strengthening Patent Agency Supervision.*

iv. The adjustment of the power lists of assessment targets covered by institutional reform was good

To meet the needs of the transformation of functions of government organs at various levels in the institutional reform and the reform of the administrative law enforcement system in the process of advancing the compilation of the list of powers and responsibilities and improving the list system, governments at various levels need to carry out the dynamic adjustment of their lists of powers and responsibilities in a timely manner. In 2020, the Project Team examined the power lists of government departments covered by the institutional reform in the previous two years, focusing on the adjustment of the power lists items of medical security departments, veterans affairs administration departments, health departments, emergency management departments and ecology and environment departments of governments at various levels. The assessment shows that, among the 31 provincial-level governments, 49 governments of larger cities and 120 county (city, or district)-level governments, 112 completely adjusted their power lists and 72 adjusted the power lists of some departments. For example, the governments of Liaoning Province and Xi'an City of Shaanxi Province did not adjust the power lists of medical insurance bureaus in a timely manner and the governments of Changsha City of Hunan Province and Fuzhou City of Fujian Province did not adjust the power list of medical insurance bureaus and veterans affairs bureaus in a timely manner; only ten assessment targets, including the governments of Chengdong District of Xining City of Qinghai Province and Binhai New Area of Tianjin Municipality, did not adjust their power lists. On the whole, the adjustment of the power lists by assessment targets covered by institutional reform had been greatly improved as compared with that in 2019.

(2) Problems identified in the assessment

i. Some assessment targets disclosed the same power lists obtained from different sources in different columns of their portal websites

The assessment shows that some county (city, or district) level assessment targets published their power lists on both their portal websites and government service platforms, but the lists published on the two different places were inconsistent with each other in content. For example, the power list published by a district government on its portal website did not include the power items of the Medical Insurance Bureau and

Veterans Affairs Bureau, and the names of the Health Commission, the Emergency Management Bureau and the Ecological Environment Bureau had not been changed according to the institutional reform, while those published in the power list column of the government service platform had been adjusted.

ii. The contents of the power lists of governments at various levels had not been updated in a timely manner

In order to strengthen vaccine administration, guarantee vaccine quality and supply, standardize vaccination, promote the development of the vaccine industry, safeguard public health, and maintain public health security, China adopted in June 2019 the Vaccine Administration Law, which officially came into force on December 1, 2019. Accordingly, in this year's assessment, the Project Team examined whether the medical and health departments of governments at various levels had timely updated the power items related to "group preventive vaccination" in their power lists in accordance with the relevant provisions of the *Vaccine Administration Law*. The assessment shows that, among the 31 provincial-level governments, 49 governments of larger cities and 120 county (city, or district)-level governments covered by the assessment, apart from the eight assessment targets that did not publish the power lists and the two assessment targets that did not gave the document basis in the power lists, only three assessment targets, namely the governments of Jiangxi Province, Hubei Province and Anshan City of Liaoning Province, updated the power item related to group preventive vaccination and changed the document basis of the power item from the already abolished *Regulations on the Administration of Circulation and Vaccination of Vaccines* to the newly adopted *Vaccine Administration Law*. Among the remaining 187 assessment targets, 63 did not include the power items related to "group preventive vaccination" in their published power lists, and 124 still listed the already abolished *Administration of Circulation and Vaccination of Vaccines* as the basis of the power items related to "group preventive vaccination" in their published power lists.

In order to regulate wage payment to migrant workers and ensure that migrant workers receive their wages on time and in full, the State Council adopted at its 73rd executive meeting the *Regulations on Ensuring the Wage Payment to Migrant Workers*, which came into force on May 1, 2020. On the basis of the *Regulations*, the Project Team carried out assessment on whether the power lists of the administrative departments of human resources and social security of county (city, or district)-level governments included the powers of these departments "to use emergency working capital to pay in advance some of the wages or basic living expenses of migrant workers in arrears by the employer if an employer is unable to pay the wages of rural migrant workers in arrears for a time, or flees while defaulting on migrant workers' wages" and "to recover from the employers that have defaulted on the wages of migrant workers in accordance with law the emergency working capital that has been paid in advance". The assessment shows that none of the 115 county (city, or district)-level governments that published their power lists included in their power lists the power items related to "advance payment of the wages of migrant workers in arrears and recovery of the wages paid in advance from the employers that have defaulted on the wages of migrant workers".

The reasons why the contents of the power lists of provincial-level governments, governments of larger cities and county (city, or district)-level governments had not been updated in time in accordance with relevant policy documents were the following: on the one hand, because the documents were promulgation and implementation only recently, the relevant government departments had not yet made arrangements or were in the process of making arrangements for the changes; on the other hand, due to the serious Covid-19 pandemic situation in the first half of the year, health and other relevant departments had to give priority to making overall arrangements for the fight against the pandemic and, as a result, the adjustment and update of the contents of the power lists was delayed.

iii. The disclosure of power lists by departments under the State Council was not satisfactory

Among the departments under the State Council, only six, including the National Forestry and Grassland Administration, the National Energy Administration, the National Railway Administration, the National Medical Products Administration, the State Taxation Administration, and the Ministry of Culture and Tourism, had published the power lists in recent two years. Among them, the National Forestry and Grassland Administration, the National Railway Administration, the National Medical Products Administration, and the Ministry of Culture and Tourism disclosed incomplete power lists, which contained only the power item of "administrative licensing"; 34 released a partial list of power items. For example, the Ministry of Natural Resources and the Ministry of Ecology and Environment released only a list of administrative approval items; and the remaining nine did not disclose the power list or the list of power items in a particular field.

4. Disclosure of government service information

The *Guiding Opinions of the State Council on Accelerating the Building of a National Integrated Online Government Service Platform* require governments at various levels to further advance "Internet plus Government Service", accelerate the construction of a national integrated online government service platform, integrate resources, optimize processes, strengthen coordination, and focus on solving hot and difficult issues that enterprises and the public are most concerned about, promote the transformation of government services from a government supply-oriented one to a public demand-oriented one, thereby further optimizing the business environment, providing more convenient services to enterprises and the public, stimulating market vitality and social creativity, and building a service-oriented government that people are satisfied with.

In the assessment of the disclosure of government service information, the Project Team mainly examined the disclosure by the 46 departments under the State Council that provided external government services, 31 provincial departments, 49 governments of larger cities and 120 county (city, or district)-level governments on their portal websites of catalogs of government service items, guides to government service items, and lists of certification items that truly need to be retained. In the assessment of the disclosure of government service information by provincial, municipal and county (city, or district)-level governments, the Project Team also examined the situation of concentrated disclosure of service guides according to the whole life cycle of individual citizens and enterprises, as well as the disclosure of documents relating to complaints made by foreign-invested enterprises. In the assessment of county (city, or district)-level governments, the Project Team also examined the promised approval period for integrated handling of real estate registration and the construction of report and complaint channels for wage arrears of migrant workers.

(1) Bright spots found in the assessment

i. The disclosure of catalogs of government service items was satisfactory

The *Guiding Opinions of the State Council on Accelerating the Promotion of the "Internet plus Government Services" Work* clearly require governments of all provinces, autonomous regions or municipalities directly under the Central Government and all departments under the State Council to comprehensively review, in light of their statutory functions, the specific service items provided by administrative organs and public enterprises and institutions directly to the public and prepare catalogs of government service items. The assessment shows that 42 departments under the State Council and all provincial-level governments, governments of larger cities and county (city, or district)-level governments had published their catalogs of government service items, with the disclosure rate of departments under the State Council reaching 91.30%, while local governments continued to maintain the disclosure rate of 100%, and the disclosure of the catalog of government service items had been improving year by year.

ii. The situation of disclosure of government service guides by provincial-level governments was good

Article 7 of the *Invoice Management Measures* stipulates that the power to print VAT invoices shall remain with entities designated by the competent department of taxation under the State Council, while the power to print other invoices shall remain with the entities designated by the tax authorities of the provinces, autonomous regions and municipalities directly under the Central Government pursuant to the relevant provisions of the competent department of taxation under the State Council. Unauthorized printing, counterfeiting or fabrication of invoices is forbidden. In this year's assessment of the disclosure of government service guides by provincial-level governments, the Project Team selected the service guide for the approval of the printing of invoices by enterprises as the object of assessment and mainly examined the disclosure of the guides for this government service.

The assessment shows that, with the exception of the government of Shaanxi Province, all the provincial-level governments disclosed the service guides for the approval of printing of invoices by enterprises, and the contents of the guides were standardized and specific, all of which contained such elements as the basis of handling, conditions of application, handling period, handling process, charging standards, and contact information or consultation channels. Among all the assessment targets, 28, or 93.33% of the total, disclosed the list of required application materials, which were clear and contained no vague catch-all requirement, 20, or 66.67% of the total, provided blank/standard application forms, 17, or 56.67% of the total, provided sample forms or instructions/reference texts for filling out application forms; and 26, or 86.67% of the total, disclosed clear and specific information about the locations of application-handling organs. The overall quality of service guide disclosure was good.

iii. The disclosure of "whole-life-cycle" government service items for market entities and individuals was satisfactory

The situation of integrated one-stop disclosure of "whole-life-cycle" government service items for market entities and individuals was good. The assessment of concentrated disclosure of "whole-life-cycle" government service items mainly examined whether provincial-level governments, governments of larger cities and county (city, or district)-level governments disclosed "whole-life-cycle" government service items in an integrated way through special topics, special columns, special illustrations and compilation of guides. The assessment shows that 30 provincial-level governments, 48 governments of larger cities, and 107 county (city, or district)-level governments were able to disclose in an integrated way "whole-life-cycle" service items for market entities (enterprises), accounting for 96.77, 97.96 and 89.17% of the total, respectively; and 24 provincial-level governments, 43 governments of larger cities, and 97 county (city, or district)-level governments were able to disclose in an integrated way "whole-life-cycle" service items for individuals, accounting for 77.42, 87.76 and 80.83% of the total, respectively. The classification of "whole-life-cycle" service items by some assessment targets was scientific, clear and easy to search. For example, the "whole-life-cycle" service items for individuals in Henan Province were divided into 11 categories of events of life, namely education, work, house purchase, marriage, childbirth, unemployment, entrepreneurship, relocation, retirement, funeral and other events; and the "whole-life-cycle" service items for legal persons in Qinghai Province were further divided into 34 items ranging from financing and credit to coping with climate change.

(2) Problems identified in the assessment

i. The service guides of departments under the State Councils disclosed in different columns on their portal websites were inconsistent with each other in content

The *Opinions of the General Office of the State Council on Establishing a System of "Positive and Negative Reviews" of Government Services to Improve Government Services* point out that, China will, in light of the list of statutory duties and powers and responsibilities and based on the basic catalog of national government service items, prepare a complete list of government service items and incorporate it into the management of the national integrated online government service platform to realize the unification of such basic elements as the name, code, basis and type of the same item, compile and improve service guides item by item, clarify application acceptance organs, handling channels, application conditions, application materials, application handling procedures, time limits for handling of applications, fee-charging basis and standards, and assessment channels, and promote the indiscriminate acceptance of applications for the same service item by the same standard.

On the homepage of the National Government Service Platform (http://gjzwfw.www.gov.cn/), two special columns, namely "Direct Links to Departments under the State Council" and "Service Window of Departments under the State Council", were set up to disclose the online service channels and service guides of departments under the State Council. Meanwhile, most departments under the State Council had also set up special columns on their portal websites to disclose in a concentrated way the guides to and channels of government service items. The assessment shows that the service guides published by only five departments under the State Council, or 10.87% of the total, including the National Medical Products Administration, the Civil Aviation Administration of China and the Ministry of Education, in the columns of "Direct Links to Departments under the State Council" and the "Service Window of Departments under the State Council "on the homepage of the National Government Service Platform were consistent in content with the same guides they published on their own portal websites; among the remaining 41 departments under the State Council, except for the three that did not disclose the guides to government service items and three that disclosed the guides only through one single channel such as their own portal websites, all had the problem of content inconsistency between the same service guide published on different platforms.

ii. The level of disclosure of service guides by some governments of larger cities and counties (cities, districts)-level governments was not high

Article 13 of the *Regulations on Household Registration* stipulates that, if a citizen resettles from one place to another place, he or the head of his household shall, within three days from the time of his arrival at his new place of residence in an urban area or within ten days from the time of his arrival at his new place of residence in a rural area, apply to the local department of household registration for move-in registration on the strength of the moving certificate. In this year's assessment, the Project Team selected the service guide for "registration of elderly retirees who live with their adult children as dependents as local non-agricultural permanent residents" to assess the disclosure of service guides by governments of larger city and county (city, or district)-level governments, mainly examining the situation and quality of the disclosure of the guide to this government service. The assessment shows that 29 governments of larger cities and 27 county (city, or district)-level governments did not disclose this service guide. This shows that the catalog of government service items compiled and published by local governments was still not comprehensive enough, and online government service could not cover all service items, resulting in obstacles to people's access to information and handling of related matters.

Among the 20 governments of larger cities and 93 county (city, or district)-level governments that had disclosed the guide, six did not disclose the basis for handling applications, and seven failed to disclose a clear basis for handling applications; four did not disclose the application conditions, three disclosed application conditions that were not clear enough, containing such vague catch-all conditions as "other conditions"; eight did not disclose the list of application materials; ten did not disclose information about the place of handling the applications or failed to provide clear information about the place of handling of applications; three did not disclose the handling process; five did not disclose the time limit for handling applications; six did not disclose the fee-charging standards; and seven did not disclose contact information or consultation channels. This shows that there was still room for improvement in the quality of disclosure of service guides.

iii. The disclosure rate of the list of certification items that truly need to be retained was low

The *Notice of the General Office of the State Council of Effectively Conducting the Review of Certification Items* requires local governments to cancel the certification items as specified in local provisions before December 31, 2018 at the latest. In accordance with the time schedule requirements of this document, all government departments should have completed the review and cancellation of self-set certification items by 2020. The assessment shows that 23 departments under the State Council, 19 provincial-level governments, 34 governments of larger cities and 38 county (city, or district)-level governments had reviewed and published the list of certification items that truly need to be retained, with a disclosure rate of 50.00, 61.29, 69.39 and 31.67%, respectively. The lists prepared by some assessment targets were not updated in a timely manner or published in a standardized form.

23 departments under the State Council only released the draft of the list of certification items that truly need to be retained in 2018, 2019 or 2020, but not the final version of the list after solicitation of public opinions. Five of the 19 provincial-level governments, 11 of the 34 governments of larger cities, and 19 of the 38 county (city, or district)-level governments disclosed the list without such content elements as justifications for establishment, requesting entities, and issuing entities.

iv. The disclosure of complaints from foreign-invested enterprises was not satisfactory

The promulgation of the *Measures for Complaints of Foreign-invested Enterprises* by the Ministry of Commerce was aimed at handling the complaints filed by foreign-funded enterprises in a timely and effective manner, protecting the lawful rights and interests of foreign investors, and continuously optimizing the environment for foreign investment. In this year's assessment, the Project Team assessed the disclosure of documents relating to complaints from foreign-invested enterprises by provincial, municipal and county (city, or district)-level governments, mainly examining whether they had disclosed the working rules, complaint methods and processing periods of complaints from foreign-invested enterprises. The assessment shows that the rates of disclosure of documents relating to complaints from foreign-invested enterprises by provincial-level governments, governments of larger cities and county (city, or district)-level governments in their respective administrative areas were only 32.26%, 12.24% and 0.83%, respectively.

Among the assessment targets that disclosed the documents relating to complaints from foreign-invested enterprises, three disclosed documents with incomplete contents, including the *Measures of Xinjiang Uygur Autonomous Region for the Implementation of the System of Joint Conference on Complaint Service for Foreign-invested Enterprises* and the *Official Letter of General Office of Shanxi Provincial People's Government on Agreeing to Establish the System of Joint Conference on Complaint Service for Foreign-invested Enterprises* in Shanxi Province, which did not provide complaint methods and processing periods, and the *Measures for Handling Complaints from Foreign-invested Enterprises in Hebei Province*, which did not provide complaint methods.

v. The degree of disclosure of the time for integrated processing of real estate registration was low

The *Notice of the General Office of the State Council of Shortening the Time for Realty Registration* requires governments at various levels to take the advancement of modernization of the national governance system and capacity as the objective and "effectively handling one thing" for enterprises and the public as the standard, strengthen departmental collaboration, integrate information sharing, process or personnel, conduct full-process optimization, shorten the handling time, and solve the problem of time-consuming and difficult realty registration. The *Notice* sets the following work objectives: effectively simplifying and optimizing the process and significantly improving the quality of realty registration data and related information, making relevant departmental information necessary for realty registration in cities at and above the prefecture level accessible by sharing, and shortening the time for transacting general registration and mortgage registration business in all cities and counties throughout the country to not more than ten days and not more than five days, respectively by the end of 2019; and improving realty registration data, effectively sharing relevant departmental information necessary for realty registration in all cities and counties, fully implementing "Internet plus realty registration" in cities at and above the prefecture level, and shortening the time for transacting general registration and mortgage registration business in all cities and counties throughout the country to not more than five days by the end of 2020.

In this year's assessment, the Project Team observed the disclosure by county (city, or district)-level governments of promised time limit for integrated online real estate registration. The assessment shows that although 48 assessment targets had set up the column of "integrated handling of real estate registration through a single service window" on their portal websites, only the governments of Changshu City of Jiangsu Province and Ouhai District of Wenzhou City of Zhejiang Province clearly disclosed the integrated handling time for real estate registration, which were five working days and seven working days, respectively.

vi. The level of disclosure of channels for filing reports and complaints against wage arrears owned to migrant workers was not high

The *Regulations on Ensuring Wage Payment to Migrant Workers* stipulate that a migrant worker whose wages are paid in arrears shall be entitled to file complaints in accordance with law or to apply for mediation and arbitration of labor disputes and bring lawsuits. Any entity or individual shall have the right to report any act of defaulting on wages for migrant workers to the administrative department of human resources and social security or other relevant departments. The administrative department of human resources and social security and other relevant departments shall disclose tip-off and complaint hotline, website and other channels, and accept tip-offs and complaints on wage arrears owned to migrant workers in accordance with law. The first inquiry accountability system shall be implemented in handling tip-offs or complaints. A department receiving a tip-off or complaint that falls within its scope of responsibility shall deal with the tip-off or complaint in a timely manner in accordance with law; a department receiving a tip-off or complaint that falls outside its scope of responsibility shall transfer it to the relevant departments in a timely manner, which shall deal with it in a timely manner in accordance with law and inform the informant or complainant of the handling results.

In this year's assessment, the Project Team examined the disclosure of the tip-off and complaint channels for wage arrears owned to migrant workers by county (city, or district)-level governments. The assessment shows that only the governments of Jiangyin City of Jiangsu Province and Gulou District of Fuzhou City of Fujian Province had disclosed the tip-off and complaint telephone numbers. For example, the Government of Jiangyin City of Jiangsu Province disclosed in detail the telephone numbers of the Construction Project Management Department, the Labor Rights Service Center, the Labor and Personnel Dispute Arbitration Court, and the Legal Aid Center in the *Special Plan for Implementing Long-term Management of the Payment of Wages to Migrant Workers in the Field of Housing and Construction.* None of the other assessment targets disclosed the tip-off and complaints telephone numbers or websites for wage arrears owned to migrant workers.

5. Disclosure of Information About "Double Random" Inspections

The *Opinions of the State Council on Comprehensively Implementing the Joint Regulatory Mechanism Featuring the Random Selection of Both Inspectors and Inspection Targets and the Prompt Release of Results of Inspection in the Field of Market Regulation* (No. 5 [2019] of the State Council) require that all relevant departments shall, in accordance with the provisions of laws, administrative regulations and government rules, establish their list of random inspection items, and specify their random inspection basis, subjects, content and methods, among others; the checklist of random inspection items shall be adjusted dynamically according to the enactment, revision, repeal and interpretation of laws, administrative regulations and government rules as well as actual work circumstances, and shall be released to the public through relevant websites and platforms in a timely manner. Random inspection results shall be publicized via the National Enterprise Credit Information Publicity System and the National Credit Information Sharing Platform, among others, according to the principle of "whoever conducts an inspection shall input and disclose information about the inspection", and accept social supervision. The mutual recognition of random inspection results among government departments shall be realized, the effective linkage between the regulation featuring the "double-random" inspection and credit regulation shall be promoted, and joint punishments shall be imposed on illegal and dishonest acts found in random inspections in accordance with law, so as to form a strong deterrence against violations of law and enhance the consciousness of market subjects to abide by laws.

This year, the Project Team carried out an assessment on the disclosure of information about the "double random" inspection by government departments at all levels. With respect to the 34 departments under the State Council with the "double random" inspection function, the assessment mainly focused on whether they had set up a special column on double random inspection on their websites and whether they had disclosed such information as lists of double random inspection items, the contents of the lists (whether the lists included such elements as the subjects, content, and methods of inspection), the results of double random inspections and related investigations and punishments of violations in 2020; and with respect to the 31 provincial-level governments, 49 governments of larger cities and 120 county (city, or district)-level governments, the assessment mainly focused on whether they had set up a special column on double random inspection or related columns on their websites, whether they had released the lists of double random inspection items of various departments at their corresponding levels, and whether the contents of the lists released by departments of ecology and environment were complete (whether they included the basis, subjects, content and method of double random inspection), and the results of double random inspections and related investigations and punishments of violations in 2020.

(1) Bright spots found in the assessment

i. Some assessment targets had set up the "double random inspection" column on their websites

The assessment shows that 12 departments under the State Council had set up a special column on "double random inspection" or related columns on their portal websites. For example, the Ministry of Transport had set up a "double random inspection" column on its website. 14 provincial-level governments had set up a special column on "double random inspection" or related columns on their portal websites. Among them, the Government of Guizhou Province had set up a special column on "double random inspection" in the "openness of government affairs in key areas" section of its website. By clicking on the icon of this column, a user can go to the "Double Random Inspection" Platform of Guizhou Province and view the lists of random spot inspection items of various departments directly under the provincial government and those of departments under provincial, municipal and county level governments in the province. The Government of Zhejiang Province had set up the "openness of double random inspection" column on its homepage. By clicking on this column, a user can go to the "double random inspection" column of the Government Service Platform of Zhejiang Province and view the lists of random inspection items and inspection results of all government departments in the whole province. 32 governments of larger cities had set up a special column on "double random inspection" or related columns on their portal websites. For example, the Government of Baotou City of Inner Mongolia Autonomous Region disclosed in a concentrated manner the lists of random spot inspection items of various departments under it in the "Administration by Law-Lists of Random Spot Inspection Items of Municipal Level Government Departments in Baotou City" column, and the Government of Fushun City of Liaoning Province had set up three sub-columns, namely "Organs Carrying out Spot Inspection", "Spot Inspection Results" and "List of Random Spot Inspection Items", under the "Double Random Inspection" column of its portal website. 80 county (city, or district)-level governments had set up a special column on "double random inspection" or related columns on their portal websites. For example, the Government of Tongzhou District of Beijing Municipality had set up the "Openness of Administrative Law Enforcement" column on its portal website to disclose in a concentrated way information about administrative inspections carried out by various departments under it and two sub-columns under this column to disclose the list of double random spot inspection and law enforcement inspection results.

ii. The situation of disclosure of lists of random spot inspection items was good

The assessment shows that 21 of the 34 departments under the State Council covered by the assessment published the list of random spot inspection items. 19 provincial-level governments disclosed in a concentrated way (in a special column on the website or a unified list of double random inspection items of various departments issued by the government) lists of random spot inspection items of departments at their corresponding level. For example, the Government of Qinghai Province disclosed the list of random spot inspection items of 31 departments directly under it in the *Notice of the General Office of Qinghai Provincial People's Government on Issuing the List of "Double Random" Spot Inspection Items of Provincial-level Departments (Units) in Qinghai Province*. The Government of Shanghai Municipality published the lists of random spot inspection items of 23 departments under it in the "double random inspection" column on its portal website. 37 governments of larger cities disclosed in a concentrated manner (in a special column on their websites or a unified list of double random spot inspection items of various departments issued by the government) the list of random spot inspection items of departments at their corresponding level. For example, the Government of Guangzhou City of Guangdong Province published a list of random spot inspection items of 39 departments under it in the column of "Lists of Spot Inspection Items" on its portal website. 81 counties (cities, districts)-level governments released in a concentrated manner (in a special column on their websites or a unified list of double random spot inspection items of various departments issued by the government) the list of random spot inspection items of departments at the corresponding level. For example, the Government of Xiuying District of Haikou City of Hainan Province published a list of random spot inspection items of 10 departments under it in the online service hall of the Government Service Platform of Haikou City.

iii. The disclosure of the results of random spot inspections and related investigations and punishments of violations by departments of ecology and environment of governments of larger cities and counties (cities, districts)-level governments in 2020 were satisfactory

36 of the 49 governments of larger cities and 77 of the 120 county (city, or district)-level governments disclosed the results of both spot inspections and related investigations and punishments of violations. For example, the "double random inspection" column on the portal website of the Government of Haikou City of Hainan Province had a jump link to the Online Government Service Hall of Haikou City, where the results of the random spot inspections carried out by various departments and related investigations and punishments of violations were disclosed; the Ecology and Environment Bureau of Sichuan Province disclosed the results spot inspections it carried out and related investigations and punishments of violations in 2020 in the column "Supervision and Law Enforcement-Disclosure of Information About Double Random Inspections" of its website on a monthly basis.

(2) Problems identified in the assessment

i. The setting of the "double random inspection" column on the portal websites of departments under the State Councils and provincial-level governments still needed to be improved

The assessment shows that 22, or 64.71%, of the 34 departments under the State Council and 17, or 54.84%, of the 31 provincial-level governments covered by the assessment did not set up a special column on double random inspection or a related column on their portal websites.

ii. The lists of random spot inspection items released by some assessment targets were incomplete in content

The assessment shows that, among the 21 departments under the State Council that had published the list of random spot inspection items, ten failed to publish the list with complete content, which should include such elements as the basis, subject, content and method of random spot inspections. Eight of the 23 provincial-level governments, 17 of the 37 governments of larger cities and 29 of the 66 county (city, or district)-level governments that had released the list of random spot inspection items of their ecology and environment departments failed to release the list with complete content, which should include such elements as the basis, subject, content and method of random spot inspection.

iii. The disclosure of the results of random spot inspections and related investigations and punishment of violations by departments under the State Council and the ecology environment departments of provincial-level governments was not satisfactory

The assessment shows that, among the 34 departments under the State Council covered by the assessment, 29 did not disclose the results of random spot inspections and related investigations and punishment of violations in 2020 and one disclosed the results of only random spot inspections, but not related investigations and punishment of violations; and among the 31 provincial-level governments covered by the assessment, 27 did not disclose the results of the random spot inspections conducted by their ecology and environment departments or related investigations and punishment of violations in 2020 and three disclosed the results of only random spot inspections, but not related investigations and punishment of violations.

iv. Some assessment targets failed to disclose the results of random spot inspections and related investigations and punishment of violations in an adequate, standardized and timely manner

The assessment shows that, although some assessment targets disclosed results of random spot inspections and related investigations and punishment of violations in 2020, the results were not disclosed in an adequate, standardized and timely manner. For example, a provincial-level government only published two results of the random spot inspections carried out by its ecology and environment departments and related investigations and punishment of violations in 2020 on the website of the National Enterprise Credit Information Publicity System (Tibet); the ecology and environment department of a provincial-level government released the monthly summary sheet of "double random inspections" under the "double random inspection" column of its website, but the sheet contained only the total number of violations discovered and investigated by the ecology and environment departments in the province, but not the results of specific spot inspections and related investigations and punishment of violations; and the disclosure of the results of random spot inspections and related investigations and punishment of violations by the ecology and environment department of another province on its website was not continuous and timely, with the results in January, February, March, May and August of 2020 missing.

6. Construction of a unified platform for the openness of administrative law enforcement

Administrative law enforcement is an important way for administrative organs to perform government functions and manage economic and social affairs. The *Decision of the CPC Central Committee on Major Issues Pertaining to Comprehensively Promoting the Rule of Law and the Implementation Outline for the Construction of a Law-based Government (2015–2020)* have made specific arrangements and put forward clear requirements for the comprehensive implementation of the administrative law enforcement publication system, the whole process recording system of law enforcement and the system of legal review of major law-enforcement decisions (hereinafter referred to as the "three systems"). Focusing on such key links as the source, process and result of administrative law enforcement and comprehensively implementing the "three systems" play a fundamental, holistic and breakthrough role in promoting strict, standardized, fair and civilized law enforcement, and are of great significance for effectively safeguarding the legitimate rights and interests of the people, upholding the credibility of the government and creating a more open, transparent, standardized, orderly, fair and efficient legal environment.

The *Guiding Opinions of the General Office of the State Council on Comprehensively Implementing the Administrative Law Enforcement Publication System, the Recording System of Law Enforcement in the Whole Process and the Legal Review System of Major Law Enforcement Decisions* require administrative law enforcement agencies to strengthen the management of information about law enforcement, promptly and accurately publish such information, achieve the recording of the whole process of administrative law enforcement and well-regulated and orderly process of legal review of major law enforcement decisions, strengthen the construction of information platform, and vigorously advance the construction of an information system for comprehensive administration of and supervision over administrative law enforcement, so as to achieve online entry of information on law enforcement, online circulation of law enforcement procedures, online supervision over law enforcement activities, real-time push of law enforcement decisions, unified publication of information about law enforcement, online search of information about law enforcement, as well as instantaneous, progressive and systematic management of administrative law enforcement activities. Meanwhile, the *Opinions* require that the basic data related to various administrative law enforcement activities should be conscientiously reorganized, a national pool of information on administrative law enforcement primarily consisting of information about the subjects of administrative law enforcement, power and responsibility lists, case handling, supervision, and statistical analyses should be established, and an administrative law enforcement data center integrating data storage and sharing functionality should be gradually built up.

In this year's assessment, the Project Team examined the construction of administrative law enforcement platforms by 31 provincial-level governments, 49 governments of larger cities and 120 county (city, or district)-level governments on their portal websites.

(1) Bright spots found in the assessment

i. Nearly half of the assessment targets had set up a standardized administrative law enforcement information disclosure platform

The assessment shows that 11 provincial-level governments, 34 governments of larger cities and 66 county (city, or district)-level governments had set up an administrative law enforcement information disclosure column on their portal websites, the website of their judicial administrative departments or government service platforms. Among them, ten provincial-level governments, 28 governments of larger cities and 54 county (city, or district)-level governments had set up standardized columns, with detailed sub-division, accurate positioning and orderly information release. For example, the Shanghai Law Enforcement Publication Platform covers all kinds of information about the law enforcement activities carried out by municipal government departments, district governments, sub-district offices, townships and town governments, administrative committees and other municipal-level administrative law enforcement organs. 14 special sub-columns had been set up under the platform to separately disclose the following 14 kinds of information: law enforcement subjects, law enforcement competencies, lists of random spot inspection items, law enforcement personnel (with Shanghai certificates), law enforcement personnel (with national certificates), procedures and flowcharts, power items and service guides, lists of powers and responsibilities, tip-offs and complaints, remedy channels, double-publication, other administrative law enforcement decisions, discretion benchmark and law enforcement data disclosure. The Government of Shanxi Province had set up a special section for the disclosure of administrative law enforcement information service on its government service platform to provide in a concentrated manner links to the administrative law enforcement column on the websites of various departments under it and those of affiliated cities. Take the special column on the website of the provincial development and reform commission as an example. A number of sub-columns had been set up under this column to disclose various kinds of information, such as "Double Publication", List of Law Enforcement Supervisors, List of Law Enforcement Items, List of Random Spot Inspection Items, List of Administrative Law Enforcement Audio-visual Recordings, List of Catalogs of Legal Review of Major Administrative Law Enforcement Decisions, Service Guides of Law Enforcement Items, and Flow Chart of Legal Review of Major Administrative Law Enforcement Decisions.

ii. The disclosure of information about administrative law enforcement work became more standardized and systematic

The assessment shows that some assessment targets took realizing "more well-regulated administrative law enforcement, more facilitative procedures for the general public, more efficient government governance, and a better business environment" as the starting point and foothold, and disclosed such information as the annual report on the overall situation of administrative law enforcement, relevant systems of administrative law enforcement, list of catalogs of law enforcement, samples of law enforcement documents, and service guides for law enforcement items.

Some assessment targets disclosed detailed information about the overall situation of their law enforcement work. For example, the Government of Guangdong Province disclosed information about the situation of administrative law enforcement in 2019 and the statistical table of the exercise of various powers of each department under it; the Government of Benxi City of Liaoning Province disclosed the work summaries and data summaries of administrative law enforcement work of each department under it. Some assessment targets established and disclosed information about relevant systems of administrative law enforcement. For example, the governments of Shijiazhuang City of Hebei Province, Benxi City and Shenyang City of Liaoning Province, Chang'an District of Shijiazhuang City of Hebei Province and Wafangdian City of Liaoning Province disclosed the information about the "three systems" of administrative law enforcement of various departments under them. The Government of Qian'an City of Hebei Province disclosed information about the training system of legal reviewers and the administrative law enforcement complaint and tip-off system. The Government of Jinan City of Shandong Province published the "Top Ten Typical Cases of Whole-Process Recording of Administrative Law Enforcement in Jinan City in 2019" to promote typical practices.

Some assessment targets prepared and published lists of law enforcement-related catalogs, including the list of administrative law enforcement items, the list of audio-visual recording items, the list of legal reviews of major law enforcement decisions, and the list of major administrative decision-making items. For example, the Government of Longsha District of Qiqihar City of Heilongjiang Province published the catalog of major administrative decision-making items, the list of items of audio-visual recording of law enforcement actions, the list of items of legal review of major law enforcement decisions and the related flow charts; the Government of Fengrun District of Tangshan City of Hebei Province published the list of administrative law enforcement items, the list of items of audio-visual recording of law-enforcement actions, the list of legal review of major law enforcement decisions and related flow charts.

Some assessment targets prepared and published samples of law enforcement documents. For example, the governments of Dalian City of Liaoning Province, Jinan City of Shandong Province, Chang'an District of Shijiazhuang City of Hebei Province, Liuyang City of Hunan Province, Wafangdian City of Liaoning Province published the detailed format samples of administrative law enforcement documents.

Some assessment targets published service guides for law enforcement items. For example, the Government of Longkou City of Shandong Province published in a concentrated manner the service guides for law enforcement items of some departments under it in the column of "Publication of Three Systems of Administrative Law Enforcement-Service Guides for Administrative Law Enforcement" on its portal website.

(2) Problems identified in the assessment

i. The setting of special columns and platforms was not standardized

The *Guiding Opinions of the General Office of the State Council on Comprehensively Implementing the Administrative Law Enforcement Publication System, the Recording System of Law Enforcement in the Whole Process and the Legal Review System of Major Law Enforcement Decisions* require that administrative law enforcement agencies should, in accordance with the principle that "who enforces the law conducts publication", clarify the duty to collect, transmit, review, and release the subject matter of publication and standardize the standards and formats of the subject matter of publication. Administrative law enforcement agencies should establish a unified law enforcement information publication platform and disclose the basic information and information on the result of administrative law enforcement to the public through government websites, new media accounts for government affairs, bulletin boards at service halls, service windows and other platforms. Information not suitable for disclosure for involving state secrets, trade secrets, or personal privacy but is required by law to be disclosed to the public should be processed appropriately before being disclosed to the public.

The assessment shows that 20 provincial-level governments, 15 governments of larger cities and 54 county (city, or district)-level governments had not set up an administrative law enforcement information disclosure platform. Among them, some published administrative law enforcement information in other columns on their websites. For example, some assessment targets release information about law enforcement personnel, law enforcement data, and law enforcement-related systems in such columns as "double random inspection", "notices and announcements", "administrative penalties" and "administrative licensing", resulting in the confusion of column information and inconvenience in inquiry.

The column setting of some assessment targets needed to be improved. The assessment shows that although some assessment targets had set up an administrative law enforcement column on their portal websites, the content in the column was not standardized and not detailed enough. For example, some local governments had set up a dynamic scroll column of "list of administrative law enforcement subjects" or "list of law enforcement personnel" in the government service section of their portal websites and placed it together with other sub-columns, making it inconvenient for inquiry. Because there is a rich variety of administrative law enforcement information, a comprehensive column system should be set up to disclose different kinds of law enforcement information. Some local governments had set up a "disclosure of administrative law enforcement information" column on their portal websites, but the column was empty with no information released in it.

The column setting on the portal websites of some assessment targets was not detailed enough and, as a result, a rich variety of information was disclosed together without classification. For example, some local governments disclosed various kinds of law enforcement information such as law enforcement subjects, law enforcement personnel, complaint and tip-off hotlines, flow charts, standards on discretion, the list of administrative law enforcement items, and law enforcement results in the "administrative law enforcement and market regulation" column; some disclosed such law enforcement information as the catalog of major administrative decision-making items, law enforcement results, law enforcement personnel, law enforcement subjects, "three systems" of administrative law enforcement, law enforcement processes, law enforcement data and service guides, all in the "administrative law enforcement notices and announcements" column on their portal websites, which was inconvenient for the inquiry by users.

ii. The administrative law enforcement information column on the portal websites of some assessment targets lacked diversity in content and failed to fully disclose the administrative law enforcement information

The *Guiding Opinions of the General Office of the State Council on Comprehensively Implementing the Administrative Law Enforcement Publication System, the Recording System of Law Enforcement in the Whole Process and the Legal Review System of Major Law Enforcement Decisions* require administrative law enforcement organs to strengthen *ex-ante* disclosure by "disclosing to the public the subjects of administrative law enforcement, personnel, duties, authority, basis, procedures, remedy channels, lists of random inspection items, and other information in a comprehensive, accurate, timely and voluntary manner, preparing and releasing their respective service guides and law enforcement flow charts and specifying the titles of law enforcement matters, acceptance agencies, approval departments, acceptance conditions, the time limit for processing, and other contents in accordance with the relevant laws and regulations and in light of their own powers and duties" and to strengthen *ex-post* disclosure of law enforcement information by "disclosing within 20 working days from the date of an enforcement decision such information as law enforcement organs, law enforcement objects, classification of law enforcement, and law enforcement results, accepting social supervision, and disclosing the information about a law enforcement decisions such as administrative licensing and administrative penalty within seven working days from the date of the law enforcement decision, unless otherwise required by any law or administrative regulation". The *Opinions* also require that an annual statistical reporting system of administrative law enforcement be established and that local administrative law enforcement agencies at all levels disclose the data on the overall administrative law enforcement situation for the previous year before January 31 each year and submit the data to the government at the corresponding level and the competent department at a higher level.

The assessment shows that the information released in the administrative law enforcement column on the portal websites of some assessment targets lacked diversity, and the administrative law enforcement information was not fully disclosed as required by the relevant documents. For example, some local governments only disclosed information about law enforcement activities or announcements in the "administrative law enforcement" column of their portal websites, some only published announcements of the loss of administrative law enforcement certificates in the "administrative law enforcement information" column of their websites, and some disclosed only information about the results of administrative licensing and administrative penalty in the "administrative law enforcement publication" column of their websites.

7. Disclosure of administrative penalty information

Effectively disclosure of administrative penalty information is conducive to improving the credit records of social subjects, establishing the mechanism for encouraging honesty and punishing dishonesty helps to improve the in-process and *ex-post* regulatory mechanism, and building the new-type market regulation mechanism with credit as its core is of great significance for accelerating the construction of the social credit system, promoting the construction of civilized cities and building a well-off society in an all-round way. The *Several Opinions of the General Office of the State Council on Strengthening the Service for and Supervision over Market Entities by Means of Big Data Analysis* clearly define the time limit for the disclosure of administrative penalty information and the publication requirements of credit platform. The *Guiding Opinions of the State Council on Establishing and Improving the System of Joint Incentives for Keeping Faith and Joint Punishment for Losing Faith and Accelerating the Development of Social Honesty* require the full implementation of the system of online disclosure of administrative penalty information. The *Regulations on the Disclosure of Government Information*, revised in 2019, clearly stipulate that administrative organs should voluntarily disclose information about the basis, conditions and procedures for the imposition of administrative penalties and administrative compulsions and about administrative penalty decisions that an administrative agency considers to have certain social influence.

In the assessment of administrative penalty information disclosure, the Project Team mainly examined the disclosure of administrative penalty information in 2020 by 37 departments under the State Council with administrative penalty power, 31 provincial-level governments, 49 governments of larger cities and 120 county (city, or district)-level governments on their own portal websites, the websites of the departments under them, or enterprise credit information platforms. Among them, 31 provincial-level governments, 49 governments of larger cities and 120 county (city, or district)-level governments were randomly selected for the assessment of disclosure of administrative penalty information by their market regulation departments.

(1) Bright spots found in the assessment

i. The disclosure rate of results of administrative penalties imposed by market regulation departments was relatively high

The assessment shows that the market regulation departments of 30 provincial-level governments, 46 governments of larger cities and 112 county (city, or district)-level governments disclosed information about administrative penalties in 2020, with disclosure rates of 96.77, 93.88 and 93.33%, respectively.

ii. A special column was set up on government websites to disclose administrative penalty results

The situation of setting up a special column for centralized disclosure of administrative penalty information by governments at various levels on their portal websites was good. The assessment shows that 24 provincial-level governments, 40 governments of larger cities and 97 county (city, or district)-level governments had set up a special column on their portal websites to disclose information about administrative penalties in 2020, with the setup rates of 77.42, 81.63 and 80.83%, respectively. For example, the "double publication" column on the portal website of the Government of Shanghai Municipality was linked to the Credit China (Shanghai) platform, which provided the functions of "double publication directory inquiry" and "double publication data inquiry". The "double publication" information in Shanghai was disclosed in the "dada openness" column on the platform in a concentrated manner and classified by legal persons, natural persons and departments, thus ensuring the consistency, clarity and comprehensiveness of information disclosed in different platforms, while facilitating the public access to administrative penalty information. The Government of Dongcheng District of Beijing Municipality had set up the column of "results of administrative licensing and administrative penalty" to disclose in an easy-to-access manner the administrative penalty information of various departments under the district government.

Among the 37 departments under the State Council, eight, including the National Bureau of Statistics, China Banking and Insurance Regulatory Commission, the Ministry of Ecology and Environment, the Ministry of Transport, the Ministry of Finance and the State Administration of Market Supervision, disclosed the administrative penalty information in the corresponding administrative penalty columns of their portal websites. Among them, China Banking and Insurance Regulatory

Commission had set up the "administrative penalty" column on its portal website to disclose in a concentrated way the administrative penalty information of the Commission. In the column, each piece of information was named after the document number of the administrative penalty decision, the key contents of the penalty were listed in the form of a table, and the elements of disclosure were comprehensive and clear.

iii. The disclosure of administrative penalty information by some assessment targets was standardized

Standardizing the content of disclosure of administrative penalty information is conducive to further improving the quality of information disclosure, giving full play to the role of public supervision and raising the levels of state governance and government services. Among the 11 departments under the State Council, the 30 provincial-level governments market regulation departments, the 46 market regulation departments of larger cities, and the 112 county (city, or district)-level government market regulation departments that disclosed administrative penalty information, 5, 13, 24 and 46, respectively, disclosed the information in the form of administrative penalty decisions. Each of the administrative penalty decisions published by them contained such elements as the person or entity subject to the penalty, the main illegal facts, the basis of the penalty, and the result of the penalty and was standardized both in content and in form.

(2) Problems identified in the assessment

i. The disclosure of administrative penalty information by departments under the State Council needed to be strengthened

The assessment shows that only 11 of the 37 departments under the State Council with administrative penalty power disclosed administrative penalty information, accounting for 29.73% of the total. Among them, four failed to release administrative penalty information in a continuous way, leaving the administrative penalty results of some months unpublished; the administrative penalty information disclosed by one assessment target did not include the basis of the administrative penalty decision; two assessment targets failed to release administrative penalty information in a timely manner, disclosing the information online seven working days after administrative penalty decisions were made; and one assessment targets did not indicate the date of administrative penalty decisions.

ii. The disclosure of administrative penalty information by some local market regulation departments was unsatisfactory

The *Several Opinions of the General Office of the State Council on Strengthening the Service for and Supervision over Market Entities by Means of Big Data Analysis* require that the information about an administrative penalty should be made public online within seven working days from the date of the making of the administrative decision, so as to improve the transparency of administrative management and the credibility of the government. If a government department makes an administrative penalty decision in the process of law enforcement, it should disclose the decision to the public in a timely manner; if no decision on administrative penalty has been made during a given period of time, the situation should be explained to the public through a regular reporting mechanism.

The assessment shows that some local market regulation departments disclosed little administrative penalty information in 2020. For example, a provincial market regulation department only released three pieces of administrative penalty information in 2020; some government market regulation departments failed to release administrative penalty information in a continuous way. For example, one provincial market regulation department released in a concentrated manner a large amount of administrative penalty information in July, but released no information during the period from January to June and in August, thus failing to normalize the release of the information.

iii. Some local market regulation departments leaked personal information in the disclosure of administrative penalty information

The *Guiding Opinions of the General Office of the National Development and Reform Commission on Further Improving the Disclosure of Such Credit Information as Administrative Licensing and Administrative Penalty* issued in 2018 require that the information involving trade secrets of enterprises or personal privacy shall undergo necessary technical processing before being disclosed to the public. The *Notice by the General Office of the State Council on Issuing the Key Tasks in Promoting the Transparency of Government Affairs* in 2018 required relevant government departments to effectively protect personal privacy in accordance with law. With the exception of announcements of penalties and mandatory information disclosure, government information involving personal privacy should be identified and appropriate methods and scope of release should be selected before it is disclosed. Therefore, when government departments disclose administrative penalty information, they should carry out necessary technical treatment of the personal information, and determine the appropriate scope of information disclosure, so as to avoid unnecessary disputes.

The assessment shows that some local market regulation departments failed to carry out necessary technical treatment of the personal information of natural persons when disclosing administrative penalty information. For example, many local market regulation departments leaked personal ID numbers when disclosing administrative penalty information.

iv. Some local market regulation departments released administrative penalty information with incomplete elements

The administrative penalty information disclosed by some local market regulation departments lacked such elements as the basis, the result and the time of administrative penalties.

The assessment shows that, among the market regulation departments of 30 provincial-level governments, 46 governments of larger cities and 112 county (city, or district)-level governments that disclosed administrative penalty information, those of county (city, or district)-level governments did not disclose the basis for administrative penalty decisions; those of nine county (city, or district)-level governments did not disclose administrative penalty results; those of two provincial-level governments, three governments of larger cities and five county (city, or district)-level governments did not disclose the time of administrative penalty decisions; and those of three provincial-level governments, three governments of larger cities and 21 county (city, or district)-level governments did not disclose the time of the online release of administrative penalty results.

v. The construction and maintenance of the administrative penalty column on the portal websites of some governments needed to be strengthened

The assessment shows that, although some governments had set up administrative penalty columns on their portal websites, the information released in these columns was incomplete and the column setting was imperfect. For example, some district governments did not disclose information about administrative penalties imposed by their market regulation department in the administrative penalty columns on their portal websites; the "double publication" column on the portal website of a municipal government released the administrative penalty information of only some departments, which did include the market regulation department; the links to administrative penalties imposed by the market regulation department on the portal websites of some local governments were invalid and inaccessible. For example, the administrative penalty data in the "administrative licensing, administrative penalty and other credit information" column on the portal website of a municipal government was inaccessible.

8. Disclosure of audit results

The *Opinions of the State Council on Strengthening the Audit Work* clearly require that audit on implementation of budgets and other financial revenues and expenditures shall be strengthened, with close attention paid to both existing and additional fiscal funds to promote the reduction of idle fiscal funds, revitalization of existing funds, rational distribution and efficient use of fiscal funds, so that the funds are used where they should be; institutions under audit shall make rectification in a timely manner and conduct serious research on problems discovered in audit and any proposals offered, report the results of the overhaul to the governments or appropriate departments at the corresponding level, and disclose them to the public while notifying the relevant audit authorities in writing; and overall coordinated arrangements for audit plans of audit authorities shall be strengthened. The distribution of audit resources shall be optimized. Audit on major projects involving overall interests shall be effectively conducted. Exploration shall be made of measures for organizing audits in stages on budget implementation programs. For major policies and measures, major investment projects, key special-purpose funds, and major emergencies, tracking audits on their whole processes may be launched.

In 2020, the Project Team carried out an assessment of the disclosure of audit information by 31 provincial governments, 49 governments of larger cities, and 120 county (city, or district)-level governments on their own portal websites and the websites of their audit departments. The assessment indices included: (a) whether the audit plan information in 2020 included audits of major policy measures, major investment projects, key special funds and major emergencies; (b) announcements of the audit results of the implementation of the government budgets at the corresponding level and other financial revenues and expenditures in 2019, including basic information, main problems found in the audit, audit opinions and suggestions, and rectifications; (c) follow-up audit reports on the implementation of major government policies and measures in 2019, including basic information and main problems found in the audits. Meanwhile, the Project Team also paid special attention to whether a whole-process follow-up audit of Covid-19 pandemic prevention and control work had been carried out in 2020 and took it as an observation index.

(1) Bright spots found in the assessment

i. The disclosure of audit information by provincial-level governments was good

The assessment shows that the situation of publication of audit reports on the implementation of budgets and other financial revenues and expenditures by provincial-level governments was good. Thirty-one provincial-level governments published audit reports on the implementation of budgets and other financial revenues and expenditures in 2019, with the disclosure rate reaching 100%. All the published audit reports in 2019 contained information about the basic situation of and the main problems found in the audit, as well as audit opinions and suggestions. Among them, the audit reports of 15 provincial-level governments included information about the rectification of problems identified in the audit in the current year. An example in this respect was part six of the audit report on the implementation of the municipal budget and other financial revenues and expenditures in Beijing in 2019, entitled "Preliminary rectifications of problems found in the audit".

The disclosure of follow-up audit reports on the implementation of major policies and measures by provincial-level governments in 2019 was satisfactory. The assessment shows that 29 provincial-level governments disclosed the results of follow-up audit of the implementation of major policies and measures in 2019, with the disclosure rate reaching 93.55%; three provincial-level governments published the results of the follow-up audit of their implementation of major policies and measures in 2019 and 2020 on a quarterly basis. For example, the Government of Liaoning Province published the results of the follow-up audit of its implementation of major policies and measures on a quarterly basis under the column "audit information (announcements and reports)" on its portal website.

ii. Some governments published their audit reports in diversified forms

The assessment shows that, among the 31 provincial-level governments, 35 governments of larger cities and 60 county (city, or district)-level governments that published audit reports on the implementation of their budgets and other financial revenues and expenditure in 2019, 11 also disclosed illustrations corresponding to audit reports. For example, the *Illustrated Audit Report on the Implementation of Municipal-level Budgets and Other Financial Revenues and Expenditures in Tianjin Municipality in 2019* used mind maps, statistical tables of data, and cartoon images to make the contents of the report vivid and easy to understand.

(2) Problems identified in the assessment

i. The disclosure of information about audit plans in 2020 was poor

The assessment shows that 19 provincial-level governments, 31 governments of larger cities and 76 county (city, or district)-level governments did not disclose the audit plan for 2020, accounting for 61.29, 63.27 and 63.33% of the total, respectively. In view of the Covid-19 pandemic situation in 2020, the implementation of the Covid-19 pandemic prevention and control plan should be included in the audit plan, but the assessment shows that some assessment targets failed to do so.

Some governments did not separately disclose standardized audit plan information in 2020. The assessment shows that seven governments of larger cities and 11 county (city, or district)-level governments did not separately disclose standardized annual audit plans, but only briefly mentioned them in the 2019 work summary and 2020 work plan.

ii. The rate of publication of audit reports on the budget implementation and other financial revenues and expenditures by governments below the provincial level was not high

The situation of publication by governments below the provincial level of their audit reports on the implementation of the budget and other financial revenues and expenditures at the corresponding level in 2019 was not good. The assessment shows that 14 governments of larger cities and 60 county (city, or district)-level governments did not publish the report. Among the 35 governments of larger cities and 60 county (city, or district)-level governments that published the reports, 26 governments of larger cities and 36 county (city, or district)-level governments did not include information about the rectifications of the problems found in the audit, accounting for 74.29 and 60.00% of the total, respectively.

iii. The situation of publication of follow-up audit reports on the implementation of major policies and measures by governments below the provincial level was not satisfactory

The assessment shows that the situation of publication of follow-up audit reports on the implementation of major policies and measures in 2019 by governments at the corresponding level was not good. 16 governments of larger cities and 70 county (city, or district)-level governments did not publish the follow-up audit reports on the implementation of major policies and measures. Among the 33 governments of larger cities and 50 county (city, or district)-level governments that published the follow-up audit reports on the implementation of major policies and measures, 30 governments of larger cities and 41 county (city, or district)-level governments did not publish the reports on a quarterly basis, and most of them only mentioned the reports in their audit reports on the budget implementation and other financial revenues and expenditures at the corresponding level in 2019, which were published on an annual basis.

iv. The audit information of some governments was disclosed not in a centralized, but in a scattered manner

The assessment shows that the audit information of some governments was disclosed not in a centralized, but in a scattered manner. Some governments and their audit departments had not set up a special column on their portal websites to disclose audit information, and it was not clear in which column they had disclosed the audit information, which was not convenient for the public to find the information. For example, a municipal audit bureau published its audit plan and audit result in the "notices and announcements" column, which is mixed with information about financial budgets and final accounts, evaluation of professional titles, and website work reports. Although some governments and their audit departments had set up an audit information column on their portal websites, very little information was disclosed in the column, or most of the information disclosed in the column was information about their daily work, rather than audit results. For example, the "Openness of Government Affairs – Openness of Five Categories of Government Affairs-Openness of Implementation-Audit Openness" column on the website of a grass-roots government contained only one piece of information, which was about the daily work of the government in 2019.

9. Annual statistical report on administrative law enforcement

The *Guiding Opinions of the General Office of the State Council on Comprehensively Implementing the Administrative Law Enforcement Publication System, the Recording System of Law Enforcement in the Whole Process and the Legal Review System of Major Law Enforcement Decisions* require that an annual statistical reporting system of administrative law enforcement be established and that local administrative law enforcement agencies at all levels disclose the data on the overall administrative law enforcement for the previous year before January 31 each year and submit the data to the people's government at the same level and the competent department at a higher level.

In this year's assessment, the Project Team examined the publication of statistical annual reports on administrative law enforcement of market regulation departments by 31 provincial-level governments, 49 governments of larger cities and 120 county (city, or district)-level governments, including whether the annual statistical report on administrative law enforcement of the market regulation departments in 2019 was published, whether the report was published online before January 31, and whether the report was complete in content.

(1) Bright spots found in the assessment

The statistical annual reports on administrative law enforcement published by some assessment targets were detailed in content. The assessment shows that the statistical annual reports on administrative law enforcement by some local market regulation departments in 2019 were substantial in content, comprehensively analyzing the overall work of administrative law enforcement. For example, the statistical annual reports on administrative law enforcement published by the market regulation departments of Guangdong Province, Guangzhou City, Shantou City, Zhuhai City, and Shenzhen City of Guangdong Province, Hangzhou City of Zhejiang Province, Haizhu District and Yuexiu District of Guangzhou City of Guangdong Province, Boluo County of Huizhou City of Guangdong Province, Huizhou District of Huangshan City of Anhui Province, Xiaoshan District of Hangzhou City of Zhejiang Province and Yuhang District of Hangzhou City of Zhejiang Province reviewed and analyzed statistical tables of law enforcement data according to the type of administrative power (administrative penalty, Administrative licensing, administrative coercion, administrative expropriation, administrative inspection, administrative adjudication, administrative payment, administrative confirmation, administrative reward, and other administrative law enforcement actions) and provided textual explanations.

The annual reports on administrative law enforcement of some local market regulation departments in 2019 not only reviewed the administrative law enforcement data but also summarizes the relevant situations of law enforcement. For example, the *Statistical Annual Report on Administrative Law Enforcement by Wuhan Municipal Market Supervision Bureau in 2019* contained the names and number of law enforcement subjects, the setting of law enforcement posts and the number of on-the-job law enforcement personnel, the situation of implementation of administrative law enforcement work such as administrative licensing, administrative penalty, administrative coercion, administrative confirmation, administrative reward and administrative adjudication, the implementation of administrative inspection plans, and the handling of complaints and tip-offs. The *Report on Administrative Law Enforcement by Harbin Municipal Market Supervision Administration in 2019* included such contents as statutory law enforcement duties, administrative law enforcement data in 2019, administrative reconsideration and administrative litigation, and cases transferred to judicial organs for handling. The *Report on Market Supervision Administrative Law Enforcement in Binhai New Area of Tianjin Municipality in 2019* included the overall situation of administrative law enforcement, cases and trend analysis of key illegal acts. The *Report of the Market Supervision Bureau of Hunnan District of Shenyang City of Liaoning Province on Administrative Law Enforcement Work in 2019* contained the following information: administrative law enforcement subjects and law enforcement personnel, the overall situation of legality review, the preparation and disclosure of the list of administrative law enforcement items, enterprise-related inspection plan management, recordation of enterprise-related inspections, training of administrative law enforcement personnel, construction of the discretion standard system, disclosure of administrative law enforcement decisions, the overall situation of recordation of major administrative penalties, allocation of equipment for audio-visual recording of administrative law enforcement activities, and implementation of the administrative law enforcement responsibility system. The *Annual Statistical Report of Beijing Municipal Market Supervision Bureau on Administrative Law Enforcement in 2019* covered such matters as the names of law enforcement subjects of administrative law enforcement agencies, the input of law enforcement forces, the handling of government service items, the implementation of law enforcement inspection plans, the handling of administrative penalty cases, administrative coercion cases and other cases, and the acceptance and classification of complaints and tip-offs. The *Report of Benxi Municipal Market Supervision Bureau on the Overall Situation of Administrative Law Enforcement in 2019* summarized the administrative law enforcement of the bureau in the following aspects: new achievements made in food safety supervision, the continuous strengthening of the safety supervision of drugs and vaccines, new breakthroughs in the special rectification campaign in the field of special equipment, product quality and safety supervision, the supervision and law enforcement in the field of fair competition, protection of intellectual property, market supervision in key fields, consumer protection, law enforcement inspection, construction of the credit system and strengthening of in-process and *ex-post* supervision.

(2) Problems identified in the assessment

i. Most assessment targets did not publish the statistical annual report on administrative law enforcement

The assessment shows that only three of the 31 provincial-level governments, 17 of the 49 governments of larger cities and 40 of the 120 county (city, or district)-level governments published the annual statistical report on administrative law enforcement by their market supervision bureaus in 2019 on their portal websites, the websites of relevant government departments or special platforms of administrative law enforcement information disclosure. The remaining 140 assessment targets, or 70% of the total, did not publish the report in 2019.

ii. The publication of administrative law enforcement statistical annual reports by some assessment targets needed to be improved

Some assessment targets failed to publish statistical annual reports of administrative law enforcement in a timely manner or to indicate the time of the online publication of the reports. The assessment shows that, among the 60 local market regulation departments that published the 2019 annual statistical report on administrative law enforcement, those of two provincial-level governments, four governments of larger cities and seven county (city, or district)-level governments failed to publish the reports before January 31.

The statistical annual reports on administrative law enforcement published by some assessment targets were incomplete in content. The assessment shows that, among the 60 local market regulation departments that published the statistical annual report on administrative law enforcement in 2019, those of one provincial-level government, seven governments of larger cities and 12 county (city, or district)-level governments published the reports that contained only text descriptions, but no statistical tables of administrative law enforcement data; those of one provincial-level government, two governments of larger cities and 14 county (city, or district)-level governments published the reports that contained only statistical tables on the administrative law enforcement data, without accompanying text descriptions.

10. The annual report on the construction of a law-based government

According to the *Implementation Outline for the Construction of a Law-based Government (2015–2020)*, issued by the CPC Central Committee and the State Council, a local government at or above the county level should report its work of constructing a law-based government in the previous year to the Party committee and the standing committee of the people's congress at its corresponding level and the government at the next higher level in the first quarter of each year, a government department should report its work of construction of a law-based government in the previous year to the government at its corresponding level and the relevant department of the government at the next higher level in the first quarter of each year, and the report should be disclosed to the public through newspapers and government websites. The *Provisions on Supervisory Inspection of the Construction of a Law-based Government and the Implementation of Responsibilities*, issued by the General Office of the CPC Central Committee and the General Office of the State Council, require local governments at all levels and government departments at or above the county level to disclose to the public their annual reports on the construction of a law-based government, except those involving any Party or state secret, through newspapers, websites and other news media before April 1 of each year and accept the supervision by the people. It can be said that the annual report on the construction of a law-based government has become an important means by which governments at all levels show their effectiveness in implementing the construction of a law-based government, and the publication of the report is also an important means to assess and supervise the construction of a law-based government.

The 2020 annual assessment covered 34 departments under the State Council with external administrative functions (including 22 component departments of the State Council, one special institution directly under the State Council, eight institutions directly under the State Council and three public institutions directly under the State Council),[4] 31 provincial-level governments, 49 governments of larger cities and 120 county (city, or district)-level governments. In the assessment, the Project Team mainly examined the publishing methods and contents of the annual reports on the construction of a law-based government in 2019. Among them, the publishing method index focused on whether the assessment targets published the annual report and whether the publishing method was convenient for inquiry by the public, including the release of the report, the time of release, channels of release, the website column in which the report was released and the form of release. According to the requirements of the *Implementation Outline for the Construction of a Law-based Government (2015–2020)* and the *Provisions on Supervisory Inspection of the Construction of a Law-based Government* and the *Implementation of Responsibilities*, the Project

[4] The third-party assessment of government transparency in China conducted by the Project Team covered 49 departments under the State Council, among which the national bureaus administered by ministries and commissions under the State Council need not to release their annual reports on the construction of a law-based government separately. Therefore, this assessment only covered 34 departments under the State Council.

Team selected some important issues in the construction of a law-based government as the indices used in this assessment.[5]

(1) Bright spots found in the assessment

i. Departments under the State Council, provincial-level governments and governments of larger cities generally published their annual reports

By July 31, 2020, 33 of the 34 departments under the State Council had released their annual reports on the construction of a law-based government in the previous year, while in 2019, only 21 of the 34 departments under the State Council released their annual reports on the construction of a law-based government in 2018. Among the governments of larger cities, 47 released the annual report on the previous year, an increase of four from 43 in 2019. As in 2019, the provincial-level governments had all published the annual reports on the previous year.

ii. The proportion of reports released in time had increased

The proportion of assessment targets releasing the report in time increased significantly in 2020 as compared with 2019, in which only five departments under the State Council, four provincial-level governments, 28 governments of larger cities and 36 county (city, or district)-level governments released the annual report on the construction of a law-based government in 2018 before April 1. The 2020 assessment shows that 17 departments under the State Council, 25 provincial-level governments, 37 governments of larger cities and 73 county (city, or district)-level governments released their annual reports for the previous year before April 1, 2020, an increase of 12 (240%), 21 (525%), 9 (32.14%) and 37 (102.78%), respectively, from the previous year.

iii. Some assessment targets had set up a special annual report column on their portal websites

Publishing the annual report on the construction of a law-based government in the previous year is an important way for government departments to test and demonstrate their effectiveness in building a law-based government. As information that needs to be released continuously, the report should be placed in a fixed location on government websites for public inquiry and access. Therefore, the annual reports on the construction of a law-based government, just like the annual reports on government information disclosure, should be published in a fixed and special column on government portal websites. The assessment shows that, among each of the four types of assessment targets, few had set up special columns on their portal website to publish the annual reports on the construction of a law-based government in the past years. They included the National Development and Reform Commission, the Ministry of Education, the State Taxation Administration, the governments of Beijing Municipality, Jilin Province, Zhejiang Province, Hubei Province, Guangdong Province, the governments of the cities of Wuxi, Hangzhou, Xiamen, Wuhan,

[5] For details, please refer to the *Blue Book of Rule of Law: Development of the Local Rule of Law in China (2019)*, Beijing: Social Sciences Academic Press, 2020, pp. 57–78.

Shenzhen, Kunming, Xi'an, Yinchuan, and Shishi, and the governments of Haizhu District and Yuexiu District of Guangzhou City of Guangdong Province, Nanhai District of Foshan City of Guangdong Province, Fengrun District of Tangshan City of Hebei Province, Daoli District of Harbin City of Heilongjiang Province, Pudong New Area, Xuhui District, Huangpu District and Jinshan District of Shanghai Municipality, Ouhai District of Wenzhou City of Zhejiang Province, Cixi City of Zhejiang Province, and Gongshu District, Jianggan District, Xiaoshan District and Yuhang District of Hangzhou City of Zhejiang Province.

iv. The overall results of departments under the State Council, provincial-level governments and governments of larger cities in the assessment of some indices were satisfactory

The assessment shows that the overall results of the departments under the State Council, provincial-level governments and governments of larger cities in the assessment of some indices were satisfactory, that is, the proportions of the assessment targets meeting the requirements of some indices were high. For example, the proportions of the departments under the State Council that released the report, disclosed the data of the adoption, revision, and abolition of department rules, and disclosed information about the situation of participation in the publicity of law reached 97.06, 97.06 and 91.18%, respectively. Among the provincial-level governments, all published reports and disclosed information about the reform of the administrative approval system and strengthening of the reform of the law enforcement system, 96.77% disclosed the data on the adoption, revision and abolition of local legislation, 96.77% disclosed information about the situation of dispute resolution, 93.55% disclosed information about the improvement of law enforcement procedures, and 90.32% disclosed information about the improvement of major administrative decision-making mechanisms. Among the governments of larger cities, 95.92% published the report, 95.92% disclosed data on the adoption, revision and abolition of local legislation, 95.92% disclosed information about the deepening of the reform of the administrative approval system, 95.92% disclosed information about the strengthening of the reform of law enforcement system, 95.92% disclosed information about the improvement of law enforcement procedures, 95.92% disclosed information about dispute resolution, and 91.84% disclosed information about the improvement of major administrative decision-making mechanisms. To a certain extent, this shows that the above matters had been attached high importance in the daily work of construction of a law-based government.

v. The overall assessment results of some assessment targets were good

The assessment shows that some assessment targets had achieved high overall rates of compliance with the content requirements of all assessment indices. Among the departments under the State Council, those with the highest overall compliance rates were the Ministry of Agriculture and Rural Affairs (85.71%), the Ministry of Commerce (78.57%), the Ministry of Justice (75.00%) and the State Administration of Market Supervision (75.00%). Among the provincial-level governments, the Government of Beijing Municipality had achieved a compliance rate of 100%.

Those that achieved a compliance rate of over 90% included the governments of Jilin Province (96.67%), Hunan Province (93.33%), Shaanxi Province (93.33%), Hubei Province (90.00%) and Qinghai Province (90.00%). Among the governments of larger cities, those with the highest overall compliance rates were: the governments of Xi'an (93.33%), Handan (90.00%), Suzhou (90.00%), Hefei (90.00%) and Chengdu (90.00%). Among the county (city, or district)-level governments, those with the highest overall compliance rates were the governments of Haidian District of Beijing Municipality (95.83%), Taicang City of Jiangsu Province (95.83%), Huangpu District of Shanghai Municipality (95.83%), Longquanyi District of Chengdu City of Sichuan Province (95.83%), Huizhou District of Huangshan City of Anhui Province (91.67%), Hongkou District of Shanghai (91.67%), Pudong New Area of Shanghai Municipality (91.67%), Putuo District of Shanghai Municipality (91.67%), Jinshan District of Shanghai Municipality (91.67%), and Gongshu District of Hangzhou City of Zhejiang Province (91.67%). Obviously, the compliance rates of local governments were higher than those of departments under the State Council, and those of provincial-level governments were higher than those of governments of larger cities and county (city, or district)-level governments. Of course, a good annual report did not necessarily mean high achievements in the construction of a law-based government, but at least to a certain extent, it showed that the relevant governments and departments attached importance to this work and achieved some results in the construction of a law-based government that can be summarized and reported.

(2) Problems identified in the assessment

i. Many assessment targets failed to publish their annual reports in time

The assessment shows that many assessment targets failed to publish their annual reports in time. In this respect, provincial-level governments, governments of larger cities and county (city, or district)-level governments did better than departments under the State Council. We cannot rule out the possibility that the publication of the annual reports by some local governments and departments under the State Council was delayed by the Covid-19 pandemic.

17 departments under the State Council, 25 provincial-level governments, 37 governments of larger cities and 73 county (city, or district)-level governments published the annual report on the construction of a law-based government in the previous year before April 1, 2020.

ii. The reports of some assessment targets were released through multiple channels, thus unnecessarily increasing the difficulty of the public inquiry

The disunity or even chaos in the release channels of the annual report can increase the difficulty of public inquiry and affect the effect of information release. The annual report on the construction of a law-based government is a relatively new form of government information. For a long time, there had been no special column for the release of the report on government websites, which easily leads to multiple release channels and difficulty of the public inquiry. Only some assessment targets had set up a special column on their own portal websites or the websites of their judicial administrative departments for the release of the annual report.

In addition to the problem of the absence of a special column, many local governments had the problem of the lack of a unified platform for the release of the annual report. Some local governments published their annual reports on their own portal websites and some published them on the portal websites of their judicial administrative departments (judicial bureaus).

Moreover, the release channels were not fixed but selected randomly. For example, the State Administration of Radio, Film and Television released its 2019 and 2018 reports under the "Announcements" sub-column of the "News" column on its website, but released its 2017 report under the column of "annual reports on government information disclosure" on its website; the Government of Luoyang City of Henan Province published its reports in 2018 and 2019 under the "Announcements" column of the "Luoyang Information" column on its portal website, but the 2017 report under the "2018" sub-column of the "Municipal Government Documents" column on its portal website; the Government of Fuzhou City of Fujian Province released the 2019 report under the "Rongcheng News" sub-column of the "Current Work" column on its portal website, but the 2018 report under the "Special Plans" sub-column of "Plannings and Plans" column on its portal website; the Government of Hongkou District of Shanghai Municipality had set up a column of "Reports on Administration by Law" on its portal website. However, it released the report in 2019 not in this column, but in the "Government Self-construction" column on its portal website; and the Government of Putuo District of Shanghai Municipality had set up a column of "Reports on the Construction of a Law-based Government" on its portal website, which was divided into sub-columns by year from 2011 to 2019, but released the Report on the Construction of a Law-based Government in Putuo District in 2019 in the column of "Catalog of Voluntary Disclosure of Government Information" on its portal website.

iii. The titles of annual reports were not uniform

The annual reports on the construction of a law-based government should use a standardized and uniform name to enhance the seriousness and identifiability of the reports. The assessment shows that the titles of the annual reports adopted by assessment targets were not uniform. The *Implementation Outline for the Construction of a Law-based Government (2015–2020)* and the *Provisions on Supervisory Inspection of the Construction of a Law-based Government* and the *Implementation of Responsibilities* both use the expression of "annual report on the construction of a law-based government", but the titles used by various assessment targets this year were still not uniform. For example, the title of the report released by the General Administration of Customs was Report on Implementing the Implementation Outline for the Construction of a Law-based Government (2015–2020) in 2019; the title used by the Government of Shenzhen City of Guangdong Province was the Situation of the Work on the Construction of a Law-based Government in 2019; the Government of Huainan City of Anhui Province used the title Report on the Situation of Construction of a Law-based Government in 2019; the Government of Zibo City of Shandong

Province used the title Work Report on the Construction of a Law-based Government in 2019; the Government of Shushan District of Hefei City of Anhui Province used the title Report of People's Government of Shushan District on the Situation of Construction of a Law-based Government in 2019; the Government of Yuexiu District of Guangzhou City of Guangdong Province used the title Work Report of the People's Government of Yuexiu District of Guangzhou City on the Construction of a Law-based Government in 2019; and the Government of Boluo County of Huizhou City of Guangdong Province used the title Report of the People's Government of Boluo County on the Work of Construction of a Law-based Government and Administration by Law in 2019.

iv. The degree of detailedness of the reports released by different assessment targets varied greatly

In the preparation of the annual report, attention should be paid not to the length of the report, but to the comprehensive introduction of the situation of the construction of a law-based government in the previous year. The quality of the annual report should not be judged by the number of words in the report. However, if a report that summarizes and analyzes the construction of a law-based government in an administrative area or a department in the past year is too short, it means either that the government organ had not done much work in the field of construction of a law-based government the past year so that there is little to report on, or that the government organ attached no importance to the annual report and prepared it in a perfunctory way. Statistics show that, among the annual reports published by the four types of assessment targets, some are quite long, consisting of more than 10,000 Chinese characters, such as those of the governments of Shanghai Municipality, Jilin Province, Qingdao City of Shandong Province, Lhasa City of Xizang Autonomous Region, Nanchang City of Jiangxi Province, Daoli District of Harbin City of Heilongjiang Province, Hongkou District and Huangpu District of Shanghai Municipality, Baotou Rare Earth High-tech Zone of Inner Mongolia Autonomous Region, while some others are very short, consisting of only two or three thousand Chinese characters, or even fewer than two thousand Chinese characters. Among the reports published by various departments under the State Council, six consist of fewer than 3,000 Chinese characters, 21 consist of more than 3,000 Chinese characters but fewer than 5,000 Chinese characters, and six consist of more than 5,000 Chinese characters, with the longest one consisting of 6,793 Chinese characters, and the shortest one consisting of 2,240 Chinese characters; among the reports of provincial-level governments, one consists of fewer than 3,000 Chinese characters, 18 consist of more than 3,000 Chinese characters but fewer than 5,000 Chinese characters, nine consist of more than 5,000 Chinese characters but fewer than 8,000 Chinese characters, and three consist of more than 8,000 Chinese characters, with the longest one consisting of 12,127 Chinese characters and the shortest one consisting of only 2,606 Chinese characters; among the reports of governments of larger cities, two consist of fewer than 3,000 Chinese characters, 14 consist of more than 3,000 Chinese characters but fewer than 5,000 Chinese characters, 20 consist of more than 5,000 Chinese characters but fewer than 8,000 Chinese characters, and 11 consist of more than 8,000 Chinese characters, with the longest one consisting of 14,741 Chinese characters, and the shortest one consisting of 2,292 Chinese characters; and among the county (city, or district)-level governments, five consist of fewer than 3,000 Chinese characters, 34 consist of more than 3,000 Chinese characters but fewer than 5,000 Chinese characters, 35 consist of more than 5,000 Chinese characters but fewer than 8,000 Chinese characters, and nine consist of more than 8,000 Chinese characters, with the longest of consisting of 14,021 Chinese characters and the shortest one consisting of 2,276 Chinese characters.

v. The disclosure rates of some contents in the report were low

The assessment shows that the rate of disclosure of some data among the annual reports of assessment targets was not high. Among them, the reports of departments under the State Council contain more contents with a low rate of information disclosure, and the reports of government departments at various levels generally disclose little information about persons in charge of the government organ appearing in court to respond to lawsuits and the management of normative documents. As far as the reports of the departments under the State Council are concerned, the contents with low information disclosure rates included: the persons in charge of government organs appearing in court to respond to lawsuits (5.88%), data of acceptance and conclusion of administrative reconsideration cases (23.53%), administrative litigation data (23.53%), public participation in major administrative decision-making (38.24%), construction of normative document management mechanism (41.18%), legality review of major administrative decisions (50.00%), problems existing in the construction of a law-based government in the previous year (52.94%), and implementation of the responsibility system of a law-based government (58.82%). Among the reports of provincial-level governments, only 16 (or 51.61% of the total) disclosed information about the construction of the normative document management mechanism in 2019, and only eight (or 25.81% of the total) disclosed information about the appearance of the persons in charge of administrative organs in court to respond to lawsuits; among the reports of governments of larger cities, only 23 (or 46.94% of the total) disclosed information about the construction of normative document management mechanism in 2019 and only 25 (or 51.02% of the total) disclosed information about the appearance of the persons in charge of administrative organs in court to respond to lawsuits; among the reports of county (city, or district)-level governments, only 44 (or 36.67% of the total) disclosed the data of administrative litigation in 2019, and only 45 (or 37.50% of the total) disclosed information about the appearance of persons in charge of administrative organs in court to respond to lawsuits in 2019.

Moreover, the annual reports of many assessment targets lacked a detailed description of the problems existing in the previous year's work and the next year's work plan. Summarizing the problems existing in the previous year's work and analyzing their causes will help governments at various levels identify the experiences gained and lessons learned in the process of building a law-based government, and then determine the work priorities of the next year, and also provide some reference for public supervision over the construction of a law-based government. However, the assessment shows that some assessment targets gave no detailed description, but only a vague and simple description, of the problems existing in the previous year's work and the plan for the next year. Some even failed to list the problems existing in the work of the previous year or the plan for the work of the next year in the report. The assessment shows that only 20 departments under the State Council, 25 provincial-level governments, 39 governments of larger cities and 69 county (city, or district)-level governments analyzed and summarized the problems existing in the previous year's work in their annual reports on the construction of a law-based government and even their reports had the problems of being too vague and brief and not targeted. As for the next year's work plan, although 35 departments under the State Council, 26 provincial-level governments, 45 governments of larger cities and 76 county (city, or district)-level governments provided an explanation of their work plans for the next year in the annual report on the construction of a law-based government, the descriptions given by many of them were too general and not targeted enough.

vi. There were repetitive or similar contents in the reports of different years or in different parts of the same report

In the annual report, which is an annual summary of the work of construction of a law-based government, it is normal that the descriptions of the annual work of different years are similar and only data are replaced. This is understandable and even worth encouraging, because only by continuously disclosing the progress and data in some aspects of the work can an effective vertical comparison be made. However, the analysis of the existing problems in the work and the description of the next year's work plan should reflect the characteristics of the year and the department, and should not be repetitive or similar in large quantities. The assessment shows that, in the annual reports of some assessment targets, the expressions used in the description of problems existing in the current year were similar to those used in the work plan for the next year.

vii. The publishing institutions of annual reports were not uniform

Similar to the assessment results of last year, the publishing institutions of local governments' annual reports were not uniform. Among the provincial-level governments, 12 published the report in the name of local governments, five published the report in the name of the general office of the government, ten published the report in the name of their judicial administration departments (judicial bureaus), and four did not indicate the publishing institution; among the governments of larger cities, 16 published the report in the name of the municipal government, ten published it in the name of the general office (office) of the government, 18 published it in the name of the judicial bureau (including one in the name of an internal organ of the judicial bureau), one in the name of the general office of the municipal Party committee, one in the name of the office of the leading group for governing the city by law of the municipal Party committee, and one did indicate the publishing organ; and among the county (city, or district)-level governments, nine published the report in the name of county (city, or district)-level governments, 26 published it in the name of the offices of the government, 28 published it in the name of judicial bureau, one published it in the name of cyberspace affairs office of comprehensive Party affairs department, one published it in the name of government information disclosure office, one published it in the name of government network correspondent, and 17 did not indicate the publishing organ.

viii. The overall publication rates and assessment results of core indices of the reports of county (city, or district)-level governments were not satisfactory

The publication rates of the reports on the construction of a law-based government by county (city, or district)-level government still needed to be raised. The assessment shows that, in 2019, 48 of the 125 county (city, or district)-level governments covered by the assessment published the annual report on the construction of a law-based government in the previous year, with a publication rate of 38.40%; in 2020, 83 of the 120 county (city, or district)-level governments covered by the assessment published the annual report on the construction of a law-based government in the previous year, with a disclosure rate of 69.17%. Although the rate was greatly improved compared with 2019, there were still 37 assessment targets that did not publish the annual report in 2020.

The assessment shows that the overall assessment results of the core indices of counties (cities, districts)-level governments were not satisfactory, and the proportion of assessment targets that meet the requirements of indices was relatively low. The indices with the highest compliance rates were the publication of the report (69.17%), improvement of law enforcement procedures (65.83%), planning for the next year (63.33%), disputes resolution (62.50%), and construction of a mechanism for major administrative decision-making (61.67%). The index with the lowest compliance rate was the setup of a special column on the portal website, which was only 13.33%. This shows that the level of disclosure of information about the construction of a law-based government by county (city, or district)-level governments still needed to be improved.

11. Disclosure of normative documents

Strengthening the formulation, supervision and management of administrative normative documents, and curbing the publication of "weird" documents is an important measure to fully implement Xi Jinping Thought on Socialism with Chinese Characteristics for a the New Era and the requirements of the 19th National Congress of the Communist Party of China on "deepening the practice of law-based governance", as well as an important starting point for implementing the arrangements and requirements of the CPC Central Committee and the State Council for promoting administration by law and building a law-based government.

In this year's assessment, the Project Team observed the situation of disclosure of information about the review and recordation of normative documents and the labeling of validity of normative documents. Observation of the disclosure of information about the review of normative documents covered the recent three years starting from 2020. The objects of assessment were the portal websites of 49 departments under the State Council, 31 provincial-level governments, 49 governments of larger cities, and 120 county (city, or district)-level governments or the websites of the legal departments under them.

(1) Bright spots found in the assessment

i. The disclosure of the results of the review of government normative documents was good

The Notice of the General Office of the State Council on Strengthening the Development and Supervisory Administration of Administrative Regulatory Documents points out that the development and issuance of administrative regulatory documents is an important way for administrative organs to perform their functions in accordance with the law and, as such, directly affects the vital interests of the people and the image of the government. The assessment shows that 31 departments under the State Council, 28 provincial-level governments, 45 governments of larger cities, and 92 county (city, or district)-level governments disclosed information about the review of normative documents in recent three years on their portal websites or the website of their legal departments. Among them, 21 departments under the State Council, 16 provincial-level governments, 40 governments of larger cities and 47 county (city, or district)-level governments released information about the review of normative documents in 2020.

Compared with that in 2019, the situation of disclosure of information about the review of normative documents by departments under the State Council and governments of larger cities had improved: 21 disclosed information about the review of normative documents in 2020 as compared to 21 in 2019. Among the governments of larger cities, 40 disclosed information about the review of normative documents in 2020, as compared to 28 in 2019.

ii. Most assessment targets labeled the validity of normative documents

The assessment shows that 18 departments under the State Council, 19 provincial-level governments, 38 governments of larger cities and 61 county (city, or district)-level governments labeled the validity of the normative documents they published on their portal websites in 2020. Compared with those in 2019, the number of assessment targets that labeled the validity of normative documents had increased by six departments under the State Council, five provincial-level governments, 12 governments of larger cities and 11 county (city, or district)-level governments in 2020.

iii. Some assessment targets disclosed information about the recordation and review of normative documents

The *Notice of the General Office of the State Council on Strengthening the Development and Supervisory Administration of Administrative Regulatory Documents* requires the strengthening of supervision over the recordation of normative documents: the system for the supervision over the recordation of administrative regulatory documents shall be bettered to achieve the recordation and review of each document and the correction of each error. Development agencies of normative documents shall submit the documents for recordation in time in accordance with the prescribed procedures and time limits and voluntarily accept supervision. The administrative regulatory documents developed by local people's governments at or below the provincial level shall be submitted to the people's government at the next higher level and the standing committee of the people's congress at the corresponding level for recordation; the administrative regulatory documents developed by a department of the local people's government shall be submitted to the people's government at the same level for recordation; and for an administrative regulatory document jointly developed by two or more departments of a local people's government, the leading department shall be responsible for the recordation. For departments under vertical management, the administrative regulatory documents developed by a subordinate department shall be submitted to the competent department at the next higher level for recordation with a copy made for the people's government at the same level in the place where the agency developing the documents operates.

The assessment shows that 14 provincial-level governments, 20 governments of larger cities and 11 county (city, or district)-level governments disclosed information about the recordation and review of normative documents in 2020. Of the 14 provincial-level governments, one filed the documents for recordation on an annual basis, five filed the documents for recordation on a quarterly basis and three filed the documents for recordation on a monthly basis. Of the 20 governments of larger cities, ten filed the documents for recordation on a quarterly basis and three filed the documents for recordation on a monthly basis. Of the 11 county (city, or district)-level governments, one filed the documents for recordation on an annual basis, two filed the documents for recordation on a semi-annual basis, and five filed the documents for recordation on a quarterly basis.

iv. Most assessment targets issued normative documents in a concentrated manner

Releasing normative documents in a concentrated and unified manner is conducive to strengthening the management of normative document development and issuance procedures, improving the relevant work mechanisms and workflows, and ensuring that the development and issuance of normative documents is carried out in a standardized and orderly manner. The assessment shows that 30 provincial-level governments, 49 governments of larger cities and 120 county (city, or district)-level governments issued normative documents on their portal websites in a concentrated and unified manner.

(2) Problems identified in the assessment

i. Some assessment targets did not disclose information about the review of normative documents

18 departments under the State Council, three provincial-level governments, four governments of larger cities and 28 county (city, or district)-level governments did not disclose the results of the review of normative documents in recent three years on their portal websites or the websites of their legal departments. The disclosure of the information by provincial-level governments was not optimistic: only 16 of them disclosed the information about the review of normative documents in 2020, as compared to 21 in 2019.

ii. Some assessment targets did not label the validity of normative documents

Administrative normative documents are an important basis on which administrative organs enforce the law. Whether an administrative normative document is valid or not concerns the law-based administration of the government and the legitimate rights and interests of the public. Labeling the validity of normative documents not only helps the public to accurately find the basis for their actions but also is an important means to strengthen the management of normative documents of government organs. The assessment shows that 29 departments under the State Council, 12 provincial-level governments, 11 governments of larger cities and 31 county (city, or district)-level governments did not label the validity of normative documents.

Moreover, some assessment targets only labeled the validity of some, but not all, normative documents, which is not conducive to the standardized development and issuance of normative documents and is detrimental to the credibility and executive capability of the government. The assessment shows that four provincial-level governments, ten governments of larger cities and 26 county (city, or district)-level governments labeled the validity of only some normative documents.

iii. Most assessment targets did not release information about the recordation and review of normative documents

The *Notice of the General Office of the State Council on Strengthening the Formulation, Supervision and Management of Administrative Normative Documents* requires government organs responsible for the recordation of normative documents to strengthen the collaboration and cooperation with their counterparts in Party committees and people's congresses and establish a connection and interaction mechanism for the recordation and review of normative documents, comprehensively implement the legality review mechanism for normative documents, so as to prevent the introduction of illegal documents at the source and promote standardized, fair and civilized law enforcement by administrative organs. The legality and validity of normative documents has a direct impact on the law-based administration by the government and the legitimate rights and interests of the public.

The assessment shows that 17 provincial-level governments, 29 governments of larger cities and 106 county (city, or district)-level governments did not disclose information about the recordation and examination of normative documents in 2020.

12. Information disclosure in the field of local government debt

The *Measures for the Disclosure of Local Government Debt Information* (for Trial Implementation), issued by the Ministry of Finance on December 20, 2018 (hereinafter referred to as the *Measures*) (FB [2018] No. 209), provide in Article 4 that information about the ceilings, balances, use arrangement and repayment of principal of and payment of interest on local government debts within the scope of disclosure of information about budgets and final accounts shall be disclosed on the portal websites of local governments and those of their financial departments. If the financial department of a local government has not set up a portal website, a special column should be set up on the portal website of the local government at the corresponding level to disclose the information. Meanwhile, Article 5 of the *Measures* provides that local financial departments at or above the county level should disclose information such as the ceiling, balance, use arrangement and repayment of principal of and payment of interest on local government debts along with budget and final accounts. The *Measures,* by further standardizing the management of local government debt, are conducive to enhancing the transparency of local government debts.

In 2020, the Project Team assessed the disclosure of government debt information in 2019 by 31 provincial-level governments, 49 governments of larger cities, and 120 county (city, or district)-level governments on their portal websites and those of their financial departments. The assessment mainly covered the following issues: (a) whether all kinds of debt information were disclosed in a concentrated way; (b) whether information about the ceilings and balances of the local government debts of the previous year (2019) in the region, at the corresponding level, and in affiliated regions had been disclosed together with the final account of the previous year (2019); (c) whether information about the amounts of issuance of local government bonds and repayment of principals and payment of interests thereof in the previous year (2019) had been disclosed together with the final account of the previous year (2019); and (d) whether information about the arrangements for the use of local government bond funds had been disclosed together with the final account of the previous year (2019).

(1) Bright spots found in the assessment

i. Some assessment targets had set up a special column on their websites to disclose information about government debts

The assessment shows that 11 provincial-level governments, 11 governments of larger cities, 26 county (city, or district)-level governments had set up a special column on their portal websites or the websites of their financial departments to disclose information about government debt, bond issuance, bond disclosure documents. They included the governments of Anhui Province, Fushun City of Liaoning Province, Suzhou City of Jiangsu Province, and Jinzhai County of Lu'an City of Anhui Province.

ii. The situation of centralized disclosure of government debt information by some assessment targets was good

The assessment shows that all 196 assessment targets had disclosed government debt information in a concentrated manner or together with the final accounts in 2019, so as to facilitate public access. With respect to the data of issuance and final accounts of repayment of principal of and payment of interest on government bonds, some assessment targets, such as the governments of Beijing Municipality, Shanghai Municipality, Nanjing City of Jiangsu Province, and Luyang District of Hefei City of Anhui Province, especially made tables of issuance of and repayment of principal of and payment of interest on government bonds for concentrated disclosure.

iii. The disclosure of information about the ceilings and final accounts of balances of government debts was good

The situation of disclosure, together with information about the final accounts, debt ceilings (including the total debt ceilings, general debt ceilings and special debt ceilings) and final accounts of debt balances (including the total debt balance, general debt balance and special debt balance) of local governments at the end of the previous year in their respective region, at their corresponding level and in their affiliated regions was good.

With regard to the disclosure of final accounts of debt ceilings, 28 provincial-level governments, 38 governments of larger cities and 96 county (city, or district)-level governments disclosed in a comprehensive and standardized way local government debt ceilings in their respective regions in 2019. 22 provincial-level governments and 37 governments of larger cities disclosed in a comprehensive and standardized way the debt ceilings of local governments at their corresponding level in 2019, and 19 provincial-level governments and 29 governments of larger cities also disclosed the debt ceilings of local governments in their affiliated regions in 2019 (among them, 11 provincial-level governments disclosed the information detailed down to those of the counties and districts under their jurisdictions).

With regard to the disclosure of final accounts of debt balances, 28 provincial-level governments, 40 governments of larger cities and 111 county (city, or district)-level governments disclosed in a comprehensive and standardized way the final accounts of local government debt balances in their respective regions in 2019; 24 provincial-level governments and 43 governments of larger cities disclosed in a comprehensive and standardized way the final accounts of local government debt balances at their corresponding level in 2019; and 20 provincial-level governments and 30 governments of larger cities also disclosed the final accounts of local government debt balances in their affiliated regions in 2019 (among them, 11 provincial-level governments disclosed the information detailed down to those of the counties and districts under their jurisdictions).

The disclosure, together with information about the final accounts, of information about the debt ceilings and final accounts of debt balances of local governments at various levels at the end of the previous year was satisfactory. The assessment shows that 31 provincial-level governments, 45 governments of larger cities and 113 county (city, or district)-level governments disclosed, together with their final accounts in 2019 (through the same link, in the same document, and on the same day), information about their debt ceilings and debt balances; one government of larger cities and two county (city, or district)-level governments only disclosed the information about the ceilings and balances of some of their debts together with their final accounts in 2019; and three governments of larger cities and two county (city, or district)-level governments disclosed their debt information, but not together with their final accounts in 2019.

iv. The situation of disclosure of information about final accounts of bond issuance by provincial-level governments was good

The situation of disclosure, together with final accounts, of information about final accounts of bond issuance by provincial-level governments at the end of the previous year in their respective region and at their corresponding level was good. The assessment shows that, among the 31 provincial-level governments that disclosed the final accounts of local government bond issuance in 2019, five disclosed the amount of debts, amount of revenue from government debts and income from on-lent debts, 23 disclosed in a comprehensive and standardized way information about the total amount of bonds issued, the final accounts of general bonds issued and the final accounts of special bonds issued; and among the 30 provincial-level governments that disclosed the final accounts of bond issuance at their corresponding level in 2019, four disclosed the amount of debts, amount of revenue from government debts and income from on-lent debts and 18 disclosed in a comprehensive and standardized way the total amount of bonds issued, the final accounts of general bonds issued and the final accounts of special bonds issued.

v. The disclosure of the final accounts of repayment of principals of local government debts and payment of interest thereon was satisfactory

The situation of disclosure, together with final accounts, of the final accounts of repayment of the principals of and payment of interest on government debts by local governments in their own region, at their corresponding level, and in their affiliated regions at the end of the previous year was good. The assessment shows that 30 provincial-level governments, 46 governments of larger cities, and 114 county (city, or district)-level governments disclosed the final accounts of repayment of the principals of government debts in their respective regions in 2019, and 30 provincial-level governments, 46 governments of larger cities, and 113 county (city, or district)-level governments disclosed the final accounts of payment of interest on local government debts in their respective regions in 2019. Among them, 20 provincial-level governments, 30 governments of larger cities and 80 county (city, or district)-level governments also fully disclosed the total amount of principal repayment, the amount of repayment of principals of general debts and the amount of repayment of principals of special debts in their respective regions, and 16 provincial-level governments, 24 governments of larger cities and 64 county (city, or district)-level governments fully disclosed the total amount of interest paid, the amount of interest paid on general debts and the amount of interest paid on special debts. 30 provincial-level governments and 48 and governments of larger cities disclosed the final accounts of the amount of repayment of principals of local government debts at the corresponding level in 2019 and 31 provincial-level governments and 49 governments of larger cities disclosed the final accounts of the amount of payment of interests on local governments debts at the corresponding level in 2019. Among them, 20 provincial-level governments and 28 governments of larger cities also fully disclosed the total amount of principal repayment, the amount of repayment of principals of general debts and the amount of repayment of principals of special debts in their respective regions, and 14 provincial-level governments and 23 governments of larger cities fully disclosed total amount of interest paid, the amount of interest paid on general debts and the amount of interest paid on special debts.

(2) Problems identified in the assessment

i. The disclosure of information about the arrangements for the use of funds raised from local government bonds needed to be improved

The assessment shows that public release, together with final accounts, of information about the arrangements for the use of funds raised from local government bonds by local governments in their respective regions, at their corresponding levels, and in their affiliated regions in the previous year needed to be improved. Only 13 provincial-level governments, 18 governments of larger cities and 81 county (city, or district)-level governments disclosed the final accounts of the arrangements for the use of funds raised from local government bonds in their respective regions in 2019. Among them, four provincial-level governments, six governments of larger cities and 13 county (city, or district)-level governments disclosed the information detailed down to only the direction of use, but not specific projects using the funds. Moreover, some of them did not distinguish between projects using funds raised from newly added bonds at their corresponding level and those using funds raised from newly added bonds in their affiliated regions.

Only 11 provincial-level governments and 19 governments of larger cities disclosed clear information about the final accounts of the arrangements for the use of funds raised from government bonds at their corresponding level in 2019. Among these, two provincial-level governments and six governments of larger cities disclosed the information detailed down only to the direction of use, but not specific projects using the funds.

ii. The statistics of government debts disclosed by some assessment targets were not standardized

Firstly, some assessment targets did not disclose the final accounts of the amounts of repayment of principals of local government debts and payment of interest thereon. We cannot rule out the possibility that some local governments had made no repayment of principals of local government debts or payment of interest thereon in the year. However, they did not make zero debt payment reports in their disclosed statistics, and the public could not know the specific situation, so they were considered as not having undisclosed the information. Secondly, some provincial-level governments disclosed only the general information about the amount of government debt income and the amount of government debts, without providing detailed statistical data of bond issuance; some others disclosed only the general information about final accounts of repayment of the principals of government debts and payment of interest thereon, without providing detailed statistical information thereof.

13. Information disclosure in the field of compulsory education

Standardizing the openness of grass-roots government affairs and strengthening and continuously raising the level of information disclosure in the field of education is of great significance to standardizing the openness of education affairs at the grassroots level, actively accepting social supervision, promoting education equity, protecting the legitimate rights and interests of the people, and modernizing the governance system and capacity in the field of education. This year, the Project Team carried out the assessment of the disclosure of information about compulsory education by 120 county (city, or district)-level governments according to the requirements of the *Implementation Opinions of the General Office of the Ministry of Education on Comprehensively Promoting the Openness of Government Affairs*, the *Guideline Standards on the Openness of Grassroots Government Affairs in the Field of Compulsory Education* and other related documents.

The assessment in 2020 covered such matters as local compulsory education enrollment policies, telephone hotlines for inquiry about compulsory education enrollment policies, the scopes, conditions and results of compulsory education enrollment in 2020, and basic information about and the enrollment guides of schools of compulsory education. It mainly examined the disclosure of relevant information on the portal websites of county (city, or district)-level governments, the websites of the education administrative departments or the competent departments of entrance examination at the corresponding level, and the websites of the education administrative departments at the next higher level.

(1) Bright spots found in the assessment

i. The disclosure of information about enrollment policies of schools of compulsory education was satisfactory

The assessment shows that 93 county (city, or district)-level governments disclosed the local enrollment work documents and enrollment implementation plans of schools of compulsory education in 2020, accounting for 77.50% of the total. Among them, 91 disclosed enrollment policies of both primary schools and junior high schools; 81 published telephone hotlines for inquiries about local compulsory education enrollment policies, accounting for 67.50% of the total. The governments of Shunde District and Nanhai District of Foshan City of Guangdong Province also disclosed the enrollment policies of compulsory education in townships and towns.

With respect to enrollment scope, 96 county (city, or district)-level governments (or 80.00% of the total) disclosed the enrollment scopes of primary schools. Among them, 86 disclosed the enrollment scope of each school in 2020; 101 county (city, or district)-level governments (or 84.17% of the total) disclosed the enrollment scope of junior high schools, among which 87 disclosed the enrollment scope of each school in 2020. With respect to enrollment conditions, 98 county (city, or district)-level governments (or 81.67% of the total) disclosed the school admission requirements for ordinary students and those for children living with their migrant working parents.

ii. Some assessment targets had set up well-designed columns on their portal websites to disclose compulsory education information

The assessment shows that some counties (cities, districts)-level governments had set up a well-designed compulsory education information disclosure column or section on their portal websites to release the relevant information in an orderly manner. For example, the Government of Chancheng District of Foshan City of Guangdong Province had set up the section "Primary School Enrollment in Chancheng District in 2020" on its portal website. The section consists of two columns: "Public Primary Schools and Junior High Schools" and "Private Primary Schools and Junior High Schools" to disclose in a concentrated manner information about compulsory education policies, application guides, enrollment locations, arrangements for school enrollment quota, etc. and provide the links to the enrollment registration system and the online consultation system. The Government of Luohu District of Shenzhen City of Guangdong Province had set up on its portal website the "Education and Training" column, which was divided into the sub-columns of "Preschool Education" and "Primary and Secondary Education" to disclose in a concentrated manner such information as enrollment policy of primary and secondary schools, questions and answers about enrollment and basic information of each school.

iii. Some school enrolment service platforms provided all kinds of information about compulsory education in a unified way

Building a school enrollment service platform by a higher-level government to provide information about compulsory education and school application entrance of various counties (cities, districts) within an administrative region is conducive to facilitating the inquiry by students and parents and realizing efficient and convenient school enrollment. The assessment shows that some county (city, or district)-level governments disclosed enrollment information of schools of compulsory education, introductions to schools of compulsory education, and online application channels through the relevant compulsory education enrollment service platforms built by higher-level governments. For example, on the Beijing Compulsory Education Enrollment Service Platform, the "Relevant Policies" column was set up to disclose in a concentrated way the enrollment policy documents of schools of compulsory education in each district, and the "Start Application Now" column was set up to provide such information as the application entrances of schools of compulsory education, the relevant policies on compulsory education, introductions to primary and junior high schools, and other information in each district of Beijing. The Compulsory Education Enrollment System of Shanghai Municipality consists of two columns: "School Enrollment Policies of Shanghai Municipality" and "School Enrollment Policies of Various Districts in Shanghai Municipality", which disclose in a concentrated way compulsory education enrollment policies, service website links, service telephone hotlines and contact addresses of various districts in Shanghai, and provide application channels and application inquiry channels to schools of compulsory education. On the Compulsory Education Enrollment Service Platform of Guiyang City of Guizhou Province, the "Municipal Policies" column discloses in a concentrated way the results of the allocation of enrollment quotas by a lottery of some schools in the city in 2020 and the enrollment policies in 2020, the "District-level Policies" column discloses in a concentrated way the enrollment policies of various counties and districts in the city in 2020, and the "School Introductions" column is divided into two sub-columns of "Introductions to Public Schools" and "Enrollment Guides of Private Schools", which disclose in a concentrated way such information as the planned enrollment number, number of classes, boarding type, addresses, leaders and enrollment consultation telephone hotlines of schools in each district.

iv. Some assessment targets adopted vivid forms of compulsory education information disclosure

The assessment shows that some local governments disclosed compulsory education information in the form of charts and videos to facilitate public understanding. For example, the Beijing Compulsory Education Enrollment Service Platform used flow charts and video demonstrations to vividly display the compulsory education enrollment process. Various district governments of Shanghai adopted the form of data sheets to disclose the basic information about primary schools and junior high schools, including school names, addresses, school scale and basic facilities, teachers, charging standards, and student dormitories, and used the combination of pictures and texts to explain the enrollment process of primary schools and junior high schools. The governments of Bobai County of Yulin City and Pingguo County of Baise City of Guangxi Zhuang Autonomous Region and Korla City of Xinjiang Uygur Autonomous Region used school district division maps to disclose information about the division of school districts in their respective areas.

v. Some assessment targets provided special school enrollment channels on their websites for children living with their migrant working parents

The assessment shows that some assessment targets had provided special channels on their portal websites and compulsory education platforms for the school enrollment of children living with their migrant working parents. For example, the portal website of the Government of Jiangbei District of Ningbo City of Zhejiang Province had set up a school application platform for children living with their migrant working parents; the compulsory education platform of Guiyang City established a special enrollment system for children who were not registered permanent residents in various counties and districts of the city; and the compulsory education enrollment service platform of Beijing Municipality provides an entrance channel for the review of the certification materials for the compulsory education of school-age children who are not registered permanent residents of the city.

(2) Problems identified in the assessment

i. The situation of disclosure of enrollment numbers in compulsory education enrollment plans was poor

The assessment shows that, among the 120 county (city, or district)-level governments, 82 did not disclose planned enrollment numbers of public primary schools in

2020, 11 disclosed only the number of classes in the enrollment plan of each public primary school in 2020, two disclosed only the total planned enrollment number of primary schools in 2020, and one disclosed only the planned enrollment numbers of some public primary schools, 77 did not disclose the planned enrollment numbers of public junior high schools in 2020, 11 disclosed only the number of classes in the enrollment plan of each public junior high school in 2020, one disclosed only the total planned enrollment number in junior high schools in 2020, and two disclosed only the planned enrollment numbers of some public junior high schools.

ii. The situation of disclosure of compulsory education enrollment results urgently needed to be improved

The assessment shows that, among the 120 county (city, or district)-level governments, 105 did not disclose the enrollment results of public primary schools in 2020 and 106 did not disclose the enrollment results of public junior high schools in 2020. Moreover, some county (city, or district)-level governments disclosed only the number of classes or the total number of students enrolled in 2020, but not the name lists of the students enrolled, and some assessment targets disclose only the information about the enrollment results of some categories of schools.

iii. The rate of disclosure of information about public schools of compulsory education was low

For the assessment of the basic information about and the enrollment guides of public schools of compulsory education in 2020, the Project Team randomly selected a public school (primary school or junior high school) in each county (city, or district) to examine its information disclosure. The assessment shows that, among the 120 randomly selected public schools, only 29 (or 24.17% of the total) fully disclosed their complete school profile (including the nature, location, scale, basic conditions, and contact information of the school); and only nine (or 7.50% of the total) disclosed their enrollment guides in 2020.

14. Policy Interpretation and Response to Public Concerns

Policy interpretation is one of the important components of government information disclosure as well as an important criterion to evaluate the transparency and openness of government affairs and the quality of government services. In 2019, the assessment of policy interpretation mainly covered issues such as the setup of policy interpretation columns on government websites, the release, the form and the content of policy interpretation, and the interpretation of policies by the principal persons in charge of policy-making organs. The Project Team adopted a stricter assessment standard for policy interpretations, which must be the interpretations by an administrative organ of its own policies. For the assessment of response to public concerns, the Project Team mainly observed the websites of departments under the State Council, governments of larger cities and county (city, or district)-level governments to see whether online interactive platforms had been set up and whether the feedback on public concern had been disclosed on websites.

(1) Bright spots found in the assessment

i. Interactive platforms were generally set up by assessment targets on their websites

A total of 98.00% of the assessment targets, including 46 departments under the State Council, 31 provincial-level governments, 49 governments of larger cities and 119 county (city, or district)-level governments had set up a special column on policy interpretation on their websites. Some assessment targets had not only set up the column but also divided it into sub-columns. For example, the governments of Anhui Province, Hefei City of Huainan City of Anhui Province, and Jinshan District of Shanghai Municipality had set up a sub-column under the policy interpretation column on their portal websites to disclose the interpretation of policies by the principal persons in charge of the policy-making organs. The Government of Guangdong Province had not only set up a policy interpretation column on its portal website but also divided it into sub-columns such as interpretations of national policies, interpretations of provincial policies and interpretations of policies of various prefecture-level cities to facilitate consultation by the public.

ii. The policy interpretations were relatively complete in terms of content elements

The assessment shows that 42 departments under the State Council, 30 provincial-level governments, 46 governments of larger cities and 64 county (city, or district)-level governments included the background and core content of the interpretation in their published policy interpretations. The contents of interpretations were relatively comprehensive, not just copying the original policy documents but giving concise and clear explanations for some of the core contents, thus making abstruse professional policy documents easy for the public to understand. Some policy interpretations published by the Government of Guangxi Zhuang Autonomous Region on its portal website not only are complete in content elements but also describe the overall situation of the opinions solicited on the policies and the adoption of the solicited opinions. The governments of Hangzhou City of Zhejiang Province, Zhengzhou City of Henan Province and Yuyao City of Zhejiang Province not only disclosed the contents of policy interpretations but also included the names of interpreters of policies and other relevant information in the interpretations.

iii. The forms of interpretation were diversified

The assessment shows that many assessment targets adopted not only the traditional policy interpretation methods such as text interpretation, graphic interpretation, video interpretation, etc. but also non-traditional methods such as H5 interpretation, cartoon interpretation, etc., thus making policy interpretation more readable and interesting to the public. For example, the Government of Hunan Province adopted diversified methods of interpretation and created a special webpage for policy interpretation; the governments of Xicheng District of Beijing Municipality, Boluo County of Huizhou City of Guangdong Province and Xi'an City of Shaanxi Province used cartoons to interpret their policies.

The assessment shows that, in addition to text interpretation, multiple policy interpretation methods were adopted by 36 departments under the State Council, 29 provincial-level governments, 39 governments of larger cities and 88 county (city, or district)-level governments. Among them, the number of county (city, or district)-level governments that used multiple methods to interpret policies increased by nearly 20 as compared with that in 2019, indicating a major raise in the level of interpretation.

iv. The positioning of the content under the policy interpretation column on government websites was basically accurate

The assessment shows that the policy interpretation column on the portal websites of 34 departments under the State Council, 26 provincial-level governments, 41 governments of larger cities and 101 county (city, or district)-level governments contained only policy interpretation information and no irrelevant information, indicating that the information positioning of the column was accurate. Accurate placement of policy interpretation information provides correct guidance to the public and facilitates their access to policy interpretation information.

(2) Problems identified in the assessment

i. There was still no linkage between policies and their interpretations disclosed by many assessment targets

In order to solve the problem of inconvenience in inquiry caused by the release of policies and their interpretations in different locations, it is necessary to establish a mutual linkage between policies and their interpretations. The assessment shows that, among departments under the State Council, seven did not establish linkages between policies and their interpretations and three established linkages only between some policies and their interpretations. Four governments of larger cities established linkages only between some policies and their interpretations, and 12 county (city, or district)-level governments did not establish any linkage between policies and their interpretations.

ii. The synchronization between policy interpretation and policy release was poor

The synchronization between policy interpretation and policy release helps the public to fully understand the background and content of policies through interpretation in a timely way after their release. The assessment shows that 26 departments under the State Councils, 22 provincial-level governments, 28 governments of larger cities, and 53 county (district, or city)-level governments did not synchronize or only partially synchronized policy interpretation and policy release. Some assessment targets did not indicate the date of policy interpretation and policy release and, as a result, we were unable to judge whether they synchronized policy interpretation and policy release.

iii. The interpretation of policies by principal persons in charge of policy-making organs was not satisfactory

The interpretation of policies by the principal persons in charge of policy-making organs improves the authority of policy interpretations and is more conducive to the implementation of policies. However, the assessment shows that seven departments under the State Council, 25 provincial-level governments, 43 governments of larger cities and 107 county (district, city)-level governments did not release policy interpretations by the principal persons in charge of policy-making organs, indicating that provincial-level governments, governments of larger cities and county (city, or district)-level governments still needed to strengthen the work of policy interpretation by principal persons in charge of policy-making organs.

iv. Many assessment targets did not classify the contents in the policy interpretation column on their websites

Although many departments had set up a policy interpretation column on their portal websites, they did not set up sub-columns under the column to classify policy interpretations, but put all the policy interpretations together, which was not inconvenient for readers to find a particular policy interpretation. The assessment shows that 37 departments under the State Council, seven provincial-level governments, 21 governments of larger cities and 76 county (city, or district)-level governments did set up sub-columns under the policy interpretation column on their own portal websites.

v. It was not convenient to view feedback on public opinions on the websites of some assessment targets

Disclosing information about the feedback on opinions and suggestions put forward by the public through website interaction is conducive to responding to and guiding people with the same demands in a timely manner and avoiding repetitive consultation and complaints. The assessment shows that, among the departments under the State Council, two did not set up interactive platforms and four did not disclose feedback on public opinions and suggestions on their interactive platforms. On the portal websites of five counties (cities, or districts)-level governments, login was required in order to view feedback on public opinions.

15. Disclosure of government information upon application

To implement the spirit of the instructions of the CPC Central Committee and the State Council on comprehensively promoting the openness of government affairs and actively respond to the people's demand for the disclosure of government information, the revised *Regulations* have improved the system, mechanism and procedure of disclosure of government information upon application. From June 6 to October 23, 2020, the Project Team assessed the disclosure of government information upon application by 120 county (city, or district)-level governments by submitting to them applications for the disclosure of information about "the actual amount of investment in buildings reconstruction projects in the district (county, or city) in 2019" either electronically or by registered mail. In electronic application, priority was given to the platform of information disclosure upon application on the portal websites of the assessment targets, followed by the e-mails published in government information disclosure guides. In the absence of electronic application channels or if the electronic application channels were not working, applications were made by registered mail. The assessment was focused on whether the government information disclosure guide (hereinafter referred to as the guide) was updated in a timely manner, whether the application channels were unblocked, and whether replies to applications for government information disclosure were standardized.

(1) Bright spots found in the assessment

i. Some assessment targets had published and updated the guide

The revised *Regulations* have improved the procedures for disclosure of government information upon application, and clarified such matters as the submission, supplementation and correction of applications, standardized forms of reply, and procedures for soliciting public opinions, so as to effectively guarantee the people's access to government information in accordance with law. The assessment shows that, among all the assessment targets, 117 disclosed the guide, 81 indicated the date or version of the guide, and 99 provided the name, address, office hours, contact telephone number and other information about their information disclosure departments.

First, updating the time limit of replies to applications for government information disclosure. Article 33 of the revised *Regulations* stipulates that "if an administrative organ cannot reply to an application for information disclosure on the spot, it shall reply within 20 working days from the date of receipt of the application; and an extension of the time limit as required shall be allowed with the approval of the head of the government information disclosure office and by notice to the applicant, and the extension may not exceed 20 working days." The assessment shows that 89 assessment targets did not update the time limit for the reply to an application for government information disclosure in the guide in accordance with the revised *Regulations*.

Second, updating the procedures for the supplementation and correction of applications. Article 30 of the revised *Regulations* stipulates that "Where an application for public disclosure of government information contains any ambiguous content, the administrative agency shall give guidance and explanation and notify the applicant of supplementation and correction at one time within seven working days from the date of receipt of the application, stating the supplementation or corrections required and a reasonable time limit for such supplementation and correction. The time limit for a reply shall start from the date on which the administrative agency receives an application as supplemented and corrected. If an applicant fails to make supplementation and correction due without good reason, the applicant shall be deemed to have waived the application, and the administrative agency shall cease to process it." The assessment shows that 49 assessment targets changed the time limit for the notification of supplementation and correction of application in the guide to seven days in accordance with the revised *Regulations*.

Third, updating the rules on the handling of repetitive applications. The revised *Regulations* regulate the applicant's improper exercise of the right to apply and clarify the results. Article 36 Paragraph 6 of the *Regulations* stipulates that "if an administrative agency has replied to an application for public disclosure of the government information made by the applicant, and the applicant makes another application for public disclosure of the same government information, it shall inform the applicant of the denial of the repetitive application." The assessment shows that the statements on the handling of repetitive applications in the guides of 59 assessment targets were consistent with the provision of the revised Regulations.

Fourth, updating the provisions on the content of information disclosure. Article 22 of the *Regulations* before the revision provided that "In case the government information applied to be disclosed contains any content that should not be disclosed, but it is possible to distinguish such content from the government information, the administrative organ shall provide those allowed to be disclosed to the applicant", whereas Article 38 of the revised *Regulations* stipulates that "... if an administrative agency has to process or analyze the existing government information other than the information which can be subject to differential treatment as prescribed in the provisions of Article 37 of these *Regulations*, the administrative agency may withhold such government information." The assessment shows that 42 assessment targets updated this expression in the guide in accordance with the revised *Regulations*. 19 assessment targets stated in the guide that "an administrative organ may withhold the government information that needs to processed and analyzed by it", without the proviso "other than the information which can be subject to differential treatment as prescribed in the provisions of Article 37 of these *Regulations*".

Article 16 of the revised *Regulations* stipulates that "an administrative agency may withhold information on its internal matters, including personnel management, logistics management, and internal workflow. An administrative agency may withhold deliberative records, pre-decisional documents, consultation communications, applies for instructions and reports, and other pre-decisional information generated in the process of its performance of government administrative functions and information on administrative law enforcement files, unless otherwise required by any law, regulation or rule." The assessment shows that five assessment targets stated in the guide that procedural information and internal information of an administrative organ "may be withheld", which is in line with the legislative intent of the revised *Regulations*.

Article 15 of the revised *Regulations* stipulates that "for government information relating to a trade secret, individual privacy or the like the public disclosure of which would harm the lawful rights and interests of any third party, an administrative agency shall not disclose such government information to the public unless the third party consents to its public disclosure, or the administrative agency deems that its withholding would materially affect the public interest." The assessment shows that the guides of 31 assessment targets mentioned the consent of the third parties and the exercise of discretion in the disclosure of government information involving trade secrets, personal privacy and other information involving a trade secret, individual privacy or the like the public disclosure of which would harm the lawful rights and interests of any third party.

Fifth, updating the contents relating to the charge of fees. Article 42 Paragraph 1 of the revised *Regulations* stipulates that "An administrative agency shall provide government information upon application free of charge, provided that if an applicant applies for the public disclosure of government information in an amount or at a frequency obviously unreasonable, the administrative agency may charge fees for information processing." The assessment shows that 55 assessment targets had updated the relevant contents in the guide in accordance with the revised Regulations.

Sixth, updating the contents relating to complaints and reports on violations. Article 51 of the revised *Regulations* stipulates that "where a citizen, a legal person or any other organization believes that an administrative agency infringes on his or its lawful rights and interests in the government information disclosure work, the citizen, legal person or other organization may submit a complaint or report to the administrative agency at the next higher level or the government information disclosure work authority, or apply for administrative reconsideration or institute administrative litigation in accordance with law." If an applicant believes that an administrative organ infringes on his legitimate rights and interests, the administrative organ should inform the applicant to solve the problem through relevant channels. The assessment shows that 55 assessment targets updated the relevant contents in the guide according to the revised Regulations.

ii. All application channels were unblocked

Unblocked application channels are the basic conditions for applicants to obtain government information. In the assessment, the Project Team submitted applications for the disclosure of government information to 120 assessment targets through different channels. Among them, the applications to 85 assessment targets were made through the relevant platforms on their portal websites and the system showed that all submissions were successful; the applications to nine assessment targets were made by e-mail, and all the e-mails were sent successfully and their reception confirmed by the assessment targets; and the applications to 26 assessment targets were sent by registered mail, all of them received by the assessment targets. The application channels for government information disclosure of all 120 assessment targets were unblocked.

iii. The penetration rate of electronic application channels had increased

With the development of "Internet plus government affairs", the efficiency of openness of government affairs for the convenience of the people and enterprises has been continuously improved. The assessment shows that the submission of government information disclosure applications had become more convenient for the public. Among the 120 assessment targets, 94 (or 78.33% of the total) had enabled the public to submit government information disclosure applications by e-mail.

iv. Many assessment targets provided the SMS reminder function

The assessment shows that 22 of the 120 assessment targets, including the governments of Chancheng District of Foshan City, Yuexiu District of Guangzhou City, Luohu District of Shenzhen City, Xiuying District of Haikou City, Yuelu District of Changsha City, Jianggan District of Hangzhou City, Wuhua District of Kunming City, Lixia District of Jinan City and Xuhui District of Shanghai Municipality, sent short messages to applicants to inform them of the progress and results of the handling of their applications.

v. Most assessment targets replied applications within the legally prescribed time limit

Government information disclosure plays an active role in ensuring public access to government information in accordance with law and promoting the transformation of government functions. With the development of a law-based society, the desire of the public to safeguard their own rights and interests has increased and it has become a basic duty of administrative organs to actively respond to the public's demand for government information within the legally prescribed time limit. The assessment shows that, among the 120 assessment targets, 96 (or 80.00% of the total) responded to applications for information disclosure within the legally prescribed time limit, which was a significant improvement from the situation in previous years.

vi. Some assessment targets gave clear information about remedy channels in the notice to applicants

Article 51 of the revised *Regulations* stipulates that "where a citizen, a legal person or any other organization believes that an administrative agency infringes on his or its lawful rights and interests in the government information disclosure work, the citizen, legal person or other organization may submit a complaint or report to the administrative agency at the next higher level or the government information disclosure authority, or apply for administrative reconsideration or institute administrative litigation in accordance with law." Listing remedy channels in the notice to the applicant is conducive to effectively protecting the applicant's rights. The assessment shows that 43 of the 120 assessment targets listed the specific names of the reconsideration organs or courts with jurisdiction over disputes resulting from the applications, among which the governments of Lixia District of Jinan City and Rongcheng City of Weihai City of Shandong Province also provided the specific addresses under the names of the reconsideration organs and courts listed in the notice.

(2) Problems identified in the assessment

i. Some assessment targets did not update the guide in a comprehensive way

First, Article 38 of the revised *Regulations* provides for the disclosure of government information that needs to be "processed and analyzed". The assessment shows that the relevant contents in the guides of 26 assessment targets were incompatible with the legislative intent of the revised *Regulations* by stating that such information "shall be withheld", rather than "may be withheld" as provided for in the revised *Regulations*. And the guides of 74 assessment targets did not contain any information relating to the disclosure of information that needs to be "processed and analyzed".

Second, Article 16 of the revised *Regulations* provides for the disclosure of the procedural information and internal information of administrative organs. The assessment shows that the guides of 24 assessment targets described procedural information and internal information as information that "shall be withheld" rather than information that "may be withheld", thus contravening the intent of the legislation. And the guides of 91 assessment targets contained no information about the disclosure of procedural information and internal information.

Third, Article 15 of the revised *Regulations* provides for the consent of the third party and discretion of government organs in the disclosure of government information relating to a trade secret, individual privacy or the like the public disclosure of which would harm the lawful rights and interests of any third party. The assessment shows that the guides of 13 assessment targets described such information as "information that shall be withheld", which is inconsistent with the legislative intent of the revised *Regulations*. And the guides of 76 assessment targets did not contain any information about the disclosure of information involving a trade secret, personal privacy or the like.

Fourth, Article 42 Paragraph 1 of the revised *Regulations* stipulates that "an administrative agency shall provide government information upon application free of charge, provided that if an applicant applies for the public disclosure of government information in an amount or at a frequency obviously unreasonable, the administrative agency may charge fees for information processing."

The assessment shows that the guides of 12 assessment targets mentioned the charge of fees on the application for the disclosure of government information; the guides of 51 assessment targets did not mention the charge of the fees; and the guides of two assessment targets contained incomplete information about the charge of the fees, without mentioning that a fee can be charged only "if an applicant applies for the public disclosure of government information in an amount or at a frequency obviously unreasonable".

Fifth, Article 51 of the revised *Regulations* provides for complaints and reports of infringements on the lawful rights and interests in the government information disclosure work. The assessment shows that 40 assessment targets did not update the relevant information in their guides; nine assessment targets did not provide the relevant information in their guides; two assessment targets provided incomplete information, mentioning only "the administrative agency at the next higher level" or "the competent authority in charge of government information disclosure work", but not both, as the competent authorities for accepting a complaint or report of violations; 21 assessment targets still listed supervisory organs as the competent authorities for accepting a complaint or report of violations, without updating this content in accordance with the revised *Regulations*. Moreover, Article 30 of the revised *Regulations* clearly stipulates the number of times that supplementation and correction can be made to an application and the time limit for each supplementation and correction, but the assessment shows that 41 assessment targets did not specify the time limit for the notification of supplementation and correction.

ii. Some assessment targets did not specify in their guides the time limit for replying to an application for government information disclosure

Article 33 Paragraph 2 of the revised *Regulations* stipulates the time limit for replying to applications for government information disclosure that cannot be replied on the spot. Government organs should further clarify the time limit for replying to an application for information disclosure in their guides, so as to reduce disputes. The assessment shows that three of the 120 assessment targets did not provide information about the time limit for replying to an application for government information disclosure in their guides.

iii. The contact telephone numbers provided by some assessment targets in their guides were incorrect

Article 31 Paragraph 3 of the revised *Regulations* stipulates that "if the applicant makes an application for public disclosure of government information through an Internet channel or the fax of the organ responsible for government information work, the date of confirmation by both parties shall be the date of receipt of the application." Therefore, the contact numbers of the information disclosure organs published in the guides are particularly important. However, the assessment shows that the contact telephone numbers published in the guides of some assessment targets were incorrect, and it was impossible to reach the relevant assessment targets by these telephone numbers.

iv. The information about working institutions in the guides of some assessment targets was incomplete

The guide should provide the name, address, office hours, contact telephone number and other details about an information disclosure organ, so as to give full play to the role of government service in the people's production, life and economic and social activities. The assessment shows that the information about relevant organs listed in the guides of 14 assessment targets was incomplete, lacking such elements as office hours and contact telephone numbers.

v. The information about channels of application for government information disclosure released by some assessment targets was inaccurate

The guide is the guidance and basis for the public to apply for government information disclosure. In practice, however, the information about channels of application for government information disclosure published in the guides of some assessment targets was inaccurate. For example, a district people's government stated in its guide that online application could be made through the "Disclosure upon Application" column on its portal website. However, it only provided the application form for information disclosure, but did not allow the users to submit application forms in this column. The information about application channels published in the government information disclosure guide of another district government was inconsistent with that published in the special column of "information disclosure upon application" on its portal website. The application channels published in the government information disclosure guide included application by mail, application by fax and on-the-spot application, while the application channels published in the special column on its portal website included application by letter, application by fax, on-the-spot application, and application by e-mail. The application channel in the guide did not include the application on the web platform, but the government had actually set up a special column on its portal website to receive applications for government information disclosure.

vi. Some assessment targets set unreasonable obstacles to applications

First, some assessment targets examined the purpose of the application and the work unit of the applicant beyond the requirements of the revised *Regulations*. The revised *Regulations* have deleted the provision on the "special needs for production, living or scientific research" in the old *Regulations* as a precondition for citizens, legal persons or other organizations to apply for the disclosure of government information. However, the assessment shows that in the information disclosure application forms of many assessment targets, the purpose of the application for information disclosure had not been deleted, even remaining as a required field in the form. Some assessment targets repeatedly asked applicants about the specific purposes of the applications, thus setting obstacles to their lawful access to government information. A district government set "work unit" as a required field in the online application form on its portal website.

Second, the online application platforms of some assessment targets were defective in function, on which applications for government information disclosure could not be successfully submitted. The assessment shows that no application for government information disclosure could be successfully submitted on the platforms of six assessment targets. For example, the platform of a county government in Guyuan City of Ningxia Hui Autonomous Region always displayed the error message of "incorrect verification code" whenever an application was submitted, and the platform of a district government displayed a rapidly flashing verification code whenever a user tried to submit an application for government information disclosure, making it impossible for the application to be successfully submitted. On the portal website of a district government, a user needed to go through a very difficult registration process before he could submit an application for government information disclosure. Members of the Project Team had made many attempts to register on the platform, but all of them failed.

The online application platforms of some assessment targets did not cover all relevant government organs responsible for disclosing government information upon application. For example, the list of government organs responsible for disclosing government information upon application on the platform of Jinzhai County in Anhui Province did not include the county government, so it was impossible to submit applications to the county government on this platform.

Some online application platforms did not send the query codes to users who had submitted an application for government information disclosure, making it impossible for them to know whether a reply had been made to their applicants.

On some platforms, users received serial numbers and passwords for their applications after successful submission, but when they tried to check the status of their applications with the serial numbers and passwords, the platforms showed that there was no record of their applications. The online application platform of a county government did not have the ID card uploading function and a user had to send a scanned copy of his ID card by email after submitting his application on the platform.

Third, some assessment targets did not update the relevant contents in online forms or application forms in accordance with the revised *Regulations*. Article 42

Paragraph 1 of the revised *Regulations* stipulates that "An administrative agency shall provide government information upon application free of charge, provided that, if an applicant applies for the public disclosure of government information in an amount or at a frequency obviously unreasonable, the administrative agency may charge fees for information processing." The assessment shows that the online application forms issued by some grassroots governments in Shandong Province were not modified according to the revised Regulations and still contained the required choice of "fee reduction and exemption".

vii. Some assessment targets failed to reply to applications for information disclosure or to reply to applications within the prescribed time limit

Administrative organs should give replies to applications for government information disclosure in light of different circumstances. Government information disclosure is an important channel to protect the public's right to know and an effective means of supervising the exercise of government power and continuously improving government work. Failure to reply to applications for information disclosure or to reply within the prescribed time limit by government organs undermines the credibility of the government. During the assessment period, among the 120 assessment targets, nine failed to reply to applications within the prescribed time limit, ten did give reply to applications, and four replied to applications through their platforms, but did not specify the time of reply, so it was impossible for the Project Team to judge whether the replies were made within the prescribed time limit.

viii. The replies given by some assessment targets were not standardized in form

Replies to applications for government information disclosure are a kind of government behavior, which should be standardized and formal. The assessment shows that, among the 120 assessment targets, five replied to applications by telephone, eight did not sign their replies, three did not fix the official seal on the written replies, and 42 replied by unofficial email.

ix. The replies given by some assessment targets were not standardized in content

Articles 36 and 37 of the revised *Regulations* clearly provide for the replies to applications for government information disclosure given by administrative organs in different situations. Replies with standardized content include the followings: first, directly disclosing the information applied for and informing the applicants of remedy channels; second, where the information has already been disclosed by an administrative organ on its own initiative, informing the applicant of the specific location of or link to the disclosed information, and the remedy channels; and third, where the information applied for does not fall within the responsibility of the administrative organ to which the application is submitted to, does not fall within the scope of governmental information, cannot be processed and analyzed by the administrative organ to which the application is submitted or cannot be disclosed for other reasons, explaining the legal basis and reasons for non-disclosure, and informing the applicant of the remedy channels. Among them, the remedy channels should include the specific names of the reconsideration organ and the court with jurisdiction. The replies are the direct carrier of government information, and the lack of standardization of their contents directly affects the timeliness of government information disclosure.

The assessment shows that, among the 120 assessment targets, 11 did not explain the legal basis for the non-disclosure; four did not explain the reasons for the non-disclosure, 26 did not give the specific names of the reconsideration organ or the court with jurisdiction, four gave incorrect information about remedy channels, and 38 did not provide remedy channels.

x. Different assessment targets gave different replies to applications for the same information

The assessment shows that different assessment targets gave different replies to applications for the disclosure of the same government information: 50 directly disclosed the information; one refused to disclose the information; one replied that the information did not fall within the scope of governmental information; 31 replied that the information applied for did not fall within their responsibility of information disclosure; three replied that information cannot be processed; 24 replied that information did not exist, and ten did not reply to the application for the disclosure of the information.

4 Prospects

In 2020, China took a unique approach to and achieved remarkable results in coping with the Covid-19 pandemic, not only showing its comprehensive national strength and ability to deal with public health emergencies, but also further demonstrating the remarkable effect in disclosing government information and responding to social concerns in a timely and effective manner. It has been shown in practice that openness of government affairs helps to protect the vital interests of the people and is an important way to realize the modernization of the state governance system and capacity. The *Implementation Outline for Building a Law-based Society (2020–2025)* issued by the Central Committee of the Communist Party of China states that China will promote the disclosure of government information. Administrative normative documents involving the rights and obligations of citizens, legal persons or other organizations, administrative licensing decisions, administrative penalty decisions, administrative compulsion decisions, administrative expropriation decisions, etc., shall be disclosed in accordance with law. With respect to promoting multi-level and multi-field law-based governance, the *Outline* requires the implementation of the Sunshine Project of Village Affairs, the improvement of the system of openness of Party affairs, village affairs and financial affairs, the review of the list of disclosure of village affairs, and the promotion of the platform of supervision over the openness of village affairs. The *Notice by the General Office of the State Council of Issuing the Implementation Plan for Effectively Solving the Difficulties Facing the Elderly in the Use of Intelligent Technologies* puts forward new requirements for promoting the openness of government affairs for the benefit of all kinds of people in the era of Internet and mobile Internet and the *Measures for Developing Measures for the Public Disclosure of Information by Public Enterprises and Institutions*, issued by the General Office of the State Council, will further promote the information disclosure by public enterprises and institutions. In light of the successful experiences and lessons learnt in the open government work in 2020, government organs need to make further efforts in the following aspects of the work in the future.

Firstly, they should take the identification and satisfaction of the needs of the public as the starting point and the focus of their open government work. Since being user-oriented is the precondition of effectively carrying out open government work, government organs should judge the public need for openness of government affairs in light of the applications for government information disclosure, the use of government websites and new media open government platforms, the hotline consultation, and the government services by the public, so as to adjust the scope and optimize the methods of openness of government affairs in a targeted manner.

Secondly, government organs should promote in a comprehensive and deep-going way the integrated development of openness of government affairs, government administration and government services. They must get openness of government affairs out of the situation of being isolated from various other kinds of government work, deeply integrate it with government administration and government services, make it an organic part of administration and service, promote administration by openness, provide service by openness, and effectively carry out the work of openness of government affairs, the work of government administration and the work of government service.

Thirdly, they should adjust relevant measures to local conditions and to different groups of people, and effectively carry out the work of openness of government affairs to people at all levels. In many small and medium-sized cities and vast rural areas, the openness of government affairs on the Internet and mobile Internet was not satisfactory, and many people, especially the elderly, are not good at obtaining information through websites or various mobile micro-platforms. Therefore, administrative organs must make good use of traditional ways and platforms such as radio and television, grass-roots bulletin boards, etc. in the openness of government affairs and at the same time pay attention to guiding the people in the above-mentioned areas and the above-mentioned groups of people to gradually learn and try to accept the openness of government affairs by means of information technology.

Moreover, they should identify and strengthen the weak points in their work and improve the overall level of openness of government affairs. There are regulations on the openness of government affairs in various fields, but the situations of openness of government affairs in different areas and departments are different. Therefore, on the one hand, all government organs need to conduct self-examination to identify and shore up weak points in their work; on the other hand, higher-level administrative organs should refine the standards of openness, strengthen supervision and assessment, promote the standardization of openness of government affairs, and guide local government departments to implement the requirements of openness.

Finally, they should continue to intensify the openness of grass-roots government affairs. Effectively carrying out open government work at the grass-roots level is the foundation of meeting the practical needs of the people. We suggest that, on the basis of the standardization of the openness of grass-roots government affairs in recent years, administrative organs should continue to increase their efforts in guiding and promoting the openness of village and community affairs, so as to lay a solid foundation for the construction of a law-based society and a law-based China.

Deepening the Openness of Government Affairs and Building a Transparent Government in Hubei Province

The Government Affairs Administration Office of the Government of Hubei Province

In recent years, government organs at all levels in Hubei Province have conscientiously implemented a series of decisions and arrangements made by the CPC Central Committee, the State Council, the provincial Party committee and the Provincial Government, improved their political stance, emphasized the problem-oriented approach to deepening the openness of government affairs, disclosed government information in an all-round way, carried out full-node interpretation of government policies and response to public concerns, highlighted all-time fingertip communication, and provided government services at all levels, thereby making positive contributions to winning the people's total war of resistance against the Covid-19 pandemic, and effectively promoting the optimization of the environment, implementation of policies and projects, and the development of a transparent government.

1 Focusing on Institutional Innovation and Strengthening Organization and Leadership

In recent years, governments at all levels in Hubei Province have adhered to the spirit of a series of important speeches and instructions given by Party General Secretary Xi Jinping as the fundamental principle to be followed in open government work and faithfully implemented it in all links of the work, including theme planning, policy formulation, policy interpretation, response to public concerns and publicity and reporting, incorporated the openness of government affairs and government services into the overall work of pandemic prevention and control and optimization of the business environment, made overall plans, innovated mechanisms and advanced the work in a coordinated way.

The Government Affairs Administration Office of the Government of Hubei Province (✉)
Research Group of Government Transparency of Hubei Province, Wuhan, China
e-mail: 13693186775@163.com

H. Tian and Y. Lv (eds.), *Assessing Government Transparency in China (2021)*,
https://doi.org/10.1007/978-981-99-9734-3_2

1. Coordinating organization and leadership

After the outbreak of the Covid-19 pandemic, the Government of Hubei Province (hereinafter referred to as "the Provincial Government") set up the Leading Group for the Construction of a Digital Government with the governor as the head of the group and all deputy governors as the deputy heads, the Expert Advisory Committee on the Construction of a Digital Government, and the Leading Group for the Openness of Provincial Government Affairs. During the pandemic, the Provincial Pandemic Prevention and Control Headquarters set up a special publicity group to coordinate the public release of relevant information. The governor convened several executive meetings of the Provincial Government to study and make arrangements for the comprehensive implementation and interpretation of the *Regulations of the People's Republic of China on the Disclosure of Government Information* (hereinafter referred to as the *Regulations*), visited the Provincial Government portal website to carry out an investigation and provide guidance, and made specific demands on the construction of government websites. The governor and the executive vice governor heard reports and gave instructions on the work many times, expressing their approval of and support for the open government and the work of government websites. The Provincial Government established working bodies on the openness of government affairs, such as the Government Affairs Administration Office and five divisions under it, including the Government Service and Openness of Government Affairs Division of the office and a big data center, thereby exercising a comprehensive leadership over the reforms of "simplifying administrative procedures, decentralizing powers, combing decentralization with appropriate control, and optimizing services", the open government work and the government website work. The general office of the Provincial Government issued the *Notice on Further Clarifying the Functions of Competent Departments in Charge of the Open Government Work at the Municipal and Prefectural Level*, requiring the general offices of governments at all levels in the province to earnestly perform their duties as the competent departments in charge of government information disclosure and further rationalize the relevant working systems and mechanisms.

2. Highlighting the theme of openness

The Provincial Government has set up the columns of "Party General Secretary in Command", "Central Leading Group", "Central Steering Group", "Implementation" and "Progress in Cities and Prefectures" on its portal website to timely disclose the major decisions on and arrangements for the open government work made by the CPC Central Committee and the implementation measures adopted by the Provincial Government. Focusing on Party General Secretary Xi Jinping's timely and decisive decision on the strategy of pandemic prevention and control in Hubei Province and Wuhan, his scientific judgment and precise arrangement made during the inspection of the pandemic prevention and control work in Hubei Province, and his important instructions on coordinating pandemic prevention and control and economic and social development, as well as the spirit of the meetings of the Political Bureau of the CPC Central Committee, the Provincial Government organized a series of press conferences, including "the work of provincial Party committee and the Provincial Government of implementing Party General Secretary Xi Jinping's instructions and forcefully advancing the prevention and control of the pandemic", "Implementing the spirit of the important speech made by Party General Secretary Xi Jinping during the inspection of the pandemic prevention and control work in Hubei Province and securing the victory of the defense of Hubei Province and Wuhan against the pandemic", "advancing pandemic prevention and control and economic and social development in a coordinated way", and "effectively guaranteeing the people's livelihood and revitalizing economy after the pandemic", so as to guide the people in the whole province to consciously align their thoughts and actions with the spirit of Party General Secretary Xi Jinping's important speeches and the decisions and arrangements made by CPC Central Committee.

3. Strengthening professional training

In the past two years, the general office of the Provincial Government has held six special training courses on the openness of government affairs in the whole province. Focusing on the publicity and implementation of the *Regulations*, the construction of government information disclosure platforms, the standardization of the openness of grass-roots government affairs and major theoretical and practical issues of government transparency, it invited experts and scholars from various parts of China to Hubei Province to carry out thematic training and academic exchange, which were participated by more than 700 backbones staff members responsible for open government work and website work in relevant departments of the municipal and prefectural governments and various departments under the Provincial Governments.

The Information Office of the Provincial Government held the Training Course on the Practical Work of Press Release in 2020, which was attended by a total of 102 persons in charge of various departments under the Provincial Government and the publicity departments of the Party committees of various cities and prefectures. In addition to inviting well-known experts from all over the country to give lectures, practical drills were also organized to enhance the effectiveness of the training course. The office also helped the Party School of the Provincial Party Committee incorporate the press release work into its regular teaching plan, and set up a special training course on this subject with no less than four class hours for students in each regular training course.

4. Improving incentives and constraints

The General Office of the Provincial Government has incorporated the open government work into the theme education on "staying true to the Party's original aspiration and the founding mission" of the Provincial Party Committee and the of the inspection and rectification work of the Inspection Team of the Provincial Party Committee, the performance appraisal system of the Provincial Government and the Grand Inspection of Business Environment Construction. In view of the problems found in the inspection, it established a problem list and a responsibility list and carried out rectifications of the problems one by one. It also established and improved the performance evaluation and accountability system, carried out third-party assessments every year, organized mutual evaluation and mutual examination, and strengthened evaluation guidance to promote the implementation of the work through evaluation. In 2020, in light of the assessment results, the Provincial Government circulated notices to commend units that had made outstanding achievements in the open government work in the province and gave each of them a reward of RMB 500,000 Yuan, thus creating a working atmosphere in which the open government work teams perform their duties in a responsible, enthusiastic and diligent manner.

2 Focusing on Pandemic Prevention and Control and Handing in a Heroic Answer Sheet in the Great Test

Covid-19 is a major public health emergency with the fastest transmission rate, the widest scope of infection and the greatest difficulty to prevent and control since the founding of the People's Republic of China and Hubei Province was a "decisive battlefield" in the fight against the Covid-19. Under the strong leadership of the CPC Central Committee with Comrade Xi Jinping as the core, the Provincial Government thoroughly implemented the spirit of the 19th CPC National Congress and the second, third, fourth and fifth plenary sessions of the 19th CPC Central Committee as well as the spirit of Party General Secretary Xi Jinping's important speeches and instructions, overcame various difficulties, and forged ahead with hard work in the three tough battles against the pandemic, flood and poverty.

While carrying out the pandemic prevention and control work in a law-based, scientific and orderly manner, governments at various levels and departments under them in the province disclosed authoritative information about pandemic prevention and control in a law-based, accurate, timely and comprehensive manner, effectively responded to public concerns, built social consensus, and made an all-out effort to provide such services as public opinion guidance, policy implementation, answering questions and dispelling doubts, and online handling of government affairs for the pandemic prevention and control, thus handing in a heroic answer sheet in the great test by winning the double victories in pandemic prevention and control and economic and social development.

1. Quickly producing authoritative and comprehensive special columns on government websites to disclose information about, publicize, and report on the work of pandemic prevention and control in the province

In the special period, the relevant leaders of the General Office of the State Council took command at the frontline of the battle against the pandemic and put forward clear requirements for the construction and content release of the anti-pandemic section on the portal website of the Provincial government. On January 20, 2020, the Provincial Government created a special column entitled "Resolutely Winning the People's Total War of Resistance against the Covid-19 Pandemic", which contains a series of special topics that cover various levels and aspects of information disclosure, publicity and reporting work on pandemic prevention and control, including "This Is How Party General Secretary Commands the War against Covid-19 Pandemic", the Central Leading Group, the Central Steering Group, Implementation, Authoritative Circulars, Press Conferences, Resumption of Work and Production, Joint Prevention and Control, Situation of the Battles against Covid-19 in Various Cities and Prefectures, Heroes in the Fight against Covid-19, Response to Public Concerns, Quick Commentaries on the War against Covid-19, Popularization of the Scientific Knowledge of Pandemic Prevention and Control, Refuting Rumors with Scientific Knowledge, etc., which not only embody the centralized and unified leadership of the Central Government over the joint prevention and control of pandemic in the whole country but also show the actual work of the Provincial Party Committee and the Provincial Government in planning, commanding and implementing the fight against Covid-19 and the efforts made by ordinary citizens in the whole province in uniting as one to fight the pandemic. As such, it was deemed the most authoritative and comprehensive special information disclosure, publicity and reporting column on pandemic prevention and control in the whole province and even in the whole country. By the end of May 2020, with this special column as the basic platform of information disclosure, the Provincial Government released more than 480,000 pieces of authoritative information on the Chinese, English and French versions of its portal website, its client-sides, the official Weibo and WeChat accounts of its portal website, the Weibo and WeChat accounts of Hubei Authoritative Release and other platforms, integrated and produced 220 special issues on policies on pandemic prevention and control and their interpretations, with the number of visits increased by up to 50 times year-on-year during the period of the pandemic; more than 1,700 pieces of information in foreign languages were released, attracting IP visits from 167 countries and regions including the United States, Germany, Britain, France, Singapore, Canada, Australia, Japan and Italy; and the reading volumes of authoritative government information such as pandemic prevention and control notices issued by the Provincial Government and community pandemic prevention and control instruction manuals launched on the official WeChat platform of the Provincial Government all exceeded 100,000. At the same time, the Provincial Government handled a large number of applications for government information disclosure relating to pandemic prevention and control in an active and prudent manner in accordance with law, and so far had not lost any related lawsuit. Through these measures, the Provincial Government fully guaranteed the people's right to know, correctly guided public opinions, and comprehensively demonstrated at home and abroad its law-abiding, open, transparent and responsible attitude towards pandemic prevention and control, thus wining the understanding of and praise from people of all walks of life and providing important support for the effectively fight against the pandemic.

2. Holding press conferences to release complete information about pandemic prevention and control

The Provincial Government has made it clear that its portal website is the legal platform for the release of information about the press conferences held by the Provincial

Government, as well as the only platform in the whole network to make whole-process live broadcasts of press conferences in the form of picture, audio and video. By July 20, 2020, The Provincial Covid-19 Pandemic Prevention and Control Headquarters had held 123 press conferences on pandemic prevention and control work in succession with unprecedented high frequency, including 40 on the progress of and measures for pandemic prevention and control, 24 on response to public concerns, 19 on paired assistance from other provinces, 32 on policy interpretation, and 8 expert special sessions; more than 300 persons, including leaders of the Provincial Party Committee and the Provincial Government, heads of various municipal and prefectural governments and various departments under the Provincial Government, relevant experts, representatives of various fronts, etc., had been invited to participate in the press conferences, with unprecedented representativeness and authority; they answered more than 500 hot questions from reporters involving such issues as pandemic prevention and control, patient treatment, pandemic prevention and control materials, daily necessities, assistance from other parts of the country, the treatment of critical cases, pandemic prevention and control in various cities and prefectures, resumption of work and production, assistance to enterprises and stabilization of employment, restoration of normal medical order, guarantee for normal urban operations, agricultural production, long-term mechanism for pandemic prevention and control, and tackling of difficulties in poverty alleviation, with unprecedented coverage and depth.

The press conferences on the prevention and control of the Covid-19 pandemic in Hubei Province completely recorded the whole process from carrying out pandemic prevention and control and medical treatment to resuming work and production and restoring economic and social development in Hubei Province and in the city of Wuhan. Based on the content of each press conference, the portal website of the Provincial Government launched a number of new media products, which became important news and information sources for other media.

3. Accurately providing government services such as information about patient treatment channels, notification of the pandemic situation, and response to hot issues

During the pandemic, the portal website of the Provincial Government reviewed and integrated the pandemic prevention and control data in the whole province gathered by the unified information resource database of the intensive platform, and launched innovative online services for pandemic prevention and control in a timely manner in light of the changes in the pandemic situation and the most urgent concerns of the public.

Firstly, to help patients faced with difficulties in getting medical tests and treatment at the early stage of the pandemic, the portal website of the Provincial Government, in conjunction with the website of Wuhan Municipal Government, developed a WeChat applet to help users get the information of designated fever clinics and hospitals in time, and timely provide information about the number of beds available in hospitals, the epidemiological investigation of "four categories" of people,[1] and the admission of patents into "mobile cabin hospitals" and other designated hospitals.

Secondly, the Provincial Government developed "One-click Pandemic Prevention and Control Service in Hubei Province", which provides the public with a comprehensive platform for "checking policies, handling affairs, looking for government responses to public concerns, and identifying rumors", and releases in an authoritative, comprehensive and timely manner various kinds of information about pandemic prevention and control, such as pandemic clue reporting, health registration, online consultation and government directories.

Thirdly, through the Provincial Government service network and its online services APP "Ehuiban", the Provincial Government provided such authoritative information and services as health status reporting channels, gas service information and online shopping information for the convenience of the people.

4. Focusing on providing policy inquiry services relating to the resumption of work and production and economic and social revitalization in the later period of the fight against the pandemic

The Government Affairs Administration Office of the Provincial Government organized the development of the data service system of "Enquiry about Policies on the Resumption of Work and Production in Hubei Province" and upgraded the platform "Chuchu the Intelligent Assistant of Hubei Provincial Government (Pandemic Edition)". At the same time, it set up special columns on "Resumption of Work and Production", "Press Conferences" and "Gazettes" on mobile terminals such as WeChat and APP to make full use of intensive platform data and intelligent search function and dynamically provide inquiry about policies on resumption of work and production, such as those on recruitment, tax and fee reduction, financing loans, spring plowing, transportation and social security in all parts of the province.

At the end of April 2020, decisive results were achieved in the pandemic prevention and control in Hubei Province. Focusing on the new emphasis of work of the CPC and the Chinese Government, namely economic and social revitalization after the pandemic, the Provincial Government set up a special column "Winning the Double Victory in Pandemic Prevention and Control and Economic and Social Development" on its portal website, which highlights the two major contents of "relentlessly preventing the resurgence of the pandemic" and "accelerating post-pandemic development", releasing in a timely manner information about press conferences and the progress of resuming work and production and reopening of schools, and focusing on providing information about the marketing of agricultural products, winning the decisive battle of poverty alleviation, and major construction projects.

5. Taking "Popularization of Scientific Knowledge about the Fight against Covid-19 in Action" as the theme to build a health knowledge popularization matrix with wide coverage, great influence and strong professionalism

[1] The "four categories of people" refer to confirmed patients, suspected patients, fever patients who cannot rule out the possibility of infection, and close contacts of confirmed patients.

First, whole-process follow-up. The provincial health department closely followed the development of the development of the human knowledge and understanding of Covid-19 and carried out the popularization of health knowledge in light of the actual needs of pandemic prevention and control at each stage; timely launch a series of popular science works with texts and pictures; took the lead in the whole country in compiling and printing popular science brochures, posters and leaflets on the prevention and control of Covid-19 pandemic to help the public understand and scientifically prevent and control the pandemic situation and avoid panic; compiled and published a series of books such as *Guide to Popularization of Scientific Knowledge about Prevention and Control of Covid-19 Pandemic* and the *Handbook on the Four Measures for the Early Prevention and Control of Covid-19 Pandemic*, and designed and published posters and other graphic popular science works in support of the implementation of pandemic prevention and control measures; and produced a variety of audio and video products, one original animation, two H5, 74 short videos and 368 audios on the pandemic prevention and control knowledge, including the popular science video series Health Protection Tips and Psychological Adjustment for Different Groups of People During the Pandemic, made in cooperation with Shangshu Doctor Team. All these rich and lively forms of publicity have made the knowledge of scientific pandemic prevention and control popular among the people and enable it to be deeply rooted in the people's hearts.

The Provincial Government timely released psychological counseling service information and held prize-winning quizzes. In view of the pandemic-related psychological problems, it established a linkage mechanism with the School of Psychology of Central China Normal University, the College Psychological Counseling Alliance of the Provincial Department of Education, and the mental health centers of Hubei Province and Wuhan City to give full play to their professional advantages, and release and receive information about online psychological free counseling service; and carried out online question-answering activities such as prize-winning quizzes on popular science knowledge of Covid-19 to help people prevent and alleviate psychological difficulties caused by the pandemic and maintain mental health.

Second, entire-population attention. To support the implementation of pandemic prevention and control measures, the Provincial Government compiled and published such books as the *Guide to the Popularization of Scientific Knowledge about the Prevention and Control of Covid-19 Pandemic*, the *Handbook on Four Measures for the Early Prevention and Control of Covid-19 Pandemic*, and the *Guide to the Prevention and Control of Covid-19 Pandemic in Communities* and designed and published 134 series containing 635 graphic and text popular science works, including posters and illustrations, held the "Campaign against Covid-19: Popular Science and Public Interest Painting Exhibition", and selected a group of "Xiaolin Comics" with healing effect and displayed them in 16 mobile cabin hospitals and designated medical institutions free of charge.

Third, whole-platform push. After the outbreak of the pandemic, a special column on the Prevention and Control of the Covid-19 Pandemic was quickly launched on the portal website of the Provincial Health Commission. Divided into such sub-columns as information release, the dynamic situation of pandemic prevention and control, health science popularization, and first-line models, it releases information about pandemic prevention and control and patient treatment in high-frequency clusters. The Provincial Government gave full play to the role of the Health Media Publicity Alliance, and invited many high-level experts and leaders to interpret the important policies of pandemic prevention and control, medical treatment and prevention and control measures of the Provincial Pandemic Prevention and Control Headquarters in the form of authoritative interviews; recorded the TV series "Authoritative Release of Anti-pandemic Popular Science", of which the "Guide to the Popular Science relating to the Campaign against the Pandemic" and "Psychological Guide to the Fight against the Pandemic" were pushed to all media in Hubei TV Station, and all programs in the series were adopted by the platform "The Learning Power" (xuexi.cn); and launched we media Light Cavalry, and released nearly 6,000 pieces of information by "Healthy Hubei" accounts in WeChat, Aauto Quicker, Douyin and Toutiao. Nearly 300 original pieces of video, picture and text from the popular science program "Direct Train to the Battle Against the Covid-19 Pandemic in Hubei Province" were released on CCTV's media platform with 400 million hits, thus ensuring that the information is seen, easily understood and accepted by the public, effectively enhancing the interaction between the government and the public, and injecting a powerful "propellant" into the campaign against the Covid-19 pandemic in Hubei Province and in Wuhan.

6. Improving the coverage and influence of government information in different regions, on different platforms and among different groups of people in an all-round way

The Provincial Government has given full play to the role of the Provincial Government Affairs New Media Matrix Management Platform in monitoring the disclosure, linked release, and featured presentation of pandemic information. Especially, the following three principles were adhered to in the concrete work.

First, the principle of giving priority to mobile media. Government affairs new media, as an extension platform of government websites, releases information from the same source and according to the same standard and arrangements as that on government portal websites. During the pandemic, mobile government platforms were given priority in the release of government data disclosed on the portal website of the Provincial Government. However, this principle was not followed indiscriminately, but the Internet thinking and the rules of information transmission of different platforms were actively applied to produce new media products that can be widely disseminated on the mobile Internet. By the end of May 2020, more than 20,000 pieces of works had been published by government affairs new media such as Provincial Government client-sides, Weibo and WeChat accounts of the Provincial Government website, and Weibo and WeChat accounts of Hubei Authoritative Release, accounting for 60.00% of the published works on the whole platform.

Second, the principle of highlighting effectiveness. Popular new media products should transmit information with genuine materials, communicate true feelings, and express opinions with insights. A platform should release, interpret and respond to important information of concern to the masses of the people and public opinion in a timely manner, and disseminate such information quickly at multiple points and multiple levels. The notices, announcements, circulars and interpretation documents issued by the Provincial Pandemic Prevention and Control Headquarters quickly arrived at the hands of the public because they highlighted the characteristics of different mobile new media platforms. The press conferences of the Provincial Pandemic Prevention and Control Headquarters were interpreted visually at multiple levels using Weibo, WeChat and other platforms, and the key points were released in a concise, adaptable and fast manner, resulting in a batch of new media products that enhance people's confidence, warm people's hearts and build consensus among the people.

Third, the principle of coordination and linkage. Firstly, the pandemic information matrix, which had become the focus of public attention, was launched. Daily pandemic data, important policies on the pandemic, etc., after being released in the new media of the Provincial Government website, were reposted simultaneously as soon as possible in all kinds of new media of governments at all levels in the province, quickly forming a public opinion field and expanding the coverage of authoritative government information to the maximum. Secondly, the linkage release of key information was realized. The mode of linkage release by provincial and municipal government affairs new media was adopted for the key information such as guidelines for the clinical diagnosis and treatment of Covid-19, mobile cabin hospitals, centralized quarantine, and refutation of rumors released by all kinds of new media at all levels. For example, information about the incident of claiming pandemic prevention materials in violation of regulations in Ezhou City and the incident of returning home in violation of traffic control in Jingzhou City was released by the subjects involved in the incidents in a timely and accurate manner, and pushed and reposted by the new media of the Provincial Government, thereby refuting rumors, spreading the truth and reassuring the people. Thirdly, information was released by various government affairs new media innovatively in light of their own characteristics. For example, in view of the practical problems and difficulties in daily life faced by people who had been quarantined in isolation for a long period of time, the Government of Wuhan City released through its Weibo and WeChat accounts a series of guiding information about community services, grocery shopping, medical treatment, and payment of gas and electricity bills; and the Huanggang Municipal Government used two unique cultural symbols of the city, namely "Su Dongpo" and "Huanggang Secret Examination Papers" to make lively and easy-to-understand Q&As on pandemic prevention and control in the Weibo account of its portal website; and the Provincial Department of Agriculture and Rural Affairs disclosed in its WeChat account the information about spring plowing and agricultural means of production during the anti-pandemic period at the spring plowing time node.

3 Focusing on Capability-Building and Strengthening Platform Construction

In recent years, the Provincial Government has incorporated the standardized construction of government information disclosure platforms into its key work, conscientiously implemented the *Notice of the Office of Government Information and Openness of Government Affairs of the General Office of the State Council on Matters Relating to the Standardization of Government Information Disclosure Platforms* (Letter No. 61 [2019] of the Office of Government Information and Openness of Government Affairs of the General Office of the State Council), and focused its efforts on strengthening the construction of government websites, government affairs new media, gazettes and hotline interactive platforms, so as to comprehensively improve its capacity for the openness of government affairs. In the performance evaluation of government websites in 2020, the digital government service capacity building, the operation of official WeChat and Weibo accounts and client-sides of the Provincial government were all rated as excellent, and the program "winning the war of resistance against the Covid-19 pandemic with the help of intensive construction of online government" was selected as one of the top ten cases of outstanding innovation.

1. Carrying out pilot work on the intensive construction of government portal websites in the whole province

The Government of Hubei Province, which was among the first batch of pilot provinces for the intensive construction of government websites in China, formulated the *Implementation Plan for the Program of Intensive Construction of Government Portal Websites* to vigorously promote the intensive construction of government websites and build the primary platform of openness of government affairs. The project of intensive construction of government portal websites in the whole province passed the completion acceptance in June 2020. Based on the concept of intensiveness, nine applications, including "one thousand people and one thousand websites" and "the government affairs new media matrix and management platform" had been developed, which effectively solved some difficult problems that had long plagued the construction, management and development of government websites. A number of results were gradually popularized and applied, laying a solid foundation for improving the construction and management of government portal websites in the whole province. They include: improving functions, raising quality and increasing efficiency; developing a unified search system in the whole province and generating scene search service topics according to real-time hotspots; developing an analysis and decision-making system of the intensive platform of government portal websites in the whole province to provide decision-making reference for the construction and administration of government websites; transforming information disclosure platforms in the whole province, updating information disclosure catalogs, and taking the lead in piloting the docking with the information disclosure platform of the website of the Central Government (www.gov.cn); establishing a unified system of disclosure of government information upon application, which have already been put into operation in various cities, prefectures and departments; and continuously deepening the integration of the Provincial Government portal website and the Provincial Government service network.

2. Promoting the healthy development of new media

The Editorial Department of the Provincial Government Portal Website has set up a special government affairs new media editorial group to be responsible for the operation of the Weibo and WeChat accounts of the website, the provincial government client-side, the government affairs new media matrix and management platform, so as to ensure that all platforms are rated as excellent in the national performance evaluation of government websites. Since the fourth quarter of 2019, the Provincial Government has organized the audit and recordation of and quarterly spot checks on government affairs new media in the whole province. In 2020, the Provincial Government carried out four inspections on the 2,797 government affairs new media that had been audited and filed for recordation in the whole province, and a total of 3,936 government affairs new media were randomly selected for spot check, resulting in a total 3,936 reports, thereby promoting the healthy development of government affairs new media in the province.

3. Creating a new platform for online news release

During the pandemic, in order to minimize the risk of infection on press conference sites, 70 online press conferences with "5G live broadcast + asking questions via remote video link" had been organized from February 2 to April 22, 2020. At these online press conferences, 470 reporters from such central media as People's Daily, Xinhua News Agency, CCTV and more than 20 provinces, municipalities directly under the Central Government and autonomous regions, such as Shandong, Liaoning, Zhejiang, Guizhou, Fujian, Hunan, Yunnan, Xinjiang, Ningxia, and Xinjiang Construction and Production Corps asked questions remotely through video link. Yangtze River Cloud of Hubei Radio and Television General Station provided live broadcast signals to all news platforms in China by using 5G signals. Central media such as China Media Group Mobile, People's Daily Online and Xinhuanet, and new media such as the Paper, Red Star, Tianmu News Network, Dazhong Network, Sichuan Online, Hainan Network, Western Network, Ningxia News Network, Xinjiang Newspaper Media Group and Mobile Jiangxi Station (Ganyun) broadcasted the press conference live every day. "5G live broadcast + asking questions via remote video link" press conferences on pandemic prevention and control in Hubei Province, as a brand-new press conference mode in a special period and environment, is not only an innovation in the form of press conference but also the first application of 5G technology in press conference work, which has attracted great attention from the whole industry and all sectors of society. Because of such characteristics as faster transmission speed, freedom from time and space constraints, and wider audience, the online conference has become a highlight of the news and publicity work on the main battlefield of the war against the pandemic. The information release mode of "5G live broadcast + asking questions via remote video link" has been taken for reference and promotion by many ministries and commissions under the State Council and governments of other provinces and municipalities, and is now widely used in the normalized pandemic prevention and control.

4. Forming an "anti-pandemic" publicity matrix through integrated transmission

In order to enhance the effect of information release, the Provincial Government adopted the method of "integrated transmission and all-media reporting" for its press conferences. On the basis of traditional information release methods such as newspaper reports and live radio and television broadcasts, multi-platform webcasting was realized. Press conferences were recorded live by Yangtze River Cloud, which sent live broadcast signals to all news platforms in China. The conferences were broadcasted in real time by the Reporting Alliance Against the Pandemic consisting of national-level new media ports such as People's Daily Online, Xinhua News Agency, CCTV News, China Net, huanqiu.com, and CGTN, and 67 local media in 30 provinces, municipalities directly under the Central Government and autonomous regions, such as Yangtze River Cloud, Lightning News, Litchi News, Cover News, Red Net, Ganyun, Audiovisual Gansu, Mammoth News, Audiovisual Hainan, etc., as well as heavyweight commercial media platforms such as the Paper and Qutoutiao. Within Hubei Province, 120 cloud series clients of Yangtze River Cloud in various cities and prefectures broadcast press conferences simultaneously every day, sending the most authoritative information about pandemic prevention and control to every corner of the province through the channels and strength of county-level media convergence. A four-level press conference transmission matrix consisting of more than 200 ports of various central and local media was formed. At the same time, in terms of new media products, Hubei Daily, Chutian Metropolis Daily, Yangtze River Cloud and other provincial mainstream media launched all-media reporting of press conferences with the combination of "live broadcast + short video + poster + in-depth reporting". In light of the needs of the audience and the characteristics of social media, new media products in various forms were developed on selected hot issues, focus issues and difficult issues that were of general nature and pushed at multiple levels on WeChat, Weibo, Douyin, Toutiao, and other ports, thereby expanding the effect and achieving a certain scale of the news release, realizing all-weather release and full-platform coverage of official information, and improving the arrival rate of authoritative information.

5. Integrating and upgrading the "12345" government-citizen interactive platform

Hubei "12345" Online Service Platform accepts and deals with the complaints and requests of enterprises and citizens submitted through various channels such as the government service hotline, Hubei Government Service Network, Ehuiban APP, WeChat account and Weibo account 24 h a day. At the same time, it undertakes the work of transferring work orders from national platforms such as the Integrated National Government Services Platform and the Chinese Government Network (www.gov.cn). Relying on the existing data resources of the "12345" hotline platform, the portal website of the Provincial Government has set up columns such as "message submission entrance" and "selection of messages for publication" to present the results of government-citizen interaction on the "12345" platform. During the Covid-19 pandemic, people's complaints and requests related to the pandemic increased sharply. On February 16, 2020, according to the requirements of the main leaders of the Provincial Party Committee and the Provincial Government, the provincial "12345" government service hotline was quickly upgraded to the provincial pandemic service hotline, to be responsible for handling complaints and requests relating to pandemic prevention and control in the whole province. The Office of Provincial Pandemic Prevention and Control Headquarters immediately established the system for handling complaints and requests relating to pandemic prevention and control submitted through "12345" hotlines in the whole province, developed a remote hotline system, and integrated the government affairs hotlines in the whole province. On March 11, 2020, Mr. Ying Yong, secretary of the Provincial Party Committee, presided over a special meeting on studying and advancing the construction of the "12345" hotlines in the whole province. At the meeting, he was debriefed by the Provincial Government Affairs Administration Office and other departments on the work of "12345" hotlines in the whole province. In order to win the people's total war of resistance against the pandemic, the Provincial Pandemic Prevention and Control Headquarters timely coordinated the "12345" teams of China Telecom and the telecom companies in the provinces of Jiangsu, Guangdong, Zhejiang and Anhui to send 171 professionals to provide remote support to Hubei "12345" hotline. At the same time, Hubei Telecom Company immediately mobilized 75 volunteers from among CPC and Communist Youth League members in the company to join the team, rapidly increasing the number of seats of operators on the provincial hotline platform to 281, and the platform was maintained in real time by a 15-member technical maintenance team to ensure the stability of its operation. The headquarters organized government departments at various levels in the province to review and provide 635 pieces of data to the databank of pandemic prevention and control knowledge, and improved the reply accuracy of hotline operators. In 2020, the "12345" hotlines in the whole province (including those of various cities and prefectures) accepted 13.72 million pandemic-related complaints and requests, increased the telephone connection rate from 68.60 to 98.50%, and kept the public satisfaction rate at above 98.30%, thereby building a "heart-to-heart bridge" between the government and the public, and enhancing social cohesion and confidence in overcoming the pandemic.

4 Reflections on Further Improving the Quality and Efficiency of Openness of Government Affairs

Improving the quality and efficiency of the openness of government affairs is an inevitable requirement for the modernization of the state governance system and capacity, an urgent need of normal pandemic prevention and control, and an essential part of deepening the openness of government affairs in the new era. In the next step, the Provincial Government will closely focus on the requirement of "deepening the openness of government affairs" put forward at the Fifth Plenary Session of the 19th CPC Central Committee, sum up experiences, consolidate achievements, solve existing problems, strengthen points of weakness, and promote high-quality economic and social development with higher quality and more efficient openness of government affairs.

1. Further improving the political stance by focusing on the spirit and requirements of the relevant documents issued by the CPC Central Committee

The Provincial Government should strictly implement the responsibility system for ideological work, carry out information disclosure work in accordance with law and discipline, and ensure the safety of ideological work; implement the responsibilities of competent authorities, working bodies and departments under local governments at various levels in strict accordance with the requirements of the Regulations; improve the quality of information disclosure upon application, and better meet the individualized and reasonable demands of the people for government information; strengthen the supervision over information disclosure work in the field of public services, optimize services, and encourage administrative organs at all levels to disclose more valuable basic data to the public; continue to effectively carry out business training and case guidance, and enhance the awareness of the rule of law, the awareness of openness and service awareness among administrative organs at all levels and their staff, especially among leading cadres, and better protect the people's right to know, right of participation and right of supervision.

2. Optimizing the business environment and promoting implementation through openness by focusing on the reforms of "simplifying administrative procedures, decentralizing powers, combining decentralization with appropriate control, and optimizing services"

The Provincial Government should stick to the implementation of major policies such as relieving difficulties for market players, stabilizing and expanding employment, accurately expanding effective investment, accelerating the release of consumption potential, and preventing and defusing economic and financial risks, disclose authoritative information in a timely manner, organize in-depth interpretation of policies, increase the quantity and improve the quality of information disclosure, and release more positive signals to help the economy recover; focus on deepening the reforms of simplifying administrative procedures, decentralizing powers, combining decentralization with appropriate control, and optimizing services, rural revitalization, tax and fee reduction, pollution prevention and ecological construction, basic livelihood guarantee, etc., further advance the openness of government affairs and promote implementation through openness; stick to the goal of "all-in-one-website", all-in-one-window", "cross-department" and "cross-province" handling of government service items, further advance the simultaneous online and offline disclosure of administrative and service information, and provide more accurate and convenient policy inquiry and consultation channels for market players; and disclose information about market rules and standards and supervision and law enforcement in a timely manner, give full play to the role of information disclosure in fair regulation, and promote the continuous optimization of the business environment in Hubei Province.

3. Comprehensively strengthening and standardizing grassroots social governance by focusing on the implementation

The Provincial Government should comprehensively promote the compilation and publication of basic catalogs of openness of government affairs by government departments at all levels, clarify the items, bases, channels, and obligations of openness, and promote the timely and accurate disclosure of government information in the pilot areas of openness of grassroots government affairs; comprehensively advance the standardized page setup of information disclosure platforms of county-level government departments and township governments, and effectively publicize and interpret at the grassroots level the policies made by higher-level governments, so as to ensure the accurate and efficient implementation of the policies; and comprehensively extend the openness of government affairs to villages and communities, guide them in the openness of village and community affairs, and ensure that they implement relevant policies in an accurate and timely manner.

4. Strengthening the disclosure of information about public health emergencies by focusing on normalized pandemic prevention and control

The Provincial Government should conscientiously sum up relevant experiences and practices, adhere to the timely, open and transparent release of pandemic information, and improve the quality and effectiveness of information disclosure, so as to provide effective support to the normalized pandemic prevention and control work; effectively carry out the work of disease prevention and early warning and strengthen the publicity of and training on various kinds of emergency plans at various levels; make greater efforts in the publicity and popularization of knowledge of protection against the pandemic, enhance citizens' awareness of prevention and control of infectious diseases and their ability to cope with the diseases, and guide them in improving their health literacy and normalizing their healthy living habits; and protect all legal rights of citizens in strictly accordance with law, especially citizens' right to their personal information collected by relevant authorities in the process of pandemic prevention and control.

5. Striving to build a high-level, multi-dimensional and integrated open government platform by focusing on improving quality and efficiency

The Provincial Government should accelerate the establishment and improvement of the institutions and rules for promoting the openness of government affairs through the application of such technologies as the Internet, cloud computing, big data, and artificial intelligence, encourage the wide application of the new generation of information technology to the openness of government affairs to make it more efficient and intelligent; further standardize government information disclosure platforms, deeply develop and utilize the achievements of intensive construction, and markedly improve such functions as data openness, interactive communication, and construction and management of government affairs new media; rely on the government service network to treat the disclosure of government information upon application as a public service item, and realize the online handling of and whole-process supervision over the disclosure of government information upon application; explore the integration of data from government information disclosure platforms and such specialized websites as Credit Hubei, Government Procurement Network, Government Service Network, Big Data Capability Platform and various government affairs new media, so as to promote the formation of a new situation of openness of government affairs characterized by authoritative release and overall voice; rely on government service halls and self-service terminals at all levels to create special offline open government service areas to realize the integration of online and offline government services; advance the deep integration of the Provincial Government website and the government service website, comprehensively optimize and upgrade the "service" column of the websites, fully embody and comprehensively display the achievements of the reforms of simplifying administrative procedures, decentralizing powers, combining decentralization with appropriate control, and optimizing services, and digital government service capacity building, continuously enhance the people's sense of gain and satisfaction with government information, and push the openness of government affairs into a new stage of development.

Investigation Report on Government Information Disclosure Litigation Cases in Guangzhou—Based on the Analysis of 1,168 Cases Tried by Railway Courts in Guangzhou from 2016 to 2020

Project Team of the Administrative Division of Guangzhou Railway Transport Intermediate Court of Guangdong Province

1 Introduction

Government information disclosure is an important system to protect citizens' right to know, and the right to participate in and supervise state governance. Article 1 of the *Regulations of the People's Republic of China on Government Information Disclosure* (hereinafter referred to as the Regulations) clearly stipulates that China guarantees citizens' right to access government information, improves the transparency of government work, and strives to construct a law-based and service-oriented government. In recent years, governments at various levels and administrative organs under them in Guangzhou have vigorously advanced the standardization, specialization and informatization of the openness of government affairs, and maintained a relatively high level of openness of government affairs. With the continuous enhancement of citizens' awareness of the rule of law, their enthusiasm for participating in social

---

Head of the project team: Jianwen Hou, the president and a judge of the Administrative Division of Guangzhou Railway Transport Intermediate Court. Other members of the project team: Jianjun Tan, Director and a judge of Research Office of Guangzhou Railway Transport Intermediate Court; Shulin Yu, a judge of the Administrative Division of Guangzhou Railway Transport Intermediate Court; Huiping Zhuang, a judge of the Administrative Division of Guangzhou Railway Transport Intermediate Court; and Yan Shao, a judge of the Third Administrative Division of Guangzhou Railway Transport Court. Authors of this report: Jianjun Tan and Yan Shao.

Project Team of the Administrative Division of Guangzhou Railway Transport Intermediate Court of Guangdong Province (✉)
The Administrative Division of Guangzhou Railway Transport Intermediate Court of Guangdong Province, Guangzhou, China
e-mail: 13693186775@163.com

H. Tian and Y. Lv (eds.), *Assessing Government Transparency in China (2021)*,
https://doi.org/10.1007/978-981-99-9734-3_3

governance is growing day by day. The number of cases involving government information disclosure has been maintained at a high level, constituting an important type of administrative litigation cases and reflecting the prominent contradiction between citizens' increasing demand for government information and the insufficient supply of government information. Some common problems have also been found in the practice of judicial review. This requires administrative organs to further improve government information disclosure work in accordance with the purposes of relevant legal norms and adjudicative standards, strive to create government transparency that matches Guangzhou as a national key central city and an international metropolis with a leading position in the whole country, and actively promote the modernization of governance system and governance capacity.

2 The Basic Situation of Government Information Disclosure Litigation Cases

1. Being large in base number, they constituted an important type of administrative litigation cases

From 2016 to 2020, Guangzhou Railway Transport Intermediate Court and Guangzhou Railway Transport Court (hereinafter referred to as "railway transport courts at two levels in Guangzhou") accepted a total of 1,099 government information disclosure cases.[1] Among them, 239 were received in 2016, 328 in 2017, 150 in 2018, 246 in 2019 and 136 in 2020,[2] with the number remaining high for a long period of time (see Fig. 1). This shows that the people's satisfaction with government information disclosure had not yet reached the ideal level. In particular, in recent years, the number of applications for government information disclosure received by Guangzhou Municipal Government has been increasing year by year, from 16,475 in 2019 to 19,017 in 2020, with a year-on-year increase of 15.40%. The number of lawsuits brought at the people's courts increased from 210 in 2019 to 258 in 2020 (including lawsuits brought after administrative reconsideration and those brought directly against administrative decisions), accounting for 1.27% and 1.36% respectively of the total number of cases received by the courts.[3] The number of cases in which applicants refused to accept the reply or notice of administrative

[1] In this report, the numbers of closed cases are calculated based on the actual numbers of accepted and closed cases each year and other statistics on the types, disclosure, reply and loss of cases are all based on the final trial results.

[2] In accordance with the arrangements made by the Supreme People's Court for carrying out the pilot reform of cross-regional concentrated jurisdiction over administrative cases in seven railway transport courts, the railway transport courts at two levels in Guangzhou formally began to accept administrative cases in Guangzhou in January 2016.

[3] See "Annual Report on Information Disclosure Work of the Municipal Government", Guangzhou Municipal People's Government Portal Website. The number of cases given in this report may be different from the statistics of people's courts.

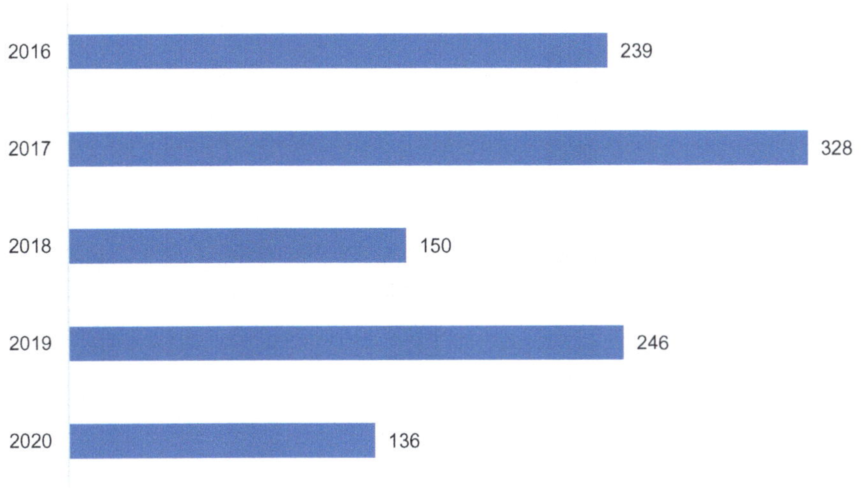

Fig. 1 Number of government information disclosure cases received by courts from 2016 to 2020

organs and filed applications for administrative reconsideration or administrative litigation accounted for only a very small proportion of all applications for government information disclosure. This is proof of the achievements made by Guangzhou in the disclosure of government information over the years. A stable balance has been formed between the supply and demand of government information. The public's right to know and to have access to government information have been well guaranteed and this fact has been highly recognized by administrative counterparts. However, due to the large base number of applications for the disclosure of government information, the absolute number of cases of government information disclosure entering litigation channels is still relatively high.

2. The range of involved administrative fields was extensive and the losing rate of administrative organs was relatively high

(1) Number of closed cases

From 2016 to 2020, railway transport courts at two levels in Guangzhou concluded a total of 1,168 government information disclosure cases (see Fig. 2).[4] Among them, 215 cases were concluded in 2016, 366 in 2017, 173 in 2018, 227 in 2019 and 187 in 2020. It can be seen from the above data that there had been some fluctuations in the number of government information disclosure cases concluded by railway transport courts at two levels in Guangzhou, but the number had remained high and such

[4] In 2016, railway transport courts at two levels in Guangzhou began to exercise cross-regional centralized jurisdiction over area administrative cases. Some second-instance cases from various districts entered the jurisdiction of the Guangzhou Railway Transport Intermediate Court in the second instance. Therefore, the number of closed cases was higher than the number of accepted cases.

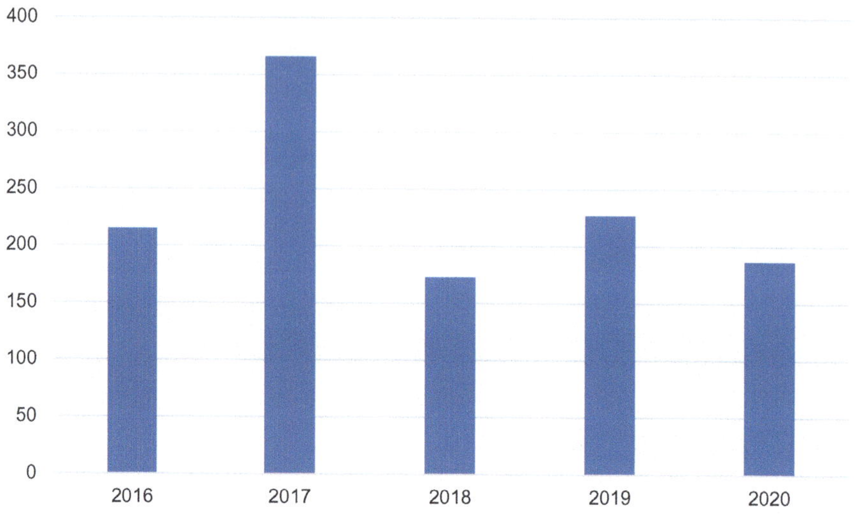

Fig. 2 Number of government information disclosure cases closed in the period from 2016 to 2020

cases constituted an important category of administrative litigation cases in railway transport courts at two levels in Guangzhou, indicating that there was still a certain tension between the public's right to know and government transparency.

(2) The wide range of fields involved in government information disclosure cases

Government information disclosure cases involve a wide range of fields, including land, housing, social security, urban management, public security, village collectives, planning, industry and commerce, tax, market, civil affairs, justice, finance, business, education, and banking (see Fig. 3). Among them, housing, land and social security are the three fields in which government information disclosure cases are most concentrated. This is the result of the comprehensive promotion of urbanization in Guangzhou in recent years. The public pays closer attention to the disclosure of information about the requisition of land and houses by government organs, and the awareness of rights protection has been continuously strengthened.

(3) The number of cases of non-disclosure of government information was far higher than the number of cases of full or partial disclosure of government information

A review of the closed cases shows that administrative organs normally make the following three kinds of decisions on the applications for the disclosure of government information submitted by citizens: disclosure, non-disclosure, and partial disclosure (see Fig. 4).

In the five years from 2016 to 2020, the decision on full disclosure of government information applied was made in 107 cases (accounting for 13.24% of the total number of cases), the decision on partial disclosure was made in 79 cases (accounting for 9.78% of the total), and the decision on non-disclosure was made in 610 cases

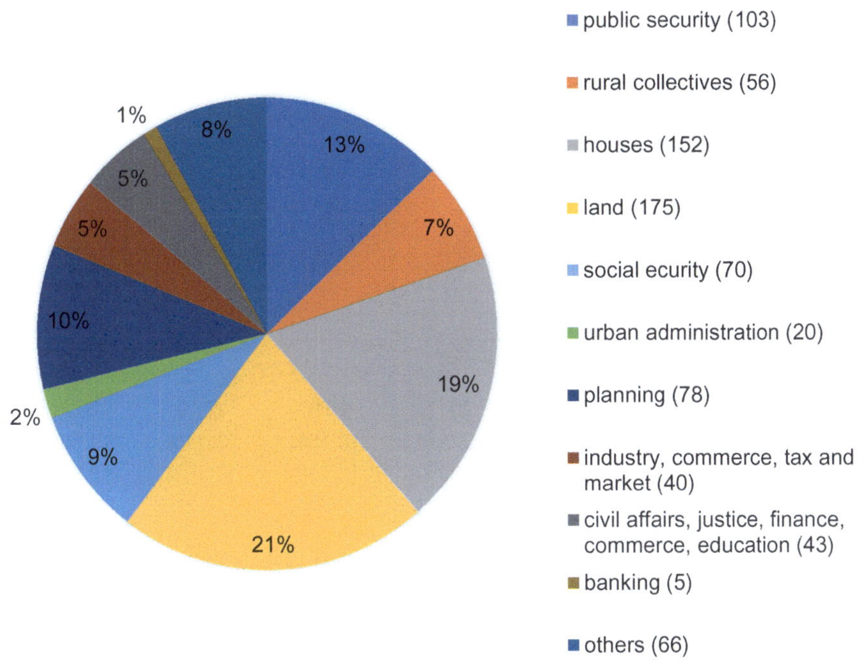

Fig. 3 Fields involved in government information disclosure cases from 2016 to 2020

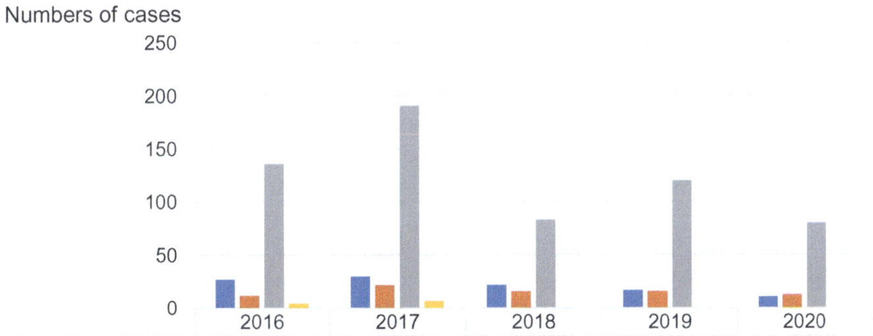

	2016	2017	2018	2019	2020
full disclosure	27	30	22	17	11
partial disclosure	12	22	16	16	13
non-disclosure	136	191	83	120	80
others	5	7	0	0	0

full disclosure partial disclosure non-disclosure others

Fig. 4 Statistics of government information disclosure cases from 2016 to 2020

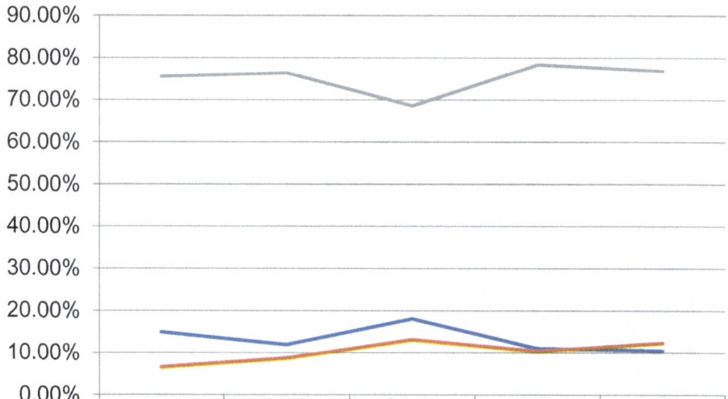

	2016	2017	2018	2019	2020
full disclosure	15.00%	12.00%	18.18%	11.11%	10.58%
partial disclsoure	6.67%	8.80%	13.22%	10.46%	12.50%
non-disclosure	75.56%	76.40%	68.60%	78.43%	76.92%

Fig. 5 Proportions of cases of full disclosure, partial disclosure and non-disclosure in government information disclosure cases from 2016 to 2020

(accounting for 75.50% of the total). The number of cases in which the decision of non-disclosure was made was 5.7 times and 7.2 times, respectively, of the number of cases in which the decision on full disclosure and partial disclosure were made.

As can be seen from Fig. 5, the proportion of cases in which the decision on non-disclosure of government information was made declined slightly in 2016 and the decline became obvious in 2018, but increased significantly in 2019 as compared with that in 2018. On the whole, the proportion of cases of non-disclosure was quite high—over 60% in each of the recent five years, which shows that the government organs need to further improve their information disclosure work.

(4) The reasons for the non-disclosure of government information given by administrative organs were diversified

Citizens who need to obtain undisclosed government information must first submit a valid application for the disclosure of the information to a competent administrative organ. After review, administrative organs divide the government information applied for into two categories: government information and non-government information. If the information applied for by citizens belongs to government information but is exempted from disclosure, the administrative organ with the information disclosure obligation makes a decision on the non-disclosure of the information; if the information applied for by citizens does not belong to government information, it will of course not be disclosed. Table 1 shows that "the administration organ having no authority to disclose the information applied for" and "the information applied for not belonging to government information" were the two most common reasons for the non-disclosure of government information, which were given in 158 cases and 241 cases respectively. "Not belonging to government information" means that the information applied for is not that "prepared or obtained by an administrative agency in the course of performing its government administration functions" as prescribed in Article 2 of the revised *Regulations*. On the whole, the reasons for the non-disclosure of government information were diversified, involving complicated situations (Fig. 6).

This report analyzes the handling of administrative cases by railway transport courts at two levels in Guangzhou in which government information applied for was not disclosed. It can be found from these cases that the top three grounds for non-disclosure of government information were "the administrative organ has no authority to disclose the information", which consisted 40% of the total; "the government information applied for does not exist", which consisted 18% of the total, and "the information involves state secrets, trade secrets, personal privacy" and "three securities and one stability" (national security, public security, economic security and social stability), which consisted of 12% of the total. The grounds that "the

Table 1 Statistics on the reasons for non-disclosure of information in government information disclosure cases from 2016 to 2020

Categories	Reasons for non-disclosure	2016	2017	2018	2019	2020	Total
Government information	No authority to disclose the information	39	41	28	32	18	158
	Information not exist	10	10	12	26	11	69
	Information not within the scope of information disclosure	3	12	1	1	0	17
	Unclear content of the application	6	6	3	0	1	16
	Privacy and security	7	11	13	7	8	46
	Information already disclosed on the initiative of the government	3	10	6	6	3	28
	Repetitive application	6	9	3	7	1	26
	Supplementation or correction of the application needed	0	2	0	0	1	3
	Application not based on special needs for production, living or scientific research	2	16	6	4	0	28
Not government information	Internal information	3	13	2	4	0	22
	Information applied for does not belong to government information	43	66	32	61	39	241
	Procedural information	5	7	5	1	0	18
	Information not saved	2	7	1	4	0	14
	Others	6	10	0	0	3	19
Failure to submit a valid application		2	2	1	2	0	7
Total		137	222	113	155	85	712

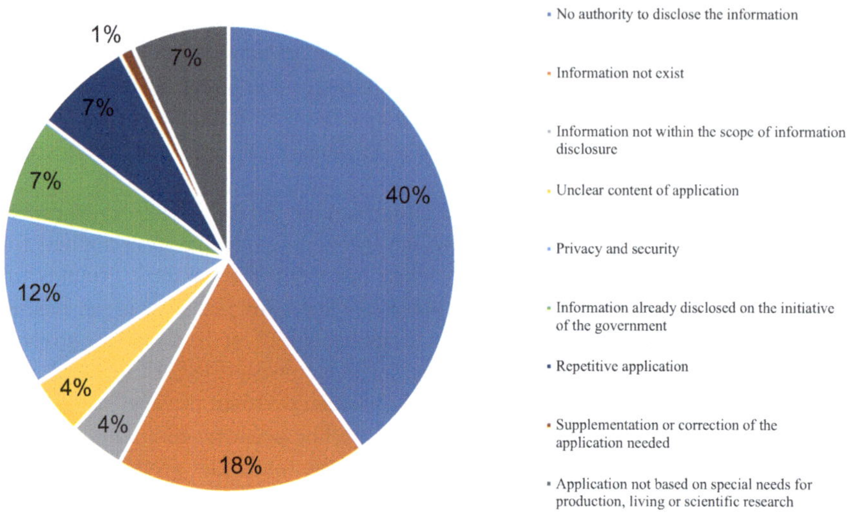

Fig. 6 Reasons for non-disclosure of government information

information applied for is not government information" consisted of 44.1% of all the grounds given for the non-disclosure of information (Fig. 7).

(5) Administrative organs tended to lose information disclosure cases in the same way and for the same reasons

In this sample, the number of cases lost by administrative organs decreased year by year, from 36 in 2016 to 20 in 2017, 18 in 2018, 17 in 2019 and 15 in 2020. But the

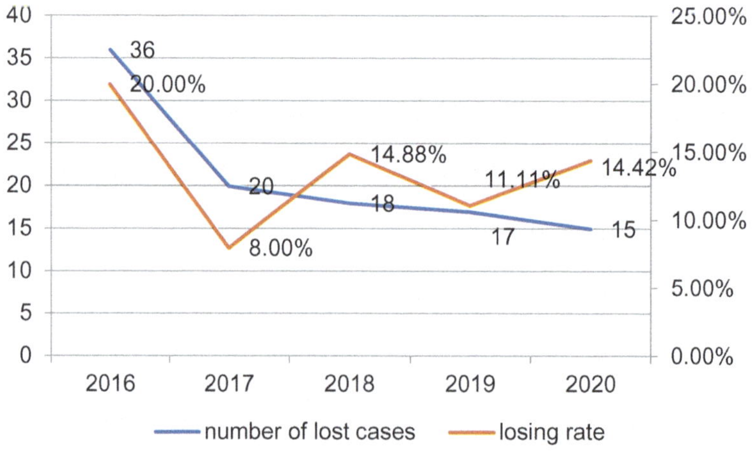

Fig. 7 The number and proportions of information disclosure cases lost by administrative organs from 2016 to 2020

losing rate was as high as 20% in the first year of the cross-regional administrative jurisdiction reform carried out by railway transport courts at two levels in Guangzhou. Although the losing rate dropped to 8% in 2017, it had been above 10% from 2018 to 2020. With the exception of 2018, the overall losing rate of administrative organs in information disclosure cases was higher than the overall losing rate of administrative organs in administrative litigation cases in general in the whole city in 2017, 2019 and 2020. The main reasons for them to lose the case were as follows: first, the lack of awareness of giving a timely reply to applications. In many cases, the overdue reply to an application was found by the court to constitute a violation of law; second, incorrect judgment of whether the information applied for belongs to government information. Some administrative organs refused to disclose the information they retained about the operation and management of town collective enterprises because they did not think that such information belongs to government information; some refused to disclose the information about the result of completed administrative procedures because they believed it is procedural information; and some had an incorrect understanding of the meaning of "internal information"; third, incorrect handling of the information involving the rights of third parties. Some administrative organs refused to disclose a piece of information involving the rights of a third party simply on the grounds that third parties did not agree to disclose it; fourth, misunderstandings about the procedures for processing information involving state secrets. Some administrative organs refused to disclose the information applied for on the grounds that it involved state secrets or that it might endanger social stability if disclosed, but failed to provide evidence that the information had been classified; fifth, inaccurate judgment by administrative organs on whether they had the duty to disclose the information applied for. With respect to applications for the disclosure of information that does not fall within the scope of their duty of information disclosure or documents not prepared by themselves, some administrative organs simply gave the reply that the information or documents did not exist, but failed to submit retrieval evidence to prove that the information did not exist and, as a result, lost the lawsuits; and some administrative organs failed to provide the information applied for due to their own improper safekeeping of the information, and as a result, were unable to resolve the disputes with the applicants.

3. The problem of abusing the litigation right by some parties was prominent

It can be seen from the government information disclosure cases tried by railway transport courts at two levels in Guangzhou that the plaintiffs in administrative litigation were relatively concentrated, and a few parties applied to administrative organs for information disclosure and brought corresponding administrative litigations against them in a repetitive and concentrated way out of some ulterior motives. In addition, some parties put pressure on the government by bringing a large number of government information disclosure lawsuits, so as to achieve some other objectives. Some applicants abused their litigation right by bringing vexatious lawsuits. For example, a couple (Tan and Lin) who were dissatisfied with the government's handling of a dispute over a medical incident involving one of their relatives submitted a large number of applications for government information disclosure to the Provincial Health Department, the Provincial People's Government and the Provincial Bureau of Traditional Chinese Medicine, and then brought corresponding administrative lawsuits at people's courts. In 2017 alone, they brought a total of 34 cases of first and second-instance lawsuits; Guo brought 12 government information disclosure lawsuits because he was dissatisfied with compensation for property expropriation and resettlement; Zhang filed 22 lawsuits against the Government of Zhongluotan Town of Baiyun District; Yang, Tang, Chen and others brought 27 lawsuits against Charao Sub-district Office, the Water Affairs Bureau and the Agriculture Bureau of Liwan District; Li brought 12 lawsuits because he was dissatisfied with the compensation for the expropriation of contracted land in Nansha; and Zhu and others brought 10 first-instance lawsuits because they were dissatisfied with the compensation for the expropriation of collective land in Huadu.

3 Main Problems in the Work of Government Information Disclosure

1. Lagging local legislation and mismatch between values of relevant laws and regulations

"Selective disclosure" is a real obstacle to the full implementation of the government information disclosure system, while "insufficient disclosure and vague transparency" are the biggest short boards. The revised *Regulations* clearly establish the basic principle of "taking openness as the norm and non-disclosure as the exception" of the government information disclosure system, and let local governments make more detailed rules on which information should be disclosed and how to disclose them. In reality, however, local regulations in this field are faced with the dilemma being lagged behind the actual needs and lack of operability. The *Provisions of Guangzhou Municipality on Government Information Disclosure* (hereinafter referred to as *Guangzhou Provisions*), the first local regulations on government information disclosure in China, was formulated in 2002. As such, they both are groundbreaking and have inevitable limitations.[5] Especially after the revision and implementation of the *Regulations* in 2019, they are no longer compatible with the spirit and connotation of the superior law. For example, the definition of government information in the *Guangzhou Provisions* is vague, being limited to "information produced, obtained or retained by people's governments at various levels and their functional departments and organizations exercising administrative functions and powers in accordance with law in the process of administration or providing public services". Therefore, compared with the revised *Regulations*, the *Guangzhou Provisions* are lagged behind in realizing the purposes of government information disclosure legislation.

[5] Zhang Wei (2021).

There are also conflicts in the concept of information disclosure among legal norms at different levels. A review of the above-mention cases shows that, if the government information applied for has been handed over to the National Archives, the administrative organ receiving the application should notify the applicant that the disclosure of the information is no longer within the scope of its duty, and guide the applicant to look for the information at the National Archives. Under this circumstance, the applicant who wants to access the information is restrained by the legislative guidelines of the *Archives Law* and the *Law on Guarding State Secrets*, and the application of the *Regulations* is no longer given priority. In other words, there is a conflict between the *Regulations*, which take the disclosure of government information as their guiding principle, and the *Archives Law* and the *Law on Guarding State Secrets*, which do not take the principle of openness as their guiding principle. An applicant who wants to access the information at the National Archives needs to comply with the *Archives Law* and the *Law on Guarding State Secrets*. Therefore, as administrative regulations, the *Regulations* need to coordinate with superior laws in the application.

2. Administrative organs are unwilling or afraid, or do not know how to disclose government information

(1) The uneven development of the information disclosure work among administrative organs at different levels

The above litigation cases reveal the problem of unbalanced development of mechanism, ability and effect of information disclosure work among administrative organs at various levels, which is mainly manifested in the positive correlation between the rate of correct handling of the applications and the administrative level: the higher the administrative level of a government organ, the better its government information disclosure work. Because municipal and district governments have specialized agencies responsible for government information disclosure, their work efficiency is high, the incidence of disputes is low, and their rate of winning related lawsuits is also high. Government organs of towns and sub-district offices have no specialized agencies for information disclosure, and most of the personnel responsible for information disclosure work are part-time and often unfamiliar with relevant laws and regulations. The procedures for information disclosure are imperfect and the results are unsatisfactory. Some administrative organs are unfamiliar with the laws and regulations that require them to disclose on their own initiative information about compensation for property appropriation, urban and rural planning, etc. and the information that has already been disclosed by the government, but refuse to disclose the information simply because they are concerned that the disclosure may bring adverse consequences to themselves; some administrative organs do not follow the statutory standards when performing their administrative payment duties and therefore are afraid to disclose related government information to the public; and some document drafting departments of administrative organs do not understand the legal requirements for government information disclosure. They arbitrarily mark the documents they drafted as "not open to the public", "work secret" or "internal information" merely based on their own subjective judgment or the will of some individual persons in charge, or do not designate a document as classified when drafting it but decide that it involves classified information when dealing with applications for the disclosure of the document. All these make it difficult for the department in charge of information disclosure to handle applications for information disclosure and often lead to their defeat in subsequent lawsuits.

(2) Tardiness and passiveness in the work of information disclosure upon application

Statistical analysis shows that the overdue reply to applications for information disclosure by administrative organs is one of the main reasons why they have lost government information disclosure litigation cases. The revised *Regulations* set a clear time limit for each link of government information disclosure upon application and impose strict statutory duties on administrative organs. A delay in any link may result in the failure to pass administrative reconsideration or judicial review and hence the finding of a violation of law. Due to various objective or subjective reasons, tardiness in the processing of applications for government information disclosure is common in practice. For example, some administrative organs were not clear about the government information disclosure system, and the chain of communication between the department accepting the applications and the department processing the applications was too long and often blocked. As a result, the latter often received the applications too late to process them in time and give a reply to the applicants within the statutory time limit, and some did not give a reply until after the case enters the litigation link; some administrative organs ignored the provisions in the *Regulations* on the competence for the approval of the extension of the time limit and postpone the handling of applications without going through the approval procedures; some deliberately delayed the handling of applications by requiring applicants to make unnecessary supplements and corrections to their applications; some lost the lawsuits because of their laziness: they gave the applicants the reply that the information applied for did not exist without performing their obligation of reasonable search, and were unable to produce the evidence that they had carried out the search in the subsequent lawsuits, which is another major reason for them to lose the lawsuits; and some grass-roots governments and sub-district offices were unwilling to disclose information about the compensation for the appropriation of houses and resettlement, even when ordered to do so, because they failed to apply a uniform standard on the compensation. The above problems show that some grassroots administrative organs had adopted a slack and negative attitude toward government information disclosure, and they had not fully accepted the idea of service-oriented administration or attached enough importance to the public's right to know.

The imperfect mechanism for sending and receiving documents by administrative organs had affected the efficiency of disclosure of government information upon application. Some administrative organs had not established a standardized procedure for receiving and handling applications for government information disclosure, resulting in poor circulation of the applications for information disclosure among different government organs and unclear responsibility for replying to the applications, which in turn led to overdue replies. For example, in the case of Jiang v. the Municipal Bureau of Planning and Natural Resources, the plaintiff sent the application for information disclosure to the defendant by express delivery and marked "Application for Information Disclosure" and gave his contact information on the envelope. But the express delivery was returned to Jiang because no one claimed it within the prescribed time period. After examination, the court found that the administrative organ had failed to reply to the application for government information disclosure, and ordered it to give a reply within a time limit.

In another case, although the administrative organ gave a reply to the applicant by mail to disclose the government information applied for, it delivered the mail by the method of freight collect payment, which did not conform to the statutory reply method and increased the burden on the applicant. It was found by the court to be a violation of law in terms of the method of reply.

In the process of institutional reform, the merger or transfer of responsibilities has objectively led to the transitional problem of the vagueness of subjects of information disclosure. The change of information disclosure responsibility of some administrative organs as a result of the change of functions and powers and the horizontal or vertical transfer of responsibility had made it difficult for applicants to obtain government information in time. For example, in the case of Jinxi Catering Company v. State-owned Assets Supervision and Administration Commission of Guangzhou City, the plaintiff, Jinxi Catering Company, applied to the Commission for disclosure of historical documents related to a demolished house for the purpose of litigation. Because the documents had been handed over to the internal archives, and the functions of the Commission of Housing and Rural-Urban Development and the State Planning Commission had been repeatedly adjusted during this period, resulting in the change of obligation for government information disclosure of administrative organs, the relevant administrative organs had been repeatedly ordered by the court to deal with the application. Some administrative organs were unable to provide the government information needed by applicants due to the incomplete transfer of data caused by institutional reform.

(3) Inconsistent judgment criteria and inappropriate handling

Incorrect determination of whether a piece of information belongs to government information: some administrative organs incorrectly identified government information that should be disclosed as internal information, procedural information or information that needed to be summarized or processed. For example, in the case of Chen v. Zhong Luotan Town People's Government of Baiyun District of Guangzhou City and Baiyun District People's Government of Guangzhou City on Information Disclosure and Administrative Reconsideration Decision (First Instance Administrative Judgment No. 586 (2019), 7101, Guangdong), the plaintiff applied to Zhong Luotan Town Government for disclosure of the information about the Contract (Agreement) on the Appraisal of Zhusan Village Kindergarten Teaching Building signed between Zhong Luotan Town Government and Guangzhou Xiangtai Housing Safety Appraisal Co.,

Ltd. and the related appraisal expenditure through the System of Guangzhou Municipality for the Disclosure of Government Information upon Application on October 12, 2018. The town government believed that this information belongs to internal management information, and decided not to disclose it. The court of the first instance held that Mr. Chen, as the person in charge of Zhusan Village Kindergarten, applied for the disclosure of information about the contract (agreement) on and expenditure of the appraisal of the teaching building of the kindergarten based on his own "special needs in production, living or scientific research" as prescribed in the Regulations, and therefore had an interest in the information. It ruled in favor of the plaintiff.

Inappropriate determination of the question of "whether a piece of government information exists": if an administrative organ receives an application for the disclosure of a piece of government information that does not fall within its responsibility of information disclosure, it should follow the provisions of Article 36 Paragraph 5 of the Regulations, namely, it shall inform the applicant and state the reasons, and if it is capable of identifying the administrative organ responsible for public disclosure of such government information, inform the applicant of the name and contact information of the administrative organ. However, some administrative organs simply replied that such information "does not belong to government information". For example, in the case, Zhu v. Xinhua Sub-district Office of Huadu District of Guangzhou City (First Instance Administrative Judgment No. 415 (2019), 7101, Guangdong), Zhu applied for the disclosure of the Detailed Rules for the Implementation of the Measures for the Compensation for Land Acquisition and House Demolition and Resettlement for the Project of Production and Plant Expansion of Dongfeng Nissan Company and the Detailed Rules for the Implementation of the Measures for the Construction and Resettlement in the Resettlement Area of the Project of Production and Plant Expansion of Dongfeng Nissan Company. Xinhua Sub-district Office replied that, after a search, it found no record of the information applied for by the applicant, and therefore the information did not belong to the scope of government information disclosure. The court of the first instance held that the two documents involved in the case were made by the defendant itself, and the defendant had the legal obligation to disclose government information. The defendant's claim in its reply to the plaintiff that there was no record of the government information applied for was inconsistent with the fact, and its claim that the government information did not belong to the scope of government information disclosure was baseless. Therefore, the court found that the defendant violated the law in its reply to the plaintiff.

Insufficient reason for the non-disclosure of government information: the Interim Provisions on the Administration of the Classification of State Secrets emphasize the principle of minimization and precision in classification and reiterate the policy of facilitating the rational utilization of information resources while safeguarding state secrets. For example, in the case of Guangzhou Jinxi Catering Co., Ltd. v. Guangzhou Municipal Bureau of Planning and Natural Resources (Final Instance Administrative Judgment No. 3482 (2018) Guangdong, 71), the court of the second instance held that, with regard to the question of whether document No. 453 involved confidential information, if the administrative organ was uncertain whether the government information can be made public, it should report the matter to the relevant competent department or the confidentiality department at the same level for determination in accordance with laws, administrative regulations or other relevant state provisions. Although Guangzhou Real Estate Archives issued a statement saying that the document was marked as a confidential document, the appellee, as the competent unit in charge of the archives, should investigate the classification procedure of the document and give a reasonable explanation in the process of re-making the administrative decision. Some administrative organs refused to provide the government information applied for by the applicants on the grounds that it endangers the "three securities and one stability", but they should bear the burden of proof in litigation, and provide the evidential materials to prove that the matter had been submitted to the relevant departments for review and approval. Some refused to disclose the information applied for on the grounds of protecting the legitimate rights and interests of a third party but failed to reasonably balance the protection of public interests and the protection of personal rights and interests, resulting in improper handling of the matter.

(4) The phenomenon of unbalance loading between active information disclosure and information disclosure upon application

According to the Regulations, government information disclosure work should be carried out in accordance with the principle of taking active disclosure, namely disclosure on the initiative of the government, as the main form and disclosure upon application as a supplement. At present, in terms of active disclosure, administrative organs generally are able to implement the requirements of the central government, take the disclosure of government information as an important part of building a law-based government, actively expand the fields of disclosure, refine the provisions on disclosure, and disclose on their own initiative government information in the fields of approval and implementation of major construction projects, allocation of public resources, social welfare undertakings, and administrative law enforcement as much as possible in a timely manner.

However, the frequent occurrence of litigation in the field of government information disclosure upon application shows that currently there is still an imbalance between the information disclosure by governments and administrative organs under them and the public's demand for government information. Although a lot of information has been disclosed by government organs on their own initiative, the amount of information that really meets the needs of the public is limited. There is a certain degree of "resource mismatch" between the supply side and the demand side. Government information resources have not been effectively allocated and circulated, especially in administrative fields such as "the reconstruction of old towns, old factories, and old villages", compensation for land and house expropriation, and allocation of houses in school districts, which involve the vital interests of the people. The information disclosed by government organs on their own initiatives cannot meet the needs of interested parties, who can obtain the information they need only through application for information disclosure, which often leads to disputes and litigation. If government organs, in the disclosure of information, fail to respond effectively to people's information needs in their work and daily life, people will have a bad personal experience of government information services. This inevitably affects their approval of and trust in the information disclosure work of the government, which in turn directly affects people's psychological perception of government transparency and their experience of public goods and services of the government, makes it difficult for government information disclosure to play its supervisory function and service function and to achieve the legislative purposes of developing economy and promoting democracy, and impedes the modernization of governance. The problem of insufficiency of effective supply shows that some administrative organs are still influenced by instrumental rationality in government information disclosure. That is to say, they regard information disclosure only as a management tool of the government and a means to achieve management objectives, rather than the construction of a law-based government itself. As a result, they over-emphasize the significance of information disclosure as a means of management, but ignore its political and legal attributes, attach no importance to such tasks as responding to the people's demands and fulfilling their own obligations, solving public problems, respecting the people's right to know, and the giving full play to democratic participation function of information openness.[6]

3. The need to further unify the application of law in judicial review

(1) The issue of notice of supplementation, correction and explanation of application issued by subjects of information disclosure

Article 30 of the revised *Regulations* takes the notice of "supplementation, correction and explanation" of the application as the procedure before the reply to an application for government information disclosure, rather than a reply to the application itself. Under normal circumstances, such a notice of supplementation, correction and explanation does not fall within the scope of administrative litigation. Under certain circumstances, however, the notice of supplementation, correction and explanation itself can be regarded as a refusal of information disclosure, that is, if the applicant thinks that the notice of supplementation, correction and explanation issued by an administrative organ has no justification, he can bring an administrative lawsuit before a court requesting the revocation of the notice or directly requesting the performance of the duty of information disclosure by the administrative organ. In handling such cases, attention should be paid to grasping the "limits" of the items of supplementation, correction and explanation. It is not necessary for the applicant to give the specific document number and title of the government information applied, as long as he enables the administrative organ to know what the information is applied for. Otherwise, he is imposed an unreasonable burden. In practice, it is not uncommon for administrative organs to make excessive demands in the notices of supplementation, correction and explanation of the application, which should be corrected by judicial review. For example, if an applicant applies for information about the compensation for the expropriation of the collective land where his homestead or contracted land

[6] See Ruoqun Xu (2020).

is located, the administrative organ should make a preliminary judgment according to the situation of land expropriation and provide the applicant with corresponding documents on compensation for expropriation.

(2) The determination of interest in the plaintiff's qualification

The revised Regulations have deleted the provisions on the requirement that the application for information disclosure must be based on "special needs for production, living or scientific research" in Article 13 of the old Regulations. Many people believe that this revision actually limits the applicant's litigation right. That is to say, the issue of admissibility of a government information disclosure case should be examined in accordance with the provisions on the conditions for instituting an action in the *Administrative Litigation Law*. Namely, the court should determine whether the plaintiff has an interest in the government information applied for. If there is no interest, the plaintiff should be deemed unqualified, and the case should not be docketed or should be dismissed. Others believe that the purpose of the deletion of the provision on the "three special needs" requirement in the revised Regulations is in essence to respond to the need for administrative reform and further strengthen the disclosure of government information. Whether the applicant has the "three special needs" should not be taken as a condition for the examination of the plaintiff's qualification or the substantive issue. This issue has caused great controversy in judicial practice. Many judges, based on their own practical experience of judicial review, tend to impose certain restrictions on the applicant's qualification and try to use "interest" as a condition to set a certain threshold for the application for government information disclosure. In view of the huge population in China, the number of potential applicants for information disclosure is very big, so it seems that the regulation of the related litigation with the administrative actions involved in government information as the connecting points is necessary.

(3) The issue of functional subjects

Article 2 of the revised Regulations adds the condition of "performing administrative functions" to the definition of government information in the old Regulations, thereby greatly limiting the scope of the originally broad concept of government information and reflecting the development of the legislation on the right to government information towards an objective law system and transition from "the need to know" to "the right to know". The administrative functions of administrative organs refer to government duties such as economic regulation, market regulation, public service, social management and environmental protection, which are different from the internal management and internal supervision duties of administrative organs. With regard to the identification of the subjects of information disclosure, the first paragraph of Article 10 of the revised Regulations stipulates, "The government information produced by an administrative organ shall be disclosed by the administrative organ that produced the government information. Government information obtained by administrative organs from citizens, legal persons and other organizations shall be disclosed by the administrative organs that retain the government information; the government information obtained by an administrative organ from another administrative organ shall be disclosed by the administrative organ that produced or first obtained the government information. Where laws and administrative regulations have other provisions on the authority of government information disclosure, such provisions shall prevail." With respect to administrative organs that produce government information, if an administrative organ refuses to provide the information applied for on grounds that it does not have the powers and responsibilities for producing the document, the matter can be examined in light of the duties and competence of the administrative organ as stipulated in the relevant laws and administrative regulations or establishment documents. However, there are many different opinions in judicial practice on the issue of the information disclosure obligation of the organs retaining the information, and little discussion on this subject has been carried out in the academic circle. Take township governments as an example. They obtain a large amount of information about village affairs and the operation and management of township enterprises each year in the performance of their function of guiding and supervising village collective economic organizations and township enterprises within their administrative areas, and they also obtain a large number of agreements on compensation and for house demolition and resettlement based on their responsibility for implementing land expropriation compensation in their respective administrative areas. If they are imposed the obligation of disclosing the huge amount of information they obtain or retain in the performance of their extensive administrative functions, their workload would become unimaginably heavy. This is a very difficult problem faced by grassroots government organs. In view of this problem, it seems necessary to set certain limitations on their information disclosure obligation in judicial practice. For example, if villagers can obtain the information through the openness of village affairs, they should no longer obtain it by applying to the town government (or sub-district office) for government information disclosure. This view has certain practical value and deserves further discussion.

(4) The issue of disclosure of information about case files

Article 16 of the revised Regulations stipulates that an administrative agency may withhold information about administrative law enforcement files generated in the process of its performance of government administrative functions. Article 2 of the *Provisions of the Supreme People's Court on Several Issues Concerning the Trial of Administrative Cases of Government Information Disclosure* stipulates that, if a party concerned or a party of interest in an administrative procedure applies for consulting case files in the name of disclosure of government information and the administrative organ has notified such a party to proceed in accordance with the relevant laws and regulations, the court shall not accept the lawsuit brought by the party concerned or the interested party. This interpretation, issued in 2011, is inconsistent with the revised Regulations, so it is doubtful whether or not it should be applied in practice. The main difference between the two is that the revised Regulations provide for great discretion of administrative subjects over the non-disclosure of information about administrative law enforcement files, regardless of the identity of the applicants, whereas the judicial interpretation limits the applicants for the disclosure of administrative law enforcement files to the parties concerned or parties of interest in a case and the time of application to during the administrative procedure. According to this interpretation and the relevant judgments of the Supreme Court,[7] after the end of the administrative procedure, the right to consult case files can be transformed into the right to apply for information disclosure and the information can be obtained without barriers by not only the parties concerned or parties of interest in a case, but any members of the public through government information disclosure. Due to the uncertain connotation of administrative law enforcement file information stipulated in the revised Regulations, almost all information about administrative management and law enforcement activities can be covered by administrative law enforcement file information. If this is taken as the grounds for non-disclosure of information, the existing right to consult case files and the right of the general public to obtain information under the old Regulations will be greatly reduced. To realize the purpose of government information disclosure legislation, namely the protection of the public's right to know, right of supervision and right of participation, the application of this provision should be appropriately limited in judicial practice.

4 Approaches to Improving Government Information Disclosure Work

1. The legislative approach: strengthening the supply of norms

Some provisions in the revised Regulations are too general. In applying these provisions, local governments should take local conditions into consideration and enhance the hard power of local norms. The Government of Guangzhou City should revise the Guangzhou Regulations in light of the new content of the revised Regulations, and make efforts to refine the new requirements and procedural norms of the revised Regulations and, on this basis, improve various supporting systems. For example, it should improve and reform Guangzhou Regulations in accordance with the new definition of government information provided for in Article 2 of the revised Regulations, so as to be compatible with the legislative design of the superior law, adjust the chapters of Guangzhou Regulations, create a new chapter on "Information Disclosure on the Initiative of the Government" in accordance with the basic principle of "taking openness as the norm" in the revised Regulations, so as to changes the mode of government information disclosure from passive disclosure to active disclosure and promote the construction of a government in the sunshine, and clarify the responsibilities of the subjects of information disclosure. The revised Regulations establish the general principle of "whoever produces or retains a piece of information shall be responsible for disclosing the information" for the subjects of information disclosure, which is too general to be operable in practice because information disclosure cases involve numerous and diversified fields. The Guangzhou Regulations are also faced with this dilemma. As the main subjects of government information disclosure,

[7] No. 2839 [2016], Administrative Petition, Supreme People's Court.

local governments should amend the relevant local regulations in a timely manner by taking the revised Regulations as reference, so as to directly respond to the practical problems of government information disclosure under the new situation.

2. The administrative approach: changing ideas and improving mechanisms

(1) Changing the idea of government information disclosure

The biggest change of the legislative idea in the revised Regulations is the transition of government information disclosure from passive disclosure to active disclosure. Currently, there is an imbalance between the understanding of government information disclosure by administrative organs and the people's growing information needs. Especially in recent years, the implementation of policies related to major social development and people's livelihood and welfare, such as urban planning, urban construction, and expropriation and requisition, have been accelerated, and the people's desire to obtain relevant information through government information disclosure has become stronger and stronger. It can be seen from the statistical data given above that, administrative organs, as machines of state governance, have unchallengeable authority and are veiled in great mystery in the eyes of ordinary citizens under the influence of traditional ideas. The rate of non-disclosure of information applied for by administrative counterparts is as high as 60%. Even if reasonable explanations have been given by administrative organs for the non-disclosure in some cases, the substantive demands of the applicants have not been met, and the mysterious veil covering administrative organs becomes even more difficult to see through, resulting in litigations. Therefore, administrative organs should change their thinking in light of the legislative spirit of the revised Regulations and adhere to the basic principle of taking openness as the norm. Information disclosure is not only an issue of supervising and being supervised but also an issue of proving the legitimacy of the government and reducing the cost of governance. The balance between supply and demand and the people's satisfaction can be regarded as the constant endogenous power source of government information disclosure. Tardy and passive information disclosure can easily cause public dissatisfaction with the work of administrative organs. In order to prevent the frequent occurrence of information blockage and poor communication between the government and the public, administrative organs should take active disclosure as their routine work, timely disclose on their own initiative information that causes high social concern or involves the vital interests of ordinary people in accordance with the legislative spirit and requirements of the revised Regulations, reduce at the source the amount of information to be disclosed upon the application, continuously expand the scope of active disclosure, determine the subjects and catalogs of government information disclosure, and pay attention to distinguishing between and strengthening the construction of the procedures and institutions of routine information disclosure and those of information disclosure in emergencies.

(2) Establishing and improving the "negative list" and doing additions and subtractions in information disclosure

The revised Regulations establish the principle of "taking disclosure as the norm and non-disclosure as the exception" and contain general provisions on the non-disclosure of government information: Article 14 stipulates that information involving national security, public safety, economic security and social stability shall not be disclosed; Article 15 stipulates that government information involving trade secrets, personal privacy, etc., the disclosure of which will cause damage to the legitimate rights and interests of a third party shall not be disclosed unless the third party consents to its public disclosure, or the administrative agency deems that its withholding would materially affect the public interest. Article 16 stipulates that an administrative agency may withhold information on its internal matters, including personnel management, logistics management, and internal workflow. An administrative agency may also withhold deliberative records, pre-decisional documents, consultation communications, requests for instructions and reports, and other pre-decisional information generated in the process of its performance of government administrative functions and information on administrative law enforcement files, unless otherwise required by any law, administrative regulations or government rules. As the main reason for the non-disclosure of information in the replies given by administrative organs, the above exemption clauses provide basic principles for administrative organs with the information disclosure obligation. Apart from that, administrative organs still need to do "additions and subtractions" in the openness of government affairs. Doing the "addition" means that they should disclose all information that should be disclosed on their own initiative, so as to effectively meet the practical needs of the people, further strengthen the disclosure of information in the field of people's livelihood and include all information that does not involve state secrets or "three securities and one stability" in the scope of information disclosure. For example, they should disclose information about the standard of compensation for property appropriation and social security, so as to respond to people's livelihood concerns in a timely manner. Doing the "subtraction" in the openness of government affairs means that administrative organs should base their information disclosure work on the spirit of the revised Regulations. By canceling the requirement of "three special needs", the revised Regulations lower the threshold of the subject qualification of applicants for information disclosure, strengthen the identification of exemption clauses, and require administrative organs to establish and improve "negative lists".[8] In short, only by clearly specifying the catalogs and standards as well as the competence and time limit for the approval of classification of information involving state secrets, trade secrets, personal privacy, national security, public security, economic security and social stability, reducing the discretionary power of administrative organs, and reducing the number of items on the "negative list" can the transparency of the operation of government information be maximize and only when the subtraction from "negative lists" is effectively carried out, can immediate result be produced in the normalization and institutionalization of government information disclosure.

[8] See *Changjiang Daily*, http://opinion.people.com.cn/n/2014/0515/c1003-25020669.html, last visited on March 3, 2021.

(3) Accelerating the construction of data platforms for government information disclosure

On October 29th, 2020, the 19th CPC Central Committee adopted at its fifth plenary session the Recommendations for the 14th Five-Year Plan for Economic and Social Development and the Long-range Goals Through 2035 (hereinafter referred to as the Recommendations). Article 24 in Chapter VI (Deepening the Reform in an All-round Way and Building a High-level Socialist Market Economic System) of the Recommendations clearly states that China will promote the standardization and facilitation of government services and deepen the openness of government affairs, "expand the orderly opening-up of basic public information and data and build an open platform for unified sharing of national data", accelerate the public data legislation, increase the scope, speed and frequency of government information disclosure through the openness of public data, meet the practical needs for protecting the public's right to know and strengthening the supervision over government work through the public's right to know, lay a solid rule-of-law foundation for "strengthening weak points, consolidating advantages and building capabilities" in the government information disclosure work, and clear out the key final hurdles to government information disclosure. It can be seen from the work of prevention and control of the Covid-19 epidemic in 2020 that public data open platforms based on big data have shown strong resource efficiency and value efficiency, providing multi-dimensional support for the exchange of and access to information by the government and the public in such fields as epidemic prevention and control, population migration, travel, and resumption of production and work. By establishing a public data platform, China will able to integrate information from multiple departments and fields, so as to further promote the transparency, high efficiency and convenience of government information disclosure by relying on such advantages of big data as large capacity, multiple types and fast access, further enhance the people's sense of participation in and the approval of government administration, and encourage them to jointly promote the construction of a law-based government.

(4) Improving the scientific evaluation and supervision mechanisms

Satisfaction and transparency are the two important indicators used to measure the quality and efficiency of government information disclosure. According to the report on indices government transparency in 2019, both the Government of Guangdong Province and the Government of Guangzhou City were in leading positions in the country in terms of openness of government affairs, and Guangzhou City had taken the lead in the whole province in compiling the standard catalog of openness of grass-roots government affairs.[9] This work will help the governments of various districts and towns and sub-district offices in the whole city overcome the randomness in government information disclosure, ensure the quality of disclosure, unify the platform of disclosure, further improve government transparency, and establish internal systems of inspection, appraisal and annual assessment. At the same time,

[9] Xu Chen and He Tian (2020).

the revised Regulations stipulate that a social appraisal system shall be established for government information disclosure. This system, as a form of external supervision, is of great significance to government information disclosure. The government should actively and effectively respond to public concerns by clarifying the cycle of social appraisal, increasing the frequency of appraisal, reducing the intermediate examination, approval and reporting links, saving time, improving the ratio between the returns and costs of supervision, enrich the forms of appraisal. In addition to carrying out questionnaire investigations and organizing appraisals by representatives, it should take advantage of the new data era to give full play to the communication power and influence of online media and news TV; the choice of appraisal by representatives should also be diversified, and different fields, ages, genders, occupations, etc. should be selected to enrich the appraisal samples; finally, the government should make the appraisal results public, ensure that the results are fair and transparent, make public the problems reported and suggestions made by the public together with the solutions to the problems provided by the administrative organs, and accept the supervision by the broad masses of the people, so as to manifest the transparency and effectiveness of government information disclosure work.

3. The judicial approach: achieving a win–win situation between legal and social effects

(1) Separating complicated cases from simple cases and effectively realizing the "quick trial of simple cases"

An analysis based on data samples shows that railway transport courts at two levels in Guangzhou have basically developed unified standards for ascertaining facts, applying laws, and analyzing the reasonableness in government information disclosure cases. Faced with the double challenges of heavy caseload and insufficient staff and the need for substantive settlement of administrative disputes, courts should separate complicated cases from simple cases in the trial of government information disclosure cases to improve judicial efficiency. According to Article 82 of the *Administrative Litigation Law*, government information disclosure cases can be tried through the summary procedure. In the five-year cross-regional administrative reform, railway transport courts at two levels in Guangzhou have applied the summary procedure in the trial of information disclosure cases, thereby greatly improving the efficiency of the trial. After the establishment of the fast-track adjudication center of railway transport courts at two levels in Guangzhou in 2020, most of these cases were tried through the summary procedure by one judge alone, thereby greatly shortening the case trial time. The judicial interpretation of the Supreme People's Court provides for four types of administrative acts against which government information disclosure litigation cases are not admissible: first, notifying the applicant to make supplementation or correction to his applications; second, refusing to provide the applicant openly circulated publications; third, refusing the applicant's request for the production, collection, summarization, analysis, or processing of certain government information; and fourth, refusing the application by a party concerned or a party of interest in an administrative procedure for consulting case files in the name of disclosure of government information. In the practice of administrative trial, some repetitive applications for information disclosure are actually complaints in essence. If such cases have been docketed, they can be directly dismissed by the judge without a hearing in court after reading case files and questioning. In order to realize the quick trial of simple cases, we suggest that administrative courts draw on the system of "one and final adjudication" in small-claim civil litigation and implement the system whereby the judgment of the first instance is final in cases of government information disclosure litigation.

(2) Preventing the abuse of the right to information disclosure through strict regulation

With respect to the protection of the litigation right, the continental law system has established "the theory of litigation interest" and "the theory of the necessity of rights protection", while the common law system has adopted the "maturity theory" and "the theory of disappearance of the cause of action".[10] The protection of the litigation right is the spiritual core of litigation anywhere and anytime, but is "litigation right" equal to "interest (right)"? Or in other words, must the lawsuit brought by a party be docketed by the court and must a lawsuit that meets the condition of admissibility enter the substantive trial? Obviously, the answer is no. In judicial review, the judge should not only safeguard the litigation right but also consider the functionality, timing and boundary of the judicial economy. The practice of various countries shows that the abuse of the right to apply for government information disclosure and litigation right is a worldwide problem. Japanese scholar Hiroshi Yano once pointed out, "Some people seem to take the application for information disclosure as a profession or as an interest or hobby. There are such people in Japan as well as in Taiwan region of China. I heard about an administrative agency in Japan. More than 80% of information disclosure cases against it have been brought by the same person. There have been discussions on how to prevent such a situation."[11] One solution to this problem is to establish a blacklist of abusers of the litigation right. China has a similar practice. Beijing No. 4 Intermediate People's Court is the first court in China to establish a list of people who abuse their litigation right. However, the scope of application of the list should not be expanded. A court can establish a list of a few individuals who have brought multiple administrative lawsuits for government information disclosure. If it finds out that someone in the list has indeed abused his litigation right, it may decide not to docket the cases brought by him.

(3) Promoting case guidance and creating a good communication environment

Today, the practice of the trial of government information disclosure cases is still at the stage of exploration. We suggest that China establish a case guidance system for the trial of government information disclosure-related administrative cases to promote the gradual improvement of government information disclosure work. The Supreme

[10] Baojian Geng (2016).

[11] Guangyu Li (2011).

People's Court should also refine and summarize the corresponding litigation rules by issuing guiding cases, so as to not only standardize the administrative activities of government agencies, but also provide unified standards for the adjudication of relevant cases. Carrying judicial review of government information disclosure cases with courts as platforms can encourage administrative organs to change their work concepts on the one hand, and strengthen the coordination and interpretation of cases, improve citizens' legal awareness, positively guide the public to rationally participate in government administrative activities, and contribute court wisdom and judicial strength to the construction of a law-based government on the other hand.

(4) Strengthening the work of judicial recommendation and promoting administration by law through information disclosure

In terms of litigation types, government information disclosure lawsuits belong to the litigation for the performance of duty. The above-mentioned case data analysis shows that, in a considerable number of cases, administrative organs refuse to disclose the government information applied for on grounds of the "non-existence of the information". According to relevant judicial interpretations, if an administrative organ can produce evidence to show that it has fulfilled its search obligation before giving the reply that the information applied for does not exist, the court can dismiss the plaintiff's claim without the need to examine the issue of whether the administrative organ has produced or retain the information. This leaves a gap between justice and administration, that is, the judicial review fails to play a role in supervising and correcting the behavior of administrative organs when they fail to perform their administrative or law enforcement duties. To close the loopholes in government information disclosure at their sources, help administrative organs to improve administrative management in related fields, and enhance the adhesion between the openness of government affairs and government administrative activities, we suggest that, if a court finds out in the judicial review that an administrative organ should prepare or retain a piece of government information in accordance with laws, administrative regulations, establishment documents or internal work standards but fails to do so, it should be able to directly recommend in the judgment that the administrative organ perform this duty in a timely manner. When necessary, it can make a finding of a violation of administrative law, so as to ensure an adequate supply of government information, compel administrative organs to rectify acts of dereliction of duty in administration and law enforcement, embed openness in all links of government administration and service, and form a "whole life cycle" management mode of government information disclosure.

5 Conclusions

Comprehensively promoting the disclosure of government information is an inevitable requirement of government administration and social governance in the new era and an important focus of the construction of a service-oriented government.

Through the judicial review of administrative litigation cases, people's courts support governments and administrative organs at all levels in the disclosure of government information in accordance with law and supervise them to rectify defective performance of duties, thereby advancing the construction of a law-based government, meeting the information needs of the public, and promoting the modernization of state and social governance. Since the railway transport courts at two levels in Guangzhou implemented the system of centralized jurisdiction over administrative cases in Guangzhou in 2016, they have tried a large number of government information disclosure cases, thus providing effective guidance for administrative organs to further standardize the work of information disclosure upon application as well as strong judicial support for building a market-oriented, internationalized and law-based business environment in Guangzhou. Guangzhou, as a thousand-year-old commercial metropolis, the center of Lingnan Culture and the core area of the Guangdong-Hong Kong-Macau Greater Bay Area, has a vibrant economy, a rich soil for the development of the rule of law, a mature civil society, and a deep-rooted civilization of the rule of law. As such, it has a solid foundation for and made remarkable achievements in the construction of a law-based government. The number of government information disclosure litigation cases in the city itself is a strong illustration of the level of the rule of law in the interaction between the public and the government and embodies the positive interaction between and organic integration of the government and society. In the surging tide of reform and opening-up and from the perspective of modernization of governance system and capacity, the Government of Guangzhou will further refine and humanize government information disclosure, standardize the operation of government power, and promote joint-construction, joint-governance and sharing, so as build a law-based, service-oriented, responsible, and efficient government.

References

Zhang Wei: "An Analysis of Approaches to Advancing Government Information Disclosure - Taking the Guangzhou Practice as an Example", 1 (2021) *Exploration*.

Ruoqun Xu, "A Study on the Imbalance Between Supply and Demand in Government Information Disclosure: from the Perspective of Modernization of Governance", *Journal of Yunnan Administration College*, No. 4, 2020.

Xu Chen and He Tian (eds.), *The Blue Book of Rule of Law in China: Report on the Development of Rule of Law in China No. 18 (2020)*, Beijing: Social Sciences Academic Press, 2020, pp. 174–210.

Baojian Geng, *The Method of Adjudication*, Beijing: People's Court Press, 2016, p. 14.

Guangyu Li, *Reader on Judicial Interpretation of Government Information Disclosure*, Beijing: Law Press China, 2011, p. 89.

Government Information Disclosure: Interest Structure, Litigation Settlement and Litigation Source Management

Huiyi Wang, Qiangli Wang, and Jia Li

1 Changes in Government Information Disclosure Cases Since the Implementation of the Revised Regulations

Since the Regulations of the People's Republic of China on the Disclosure of Government Information (hereinafter referred to as the Regulations) came into effect on May 1, 2008, the application for disclosure of government information has become a hot issue in the field of non-traditional administrative management. Administrative organs, which previously rarely had administrative disputes with administrative counterparts over external administrative management, have generally encountered a large number of applications for government information disclosure and resulting administrative disputes. Take Shenzhen as an example. There had been an outburst of applications for government information disclosure and a continuous rise in the number of cases in which administrative disputes entered reconsideration and litigation procedures in the first four years of the implementation of the Regulations, then the increase of the number gradually slowed down, and now reached a state of stable fluctuation at a relatively low level. The revised Regulations of the People's Republic of China on the Openness of Government Information (hereinafter referred to as the revised Regulations), which came into effect on May 15, 2019, further facilitate and standardize the application for government information disclosure. However, there was no explosive increase in the number of applications, which was basically in a reasonable fluctuation range, in 2019 and 2020. From 2018 to 2020, the numbers of administrative reconsideration and litigation cases resulting from administrative

Huiyi Wang—Chief Judge of the Administrative Division of Shenzhen Intermediate People's Court, Guangdong Province; Qiangli Wang, a judge at the Administrative Division of Shenzhen Intermediate People's Court, Guangdong Province; Jia Li, judge assistant at the Administrative Division of Shenzhen Intermediate People's Court, Guangdong Province.

H. Wang · Q. Wang · J. Li (✉)
Administrative Division of Shenzhen Intermediate People's Court, Shenzhen, Guangdong, China
e-mail: 13693186775@163.com

H. Tian and Y. Lv (eds.), *Assessing Government Transparency in China (2021)*,
https://doi.org/10.1007/978-981-99-9734-3_4

Table 1 Cases of applications for information disclosure handled by administrative organs over the years[a]

Year	Number of applications received	Number of cases in which a decision to disclose the information applied for was made	Number of cases in which a decision not to disclose the information applied for was made	Number of cases in which a decision other than to disclose or not to disclose the information applied for was made	Number of administrative reconsideration cases	Number of litigation cases
2009	76,026	/	/	/	7	3
2010	45,141	/	/	/	13	2
2011	37,672	/	/	/	69	33
2012	38,374	/	/	/	114	224
2013	5,747	/	/	/	91	40
2014	6,093	/	/	/	100	36
2015	5,816	/	/	/	51	15
2016	6035	2734	483	1939	113	19
2017	8987	/	/	/	79	53
2018	4411	2955	329	1091	114	146
2019	3781	2207	213	1380	115	104
2020	5915	2695	517	2638	108	133

[a] The data in this table are quoted from the annual report on government information disclosure published on the website of Shenzhen Municipal People's Government, which was accessed on March 25, 2021 at http://www.szgovcn/cn/xxgk/ndxxgkbg/. The slash in a cell ("/") means that there were no statistics in that year. The number of applications accepted in a year is inconsistent with the total number of three types of cases in that year because the handling of some applications accepted in that year was not completed and carried forward to the next year

organs' replies to government information disclosure applications also fluctuated at low levels, with reconsideration rates of 2.6%, 3.0% and 1.8% and litigation rates of 3.3%, 2.7% and 2.2% in 2018, 2019 and 2020. Wider-range empirical analyses conducted by other researchers also show that the rate of administrative disputes resulting from government information disclosure was generally low during this period of time (Table 1).[1]

From the above changes, it can be seen that, except for the initial pioneering years in which a massive number of applications were submitted, the right to government information provided for and guaranteed by legislation does not necessarily lead to a large number of applications for government information disclosure under normal

[1] Yunkai Xu, "Empirical Analysis and System Reconstruction of Administrative Reconsideration Cases of Government Information Disclosure", 2 (2020) *Chinese Public Administration*.

circumstances. From the actual cases of reconsideration and litigation, we can see that people exercise the right to know and then resort to administrative reconsideration and litigation not merely because they have this right. The greatest motive for them to exercise this right is to strive for practical interests. At the same time, the biggest reason for them to have disputes with administrative organs and to apply for reconsideration and bring litigation is that they failed to obtain the government information needed for safeguarding their own interests.

2 The Interest Structure of Government Information Disclosure Cases

Government information disclosure has multiple functions, such as guaranteeing the right to know, improving the transparency of government work, building a law-based government, and serving the people in their work, daily life, and economic and social activities. Sufficient discussions have already been carried out on the macro functions of government information disclosure.[2] Based on the basic task of judicial settlement of individual cases and research of similar cases, we pay special attention to the problems at the case level in this study. Some researchers believe that: "The original intention of the government information disclosure system is to protect the public's right to know in the sense of public law. In practice, however, the primary driving force for the public to obtain government information is still their own needs, the manifestation of which is that the number of information disclosure applications in the fields of demolition and land acquisition, social security, etc. is far bigger than in other fields."[3] Researchers who carry out empirical analyses of precedents also come to the same conclusion. Firstly, from the perspective of geographical characteristics of case distribution, government information disclosure applications and related litigation cases are concentrated in regions with a developed economy, complex interest relations and a large population, such as Jiangsu Province, Chongqing Municipality, Zhejiang Province, Guangdong Province, Shandong Province and Beijing Municipality. Secondly, from the perspective of the fields involved in the information, the information applied for mainly relates to property rights such as planning, housing and land.[4] The government information disclosure litigation cases in the region in

[2] Hanhua Zhou, "Building an Upgraded Open Government System—On the Basic Orientation of the Revision of the Regulations on Government Information Disclosure", 3 (2016) *Administrative Law Review*; Chun Peng, "Constitutional Logic of China's Government Information Disclosure System in China", 2 (2109) *Law Science*; Lin Tao, "A Review of Researches on Government Information Disclosure from the Perspective of Modernization of State Governance", 1 (2020) *Journal of Taishan University*.

[3] Xiumei Qi, "On the Conflict of Values in Government Information Disclosure", 1 (2020) *Journal of Hebei Youth Administrative Cadres College*.

[4] Yan Dong, "Analysis of Judgments in Government Information Disclosure Cases—Based on the Interpretation of the Second Instance Judgments of Local High Courts", *4 (2016) Journal of Shanghai University of Political Science and Law (The Rule of Law Forum)*; Yuan He and Jieying

which the authors of this report work also have the above-mentioned two characteristics. They mostly involve planning and land (land and real estate registration, confirmation of housing property right, house demolition and relocation, compensation, urban renewal, housing, investigation and punishment of illegal construction), as well as a wide range of other fields, such as public security administration (public security and transportation), tax administration, market regulation, etc., all of which are directly related to the personal and property interests of applicants.

We can see from the above that the right to know guaranteed by government information disclosure is only a superficial right protected by government information disclosure. People apply for government information disclosure in the name of their right to know, but not simply to satisfy the right to know. To sum up, the deep interest demands of the applications for government information disclosure mainly include the applicants' need for safeguarding their personal rights and interests, affirmation of their property ownership, the fair distribution of wealth, the increase of the value of their properties, and understanding the government's rules and activities in dealing with matters involving their vital interests. Remedies such as administrative reconsideration and litigation are only the means to realize these interest demands. Therefore, there is a behavior and relationship structure of "interest-information-remedy" in the field of application for government information disclosure. Under this structure, the direct cause of government information disclosure reconsideration and litigation cases is the failure of administrative organs handling the applications for government information disclosure to protect the applicants' information interests, while the root cause is their failure to help the applicants safeguard their own rights and interests through information disclosure.

3 The Optimized Handling of Government Information Disclosure Litigation

Although the replies to applications for government information disclosure given by administrative organs do not directly affect the interests that citizens, legal persons and other organizations ultimately pursue by applying for government information, based on the "interest-information-remedy" structure in government information disclosure cases and the purpose of protecting the legitimate rights and interests of citizens, legal persons and other organizations stipulated in the Administrative Litigation Law of the People's Republic of China, it is reasonable to assume that the purpose of government information disclosure litigation system should be to protect the legitimate right of citizens, legal persons and other organizations to safeguard their own interests through the application for government information disclosure.

Zhang, "Current Situation of Judicial Trial of Government Information Disclosure Cases—An Evaluation and Analysis Based on Judicial Cases", *4 (2016) Journal of Shanghai University of Political Science and Law (The Rule of Law Forum).*

1. Conducting typified trials of cases based on the typification of decisions in the revised regulations

The revised Regulations classify applications for government information disclosure into the following types: the information applied for should be disclosed by the government on its own initiative, the information applied for should not be disclosed, the information applied for may be disclosed, and the application is not an application for information disclosure, and provided for the corresponding reply methods. Based on these provisions, the authors of this report reviewed and summarized the different methods of handling applications for information disclosure, and put forward targeted judgment proposals in accordance with the Provisions of the Supreme People's Court on Several Issues Concerning the Trial of Administrative Cases of Government Information Disclosure (hereinafter referred to as the Judicial Interpretation) and the Administrative Litigation Law. Typification helps administrative organs to find out the reply methods, grounds and basis for handling various applications and give well-founded replies to applicants and improve their acceptance of the replies. It also helps reconsideration organs and judicial organs optimize case-handling procedures, quickly and accurately carry out legality reviews, and properly resolve disputes over government information disclosure (Table 2).

2. Substantively resolving disputes and meeting needs through judicial goodwill and judicial activism

As a new judicial concept, judicial goodwill has been advocated in the fields of criminal and civil preservation, enforcement and other profit-and-loss judicial activities with a view to achieving judicial objectives by judicial means that causes the least damage.[5] In the authors' opinion, judicial goodwill means not only adopting the judicial means that not only minimize damage but also maximize interests. In government information disclosure and judicial review, administrative and judicial organs should both uphold the principle of not interfering in the interest relations of citizens, legal persons and other organizations in government information-related social life and economic activities, provide information disclosure services and judicial services to the greatest extent in accordance with law, and allow social subjects to independently handle various kinds of legal relations. When handling information disclosure litigation cases in which the applicant has an actual interest in and need for the government information applied for, a court can adopt various active case-handling methods, such as pre-litigation mediation, litigation coordination, judicial recommendation, direct pulling of information, and adjudication, to give full play to its judicial initiative, rectify the non-disclosure reply given by administrative organ without justification, avoid idling and procrastination of procedures, and meet the information needs of the parties.

3. Controlling the abuse of litigation based on the effective and limited remedy of litigation

---

[5] Chun Wang, "The concepts of 'modesty, prudence and goodwill' have become guides to action", *Legal Daily*, July 26, 2017, p.1.

Table 2 Types of handling of applications for information disclosure provided for in the revised Regulations and the contents of related court review[a]

Types of handling of applications provided for in the revised Regulations		Emphases of review		Types of judgments provided for in the Administrative Litigation Law and the Judicial Interpretations	
Types	Concrete case-handling methods	Procedural matters	Substantive matters	Judgment in favor of the defendant	Judgment in favor of the plaintiff
Refusing to process the application	Notifying the applicant to supplement or correct the application or of his failure to supplement or correct the application within the prescribed time limit (A.30)	Whether the plaintiff meets the conditions for instituting an action	1. Whether the plaintiff has a lawful interest to be upheld through the application for government information disclosure 2. The legality of the reply given by the defendant to the application for information disclosure	Rejecting the action brought by the plaintiff (A2)	Handling the case in accordance with Administrative Litigation Law
Notification of non-disclosure of the information applied for and the reasons thereof	The information applied for does not belong to government information (A.2)			Rending a ruling to dismiss the plaintiff's claim (A12)Rending a ruling to dismiss the plaintiff's claim (A12)	A9 and A1
	Classified state secret (A. 14)			Rending a ruling to dismiss the plaintiff's claim (A12) Rending a ruling to dismiss the plaintiff's claim (A12)	
	The disclosure of the information applied for is prohibited by law or administrative regulations (A.14)			Rending a ruling to dismiss the plaintiff's claim (A12)	
	"Three securities and one stability" (A.14)			Rending a ruling to dismiss the plaintiff's claim (A12)	
	Lack of consent by the third party (A.15)			Rending a ruling to dismiss the plaintiff's claim (A12)	

(continued)

Table 2 (continued)

Types of handling of applications provided for in the revised Regulations		Emphases of review		Types of judgments provided for in the Administrative Litigation Law and the Judicial Interpretations	
Types	Concrete case-handling methods	Procedural matters	Substantive matters	Judgment in favor of the defendant	Judgment in favor of the plaintiff
Notification that the information applied for can be withheld and the reasons thereof	Information about internal affairs of an administrative organ (A.16)			Rending a ruling to dismiss the plaintiff's claim (A12)	
	Procedural information (A. 16)			Rending a ruling to dismiss the plaintiff's claim (A12)	
	Information about administrative law enforcement files (A. 16)			Rending a ruling to dismiss the plaintiff's claim (A12)	
Disclosure of the information applied for	Information about the internal affairs of an administrative organ disclosed with the consent of the administrative organ (A. 16)			Rejecting the action brought by the plaintiff (A2)	
	Procedural information of an administrative organ disclosed in accordance with legal provisions or with the consent of the administrative organ (A. 16)			Handling the case in accordance with Administrative Litigation Law	Handling the case in accordance with Administrative Litigation Law
	Information about administrative law enforcement files disclosed in accordance with legal provisions or with the consent of the administrative organ (A. 16)			Handling the case in accordance with Administrative Litigation Law	Handling the case in accordance with Administrative Litigation Law

(continued)

Table 2 (continued)

Types of handling of applications provided for in the revised Regulations		Emphases of review		Types of judgments provided for in the Administrative Litigation Law and the Judicial Interpretations	
Types	Concrete case-handling methods	Procedural matters	Substantive matters	Judgment in favor of the defendant	Judgment in favor of the plaintiff
	Information about a third party the withholding of which may materially affect public interest (A. 32)			Handling the case in accordance with Administrative Litigation Law	Handling the case in accordance with Administrative Litigation Law
	Notifying the applicant that the information applied for has already been disclosed on the initiative of the government (A36, and A19-21)			Handling the case in accordance with Administrative Litigation Law	Handling the case in accordance with Administrative Litigation Law
	Directly providing government information applied for (A.36)			Handling the case in accordance with Administrative Litigation Law	A1
	Informing the applicant of the method of obtaining the information (A.36)			Rending a ruling to dismiss the plaintiff's claim (A12)	Handling the case in accordance with Administrative Litigation Law

(continued)

Table 2 (continued)

Types of handling of applications provided for in the revised Regulations		Emphases of review		Types of judgments provided for in the Administrative Litigation Law and the Judicial Interpretations	
Types	Concrete case-handling methods	Procedural matters	Substantive matters	Judgment in favor of the defendant	Judgment in favor of the plaintiff
Other notifications	Invalidity of the objection by a third party (A.32)			Rending a ruling to dismiss the plaintiff's claim (A12)	Handling the case in accordance with Administrative Litigation Law
	Refusal to process the application on grounds of the unreasonable number and frequency of application (A.35)			Rending a ruling to dismiss the plaintiff's claim (A12)	Handling the case in accordance with Administrative Litigation Law
	The information applied for does not exist upon search (A. 36)			Handling the case in accordance with Administrative Litigation Law	Handling the case in accordance with Administrative Litigation Law
	The disclosure of the information applied for does not fall within the responsibility of the administrative organ to which the application has been submitted			Rending a ruling to dismiss the plaintiff's claim (A12)	Handling the case in accordance with Administrative Litigation Law
	Repetitive application for the same information (A.36)			Handling the case in accordance with Administrative Litigation Law	Handling the case in accordance with Administrative Litigation Law

(continued)

Table 2 (continued)

Types of handling of applications provided for in the revised Regulations		Emphases of review		Types of judgments provided for in the Administrative Litigation Law and the Judicial Interpretations	
Types	Concrete case-handling methods	Procedural matters	Substantive matters	Judgment in favor of the defendant	Judgment in favor of the plaintiff
	The information applied for is registration materials to which the access is specially provided by relevant laws or administrative regulations (A.36)			Handling the case in accordance with Administrative Litigation Law	Handling the case in accordance with Administrative Litigation Law
	The information applied for needs to be processed or analyzed (A.38)			Rejecting the action brought by the plaintiff (A2)	Handling the case in accordance with Administrative Litigation Law
	The applicant makes a public complaint or report of violation of law in the form of an application for government information disclosure, in which case the applicant is informed of the appropriate channels through which the complaint or report can be submitted (A.39)			Handling the case in accordance with Administrative Litigation Law	Handling the case in accordance with Administrative Litigation Law
	The information applied for belongs to openly circulated publication, in which case the applicants should be informed of the access channels (A.39)			Rejecting the action brought by the plaintiff (A2)	Handling the case in accordance with Administrative Litigation Law

(continued)

Table 2 (continued)

Types of handling of applications provided for in the revised Regulations		Emphases of review		Types of judgments provided for in the Administrative Litigation Law and the Judicial Interpretations	
Types	Concrete case-handling methods	Procedural matters	Substantive matters	Judgment in favor of the defendant	Judgment in favor of the plaintiff
	There is inaccuracy or error in the government information provided by an administrative organ related to a citizen or legal person, in which case the administrative organ should make corrections, or refer the information to the administrative organ with the authority to make the corrections			Rending a ruling to dismiss the plaintiff's claim (A12)	A9
				Judicial Interpretation: Rending a ruling to dismiss the plaintiff's claim in cases where the information applied for has already been transferred to the national archives at any level (A.7)	Handling the case in accordance with Administrative Litigation Law
				Judicial precedent: consultation does not belong to the application for government information disclosure[b]	Handling the case in accordance with Administrative Litigation Law

(continued)

Table 2 (continued)

Types of handling of applications provided for in the revised Regulations		Emphases of review		Types of judgments provided for in the Administrative Litigation Law and the Judicial Interpretations	
Types	Concrete case-handling methods	Procedural matters	Substantive matters	Judgment in favor of the defendant	Judgment in favor of the plaintiff
Other methods of processing the applications	Charging fees on the application for disclosure of government information which is in an amount or at a frequency obviously unreasonable (A.42)				Handling the case in accordance with Administrative Litigation Law
	Processing of suggestions on changing the nature of a piece of information from government information disclosed upon application into government information disclosed on the initiative of the government (A.44)				Handling the case in accordance with Administrative Litigation Law
	Processing of complaints and reports of derelict of duty or violation of rights in the government information disclosure work A.47 and A.51)				Handling the case in accordance with Administrative Litigation Law

[a] This form draws on the typified table of decisions on the handling of applications for information disclosure made by Baojian Geng and Mi Zhou in their published article. We adjusted and reconstructed the table to comprehensively reflect the types of disclosure of information upon application and the thinking behind the trial and judgment of relevant cases. Among them, "A.30" and other serial numbers indicate the articles in the revised Regulations and relevant judicial interpretation provisions. Baojian Geng and Mi Zhou, "Analysis of the Changes of Government Information Disclosure Litigation under the Institutional Environment of the Revised Regulations", 2 (2020) *Chinese Public Administration*

[b] Jiayi Wu, "'Consultation': Negative Determination of Government Information Disclosure Application—Based on the Analysis of 149 judgments in Shanghai", in *Public Law Studies*, vol. 19, Hangzhou: Zhejiang University Press, 2019, pp.146–162. However, the revised Regulations do not explicitly list consultation as the identification standard for non-government information disclosure, because the legal meaning of consultation is too vague, and applications that meet the requirements for government information disclosure application may also take the form of consultation. Whether consultation can be recognized as a form of government information disclosure application should be judged on a case-by-case basis

Controlling the abuse of the right of application for government information disclosure, and the related rights to administrative reconsideration and litigation is a hot spot and focus of the research on government information disclosure. Some individuals apply for government information disclosure and related administrative reconsideration or file related lawsuits in a repeatedly and harassing way without actual interest basis. This practice, which wastes administrative and judicial public service resources without bringing any actual benefit, constitutes an abuse of rights. When handling litigation cases of government information disclosure, courts need to suppress the abuse of litigation rights in accordance with law out of the judicial policy consideration of maintaining normal litigation function. The case of Lu Hongxia v. Nantong Municipal Development and Reform Commission has set a judicial precedent of controlling the abuse of litigation that has not only guiding significance for cases in the field of government information disclosure but also pioneering significance in the whole field of administrative litigation. It representatively embodies the judicial policy that "At the primary stage of the development of the rule of law, judicial organs, under heavy pressure, should only remedy the rights in need of remedy, protect the members of the public worthy of protection, and solve the disputes that can be solved".[6] But at the same time, it should be noted that, with the exception of some typical subjects and cases, abuse of the right to apply for government information disclosure and the right to remedy is still rare in practice. We must still make it clear that controlling the abuse of litigation is a negation of only the way the parties claim interests, not the interests claimed by the parties. For people's courts, supervising the government information disclosure work of administrative organs and correcting their unlawful acts, and protecting to the greatest extent the legitimate rights and interests of applicants to obtain government information is still more important than controlling the abuse of the right to apply for government information and the right to remedy.[7]

4 Managing Government Information Litigation at Its Sources

The practice of government information disclosure litigation shows that some administrative organs have failed to properly handle the application for government information disclosure: subjectively, they have failed to faithfully implement the concept and system of government information disclosure in the revised Regulations, and

[6] Baojian Geng and Mi Zhou, "Abuse of the right to sue in the field of government information disclosure and its regulation-also on the value of the case of Hongxia Lu v. Nantong Development and Reform Commission (government information disclosure case), 3 (2016) *Administrative Law Review*.

[7] Some empirical studies conclude that "in practice, some administrative organs one-sidedly stress that the right to apply for government information disclosure has been abused, which seems to be an exaggeration". See Yunkai Xu, "Empirical Analysis and Institutional Reconstruction of Administrative Reconsideration Cases of Government Information Disclosure", 2 (202) *Chinese Public Administration*.

objectively, they have failed to effectively coordinate important supporting and diversion mechanisms. They will be able to reduce the amount of government information disclosure litigation at its sources if they can overcome these obstacles.

1. Effectively implementing the concept and system of government information disclosure

The report to the 19th National Congress of the Communist Party of China pointed out that: "Socialism with Chinese characteristics has entered a new era and the principal contradiction in Chinese society has evolved into one between unbalanced and inadequate development and the people's ever-growing need for a better life." Providing balanced and sufficient government information disclosure services to help people pursue their own better life and uphold their legitimate rights and interests is conducive to resolving major social contradictions in the new era.[8] One of the important contents of Xi Jinping Thought on the rule of law is to adhere to the integrated construction of a law-based state, a law-based government and a law-based society. It is conducive to the construction of a law-based society if the government provides government information in accordance with law and social subjects deal with the interest relations between them in accordance with law under the condition of information equality. The revised Regulations further standardize the disclosure of government information upon application by deleting the provision in the old Regulations on the requirement of the relevance between the information applied for and the "production, life or scientific research" of the applicant, which is understood as a restriction on the qualification for application and clearly defining various kinds of information, such as those that should be disclosed by the government on its own initiative, those that may not be disclosed, and those that may be withheld, as well as applications that should not be treated as application for government information disclosure, and imposing restrictions on unreasonable applications, thereby providing a standardized and clear operational basis for the work of government information disclosure upon application. Administrative organs should implement the ideas, principles and requirements of "taking disclosure as the norm and non-disclosure as the exception", "justice, fairness, legality, and convenience for the people" and "timeliness and accuracy", follow the provisions of the revised Regulations on typed reply to applications, and practice good governance in accordance with good laws, so as to meet people's needs for government information.

2. Improving the supporting mechanisms to ensure access to relevant information by the public

In judicial practice, there are two kinds of situations in which the information applied for does not fall within the scope of government information disclosure according to law, but the applicant does have an objective information need that is not met. In such situations, it is necessary to improve the corresponding supporting mechanisms

---

[8] Xi Jinping, *Secure a Decisive Victory in Building a Moderately Prosperous Society in All Respects and Strive for the Great Success of Socialism with Chinese Characteristics for a New Era—Report to the 19th National Congress of the Communist Party of China*, Beijing: People's Publishing House, 2017, p. 17.

and straighten out their relationship with government information disclosure, so as to ensure that applicants can properly obtain the relevant information.

(1) Rationalizing the relationship between government information disclosure and access to administrative law enforcement case file information

According to Article 16 Paragraph 2 of the revised Regulations, an administrative organ may decide whether to disclose or withhold information about administrative law enforcement case files, unless otherwise required by any law, regulation or rule. The revised Regulations contain no definitions of the connotation and extension of administrative law enforcement case file information. Nor is there any conclusive definition of "administrative law enforcement" or "administrative law enforcement case file" in the general theory of administrative law.[9] Article 2 of the Judicial Interpretation stipulates that "Under the following circumstances, a people's court shall not accept the administrative lawsuit brought by a citizen, a legal person or any other organization against the administrative organ... (4) The party concerned or a party of interest in an administrative procedure applies for consulting case files in the name of government information disclosure, and the administrative organ notifies such a party to proceed in accordance with the relevant laws and regulations." In the opinion of the authors of this report, this article can be understood at the following levels: first, this provision is directly applicable to situations where there are channels and practical conditions for a party or a party of interest to an administrative procedure to consult case files stipulated by laws and regulations, and the administrative organ informs him to obtain the information by way of consulting case files; second, in situation where there are no laws and regulations or practical conditions that permit a party or a party of interest to an administrative procedure to obtain case file materials referred to in this provision, the right of a party to the administrative procedure or a party of interest to apply for government information disclosure is not excluded; third, persons other than the parties to the administrative procedures referred to in this provision and parties of interest may apply for the disclosure of the government information involved in the case file, and the administrative organ may provide the information by allowing them to consult case file information, or by replying their applications for case file information as applications for the disclosure of government information; fourth, the level of protection of the right of parties to administrative procedure and parties of interest to access to relevant information, whether through consultation of case files or through government information disclosure, should not be lower than that of others. On the basis of the Judicial Interpretation, the revised Regulations clearly provide for the system of relative non-disclosure of the information about administrative law enforcement case files, thereby leading to the issue of the choice between the right to apply for information disclosure and the right

[9] Yi Liang, "Interpretation and Application of Administrative Law Enforcement File Information-A Preliminary Observation Centered on Article 16 of the Regulations on the Disclosure of Government Information", 2 (2020) *Political Science and Law*.

to consult case files.[10] According to Article 16 Paragraph 2 of the revised Regulations and Article 2 Paragraph 4 of the Judicial Interpretation, if the application for government information disclosure involves information about administrative law enforcement files, the administrative organ shall produce evidence to show that such information belongs to the administrative law enforcement files and that such files do exist. The so-called administrative law enforcement case files refer to files formed in the process of acceptance and handling of administrative law enforcement cases by administrative organs in accordance with specific laws, regulations and rules. The parties and parties of interest in administrative law enforcement cases should first try to obtain the information by consulting the case files in accordance with relevant laws and regulations. If they are unable to obtain the information by this means, they may apply for government information disclosure, and the administrative organ should give a reply on whether or not to disclose such information.

(2) Rationalizing the relationship between government information disclosure and openness and utilization of archives

In practice, there are more and more cases in which administrative organs reject the application for government information disclosure on the grounds that the government information applied for has been transferred to national archives at various levels. Because the time limits imposed by the Archives Law and the Measures for the Implementation of the Archives Law on the disclosure of the government information handed over by administrative organs to archives make it basically impossible to meet the applicants' demand for the disclosure of government information that dates a little back in time, many lawsuits have been brought by applicants against administrative organs, archives or competent archives departments.[11] Article 7 of the Judicial Interpretation makes a distinction between the government information kept by the archives or archivists of administrative organs, which shall be dealt with in accordance with the procedures for the disclosure of government information, and the government information that has been transferred to the national archives at any level, which shall be dealt with in accordance with the procedures for the utilization of archives. However, the revised Regulations do not directly absorb the rules of the Judicial Interpretation, but provide in Article 25 that people's governments at all levels should set up government information consultation places in national archives, public libraries, and places of government services, and equip them with appropriate facilities and equipment, and that administrative organs should promptly provide national archives and public libraries with government information disclosed to the public on their own initiatives—which can easily give people the idea that administrative organs still have the obligation to disclose government information kept by

[10] Wenbo Dai and Xiaoyu Zhang, "The Right to Apply for Information Disclosure and the Right to Consult Files: Boundaries, Competition and Cooperation, and Way out" in, He Tian and Yanbin Lv (eds.), *Transparency of Chinese Government 2020*, Beijing: China Social Sciences Press, 2020, pp. 139–150.

[11] Research Group on Archives-related Administrative Litigation Resulting from Government Information Disclosure, "Government Information Disclosure Is the Legal Obligation of Archives Departments", 11 (2017) *Archives and Construction*.

national archives. The Archives Law of the People's Republic of China, revised in 2020, stipulates in Article 15 Paragraph 2 that "Where archives are handed over to archives in advance for preservation with the consent of the archives, the matters of the public disclosure of government information involved in the archives shall, before the expiration of the handover period provided for by the state, still be handled by the entity that originally prepares or retains such government information. When the handover period expires, matters of the public disclosure of government information involved in the archives shall be handled according to the provisions on the use of archives", in Article 29 that "Organs, groups, enterprises and public institutions, other organizations and citizens may, as required for economic construction, national defense construction, education and scientific research and other work, and in accordance with the relevant provisions of the state, use the archives kept by an archives which are not yet available to the public and the archives which are preserved by relevant organs, groups, enterprises and public institutions, and other organizations", and in Article 31 that "An entity or individual that has handed over or donated archives to an archives or deposited archives with it may have the priority in the use of such archives and may propose restrictions on the use of parts of the archives that are inappropriate for public access, and the archives shall provide support and convenience." Therefore, administrative organs have the basis and conditions to use the archival government information that has already been transferred to archives and there is still the issue of whether an administrative organ has the obligation to use the archival information in national archives that is not yet open to the public to disclose government information to the applicants in light of the needs of government information disclosure work. In the opinion of the authors of this report, the differences between government information kept in administrative organs and that transferred to archives for safekeeping are mainly in the custody subject, legal attribute and management system. If an applicant has a practical need for the government information that has been handed over to the archives, and there are no other reasons for not disclosing it, then it is necessary for the administrative organs and archives to establish a smooth mechanism for opening and utilizing individual archives in advance to meet the information need of the applicant. Meanwhile, since modern government administration has been fully informatized, a lot of government information has more than one carrier. An administrative organ does not stop keeping a piece of government information because of its transfer to the archives, and the Archives Law does not prohibit an administrative organ from disclosing by itself the government information that has been transferred to the archives. As long as the administrative organ still keeps the government information and is not prohibited by law to disclose the information, it should still be deemed to have the obligation to disclose the information.

Characteristic Mechanisms for and Innovative Explorations of Openness of Government Affairs in Xicheng District of Beijing Municipality

Project Team on the Openness of Government Affairs in Xicheng District of Beijing Municipality

In recent years, the Government of Xicheng District of Beijing Municipality (hereinafter referred to as "the district government") has focused on the positioning of the district as a core functional area of the capital, vigorously promoted the "national capital standard", cultivated the "red wall consciousness", advanced the comprehensive, standardized and sophisticated development of openness of government affairs, strengthened institutional building, refined policy interpretation, deepened the openness in key fields, and ensured the high-quality development of open government work.

1 New Opportunities for the Openness of Government Affairs Brought by the New Reform Pattern

1. The new positioning of the strategic planning of the capital

In August 2020, the Regulatory Detailed Planning of the Functional Core Areas of the Capital (Block Level) (2018–2035) was officially approved by the CPC Central Committee and the State Council, indicating that the planning and construction of the capital city entered a new historical stage. Xicheng District, as one of the functional core areas of the capital city, is a core area of the national political center, cultural center and international exchange center, a key area for the protection of the historical

Project Team on the Openness of Government Affairs in Xicheng District of Beijing Municipality (✉)
Xicheng District of Beijing Municipality, Beijing, China
e-mail: 13693186775@163.com

H. Tian and Y. Lv (eds.), *Assessing Government Transparency in China (2021)*,
https://doi.org/10.1007/978-981-99-9734-3_5

and cultural city, and an important window area for displaying the image of the national capital.

2. The new pattern of institutional reform in Xicheng District

In March 2019, the Party Committee and the Government of Beijing Municipality officially approved the Institutional Reform Plan for the Xicheng District of Beijing Municipality. The institutional reform created new opportunities for the openness of government affairs in Xicheng District: the Government Service Bureau of Xicheng District was officially established as a new department under the district government. The Openness of Government Affairs Division and the Information Disclosure Division, which were under the General Office of the District Government before the institutional reform, now become two divisions under the Government Service Bureau of the District Government, responsible for coordinating and promoting information disclosure and openness of government affairs in the whole district. Their main responsibilities include coordinating the work of "Internet plus government service" and promoting, guiding, coordinating and supervising the information disclosure and openness of government affairs work in the district. The Government Service Bureau is responsible for not only carrying out the top-level design for the reforms but also promoting the reforms and coordinating services in the district. In carrying out the open government work, the Bureau has focused on optimizing the business environment in the district and fulfilling the obligation of disclosing government information in accordance with law, and removing the last obstacles in servicing the people.

3. Seizing new opportunities in the openness of government affairs

The new reform pattern brings new opportunities. During the institutional reform, which coincided with the promulgation and implementation of the revised Regulations on the Disclosure of Government Information (hereinafter referred to as the revised Regulations) in 2019, the district government seized the opportunity of the transformation of openness of government affairs and launched the "Xicheng Model" of integrating "government services, government websites and government new media".

Firstly, it realized the integration of openness of government affairs and government service by accurately grasping the new requirements of openness of government affairs under the new situation, taking the implementation of the revised Regulations as the main line that runs through the reforms aimed at "simplification of administrative procedures, decentralization of powers, combination of decentralization with appropriate control, and optimization of services", the optimization of the business environment, and the effort to meet the needs of the citizens and enterprises, giving priority to openness in providing law-based, accurate and efficient government services, and making every effort to build a service-oriented "sunshine government".

Secondly, it realized the integration of openness of government affairs and government website work by deepening the "Internet plus openness of government affairs", promoting the online openness of government affairs, giving full play to the role of government portal website as the main channel of openness of government affairs, building an online governance platform for the performance of duties, realizing the function of "all-in-one website" online duty-performance function, and providing authoritative and convenient policy inquiry services for enterprises and citizens.

Thirdly, it realized the integration of openness of government affairs and new media work by giving full play to the advantages of government new media, such as fast dissemination, wide audience and strong interactivity, taking content construction as the foundation to continuously strengthen the functions of publication, dissemination, interaction, guidance and handling of affairs, so as to provide more convenient and practical mobile services for enterprises and citizens, building a website and new media integration platform, promoting the integrated development of websites and new media, striving to build an "online government at your fingertips", and actively use government new media to promote the openness of government affairs and optimize government services.

2 Main Practices and Experiences of Xicheng District in Promoting the Openness of Government Affairs

1. Strengthening the openness of decision-making and enhancing the public's sense of participation and satisfaction

Firstly, adhering to the high-level overall planning by district leaders and implementing the system of normalized live broadcasting of government executive meetings on Weibo. The district government has set up a leading group for information disclosure and openness of government affairs with the district head as the group leader and refined the responsibilities of the main leaders and leaders in charge of specific aspects of the work. All departments and sub-district offices have set up leading groups for the openness of government affairs according to the district-level model and a working mechanism with the "top leaders" serving as the group leaders and coordinating the advancement of open government work, and all units fully staffed with full-time professionals. In recent years, in accordance with the principle of "promoting the construction of service-oriented government and guaranteeing citizens' right to participation and expression" and in order to expand public participation and strengthen the openness of government affairs, the district government has established the system whereby representatives of the public attend the executive meetings of the district government as observers and the system of live-broadcast of the executive meetings of the district government in Weibo, which enable deputies to people's congresses, CPPCC members and representatives of the public to participate in the discussion of major government decisions by attending the online and offline executive meetings of the government as observers, thereby creating an open decision-making environment, and increasing government transparency year by year. In 2020, a total of 16 deputies to people's congresses, CPPCC members, community residents, experts and scholars were invited to attend four executive meetings of the district government as observers and participate in discussions on ten items on the agendas of the executive meetings. The discussions of 25 agenda items at 15 executive meetings of the district government were broadcast live on Weibo.

Secondly, adhering to the performance by the district head of his duty as "the primary interpreter of policies" and carrying out high-quality activities of "reporting work to the public by district government". In 2017, the district government took the lead in the city in formulating the Implementation Opinions of People's Government Xicheng District of Beijing Municipality on Reporting Its Work to the Public, which has become an important measure for building a bridge of "social communication" and promoting joint governance and realizing sharing, an exploration in comprehensively promoting the openness of decision-making, implementation, management, service and results, a new form of public communication in addition to open meetings, open government days, and government-people interaction centers, and an extension and supplement to such forms of openness as reports to the people's congresses and CPPCC, and website and the media. By 2020, the district government had organized high-standard activities of reporting its work to the public for four consecutive years, with a total of more than 2,800 participants. At these activities, more than 50 questions raised by representatives from all walks of life were answered by the district head and deputy district heads and over 200 suggestions and proposals relating to the themes of the reports had been collected from people of all walks of life by various government departments and sub-district offices in the district. The district government has developed a long-term mechanism for reporting its work to the public, which has been highly praised by the Government of Beijing Municipality and become a model of "reporting government work to the public" in the open government work in the whole country. On the morning of November 15, 2020, the head of the district government led seven deputy heads to participate in the fourth "reporting government work to the public" activity in 2020 with the theme of "Responding to Challenges and Creating the Future Together". Affected by the Covid-19 pandemic, the event was held at one main venue and 16 sub-venues to ensure the health and safety of participants and maximize participation. This activity was divided into two links: in the first link, the district head reported the annual work of the district government and the direction of future development of the work to more than 650 representatives from all walks of life, including representatives of community residents, experts and scholars, United Front organizations, central state organs, units of the armed forces, central enterprises stationed in the district, and the media, who attended the activity either online or offline. In the second link, the representatives from all walks of life, after listening to the government work report, raised questions about epidemic prevention and control, security and stability, economic development, social governance and other aspects of the government work. The district leaders interacted with the representatives on the spot, answering their questions, and responding to their concerns. To enhance the effectiveness of policy interpretation, the district government produced and published H5 interpretations of relevant policies in the policy interpretation column of its website, broadcast live the whole event in text and picture on its official Weibo account "Beijing Xicheng", and released the video recording of the whole the event on the CCTV video APP. The activity was also covered by more than ten Internet media. Through all-around and all-link publicity, the district government provided the public who did not participate in the event with channels to understand its work.

Thirdly, creating high-end services of "Double Housekeeper" and promoting the implementation of policies through publicity work led by district leaders. Xicheng District is the district where Financial Street and the National Financial Management Center are located. In order to attract more foreign-funded financial institutions to set up their branch offices in Beijing, the "Double Housekeeper" Team, jointly set up by Beijing Financial Street Service Bureau and Beijing Financial Street Service Center Co., Ltd., has established a complete set of working mechanisms, forming a one-stop, "many-to-one" and multi-field individualized service mode. "I am your prime service housekeeper" is the commitment made by the "Double Housekeeper" Team in Xicheng District to its customers as well as its own positioning, which gives Financial Street not only height but also warmth. To seize the important historical opportunity of the construction of the "two zones", namely the National Comprehensive Demonstration Zone for Expanding Opening up in the Services Sector and China (Beijing) Pilot Free Trade Zone, the "Double Housekeeper" Team visited 131 financial institutions, established connection with more than 400 of them and negotiated reserve projects with ten of them. 19 high-quality financial institutions have landed in Xicheng District and Financial Street has become a strategic place to attract various financial institutions. Focusing on the theme of "Financial Cooperation and Reform in the Global Change", the "Double Housekeeper" Team enabled the financial institutions to make their voice heard in a concentrated way and communicate and interact with each other, thereby raising the number of hits on its website to over 1.3 billion and further enhancing the international influence of Financial Street. It hosted the Third Seminar on the Creation of a Financial Legal Environment in Beijing; provided service for the establishment of new sectors of the financial industry, and introduced 45 key financial institutions such as Galaxy Assets, Fengyu Huili and China Grain Storage Finance, with a registered capital of 117.7 billion yuan, organized the second exchange activity with the theme of enterprise listing, promoted the successful listing of Qianxin Technology Group Co., LTD and Financial Street Properties, and helped GrandTech to become one of the first elected enterprises of the New Third Board. As a result of its efforts, the financial industry in the district achieved an added value of 193.05 billion yuan in GDP, accounting for 52.90% of the regional GDP, in the first three quarters of the year, and its pillar position became even more prominent; nineteen global top 500 foreign-funded enterprises, including Goldman Sachs, UBS, Credit Suisse, Daiwa Securities, SWIFT, Crédit Agricole Corporate and Investment Bank and other internationally renowned financial groups, investment banks, asset management companies and international financial organizations, as well as 19 of the top 500 foreign-funded enterprises in the world, had established branch offices in Xicheng District, and the Financial Street has achieved fruitful results in gathering high-quality financial resources, opening up a new situation in creating the open highland of the financial industry with the most comprehensive categories, the widest fields and the most complete system.

2. Strengthening the standardized management of openness of government affairs and promoting the whole-chain openness of policy release

Firstly, taking the lead in the whole city in completing the standardized production and refined management and application of the "full lists". In 2018, the district government, as a pilot unit of the State Council, took the lead in completing the production and disclosure of three types of lists in the whole city and the whole country. First of all, it completed the review of nine types of lists, including those of major construction projects, financial budgets and final accounts, and tax administration, in accordance with the requirement of the pilot plan of the State Council; second, it took the opportunity of constructing the three-level lists in key fields in Beijing to completed the compilation of the two-level lists in 51 key fields; and third, according to the responsibilities of various departments as specified in relevant laws, regulations, and provisions, it carried out a comprehensive review of the information generated by 83 units in the whole district, including 15 sub-district offices, in the performance of their duties, and classified the information according to the attribute of openness, and established the "Database of Government Information Catalogs and Lists of Xicheng District".

At the same time, in line with the requirements of "getting a clear picture of the basic situation of government information, clarifying the responsibilities of the staff, being based on standards of openness, and making visible results in the openness" and under the leadership of the Division of Openness of Government Affairs of the district government, various departments and sub-district offices quickly followed up, and after repeated polishing, comparison and review, completed with high quality the "full lists of voluntary information disclosure" of 49 units (34 departments + 15 sub-district offices) under the district government, which, after being standardized with the municipal standards as the benchmark, were disclosed in the "Full Lists of Openness of Government Affairs" column on the portal website of the district government. Due to the outstanding achievements in the production of the full lists, the district government was entrusted by the Open Government Office of the General Office of Beijing Municipal Government to exchange experiences at the pilot work promotion meeting organized by the General Office of the State Council. Currently, each government organ has designated a staff member to be responsible for the timely updating of the "full list of voluntary information disclosure".

Secondly, promoting the whole-life-cycle openness of policies, establishing a supporting interpretation mechanism, and relying on the "openness of government affairs" column on government websites to create a centralized and unified platform for the openness of policies. The Office of the District Government, the District Administrative Service Bureau and the District Judicial Bureau have jointly established a coordination mechanism for policy formulation and interpretation and compile a catalog of interpretations of district government documents at the beginning of each year in light of the pre-arrangement for topics to be discussed at government executive meetings. By closely combining various links of policy-making, including the solicitation of opinions, formulation and deliberation, public release, interpretation and application, it realized the whole-life-cycle openness of all non-confidential policy documents, established a policy interpretation and recordation process for policy documents before their release, and achieved the synchronized release of policy documents and their interpretations.

Third, building a high-quality intensive website to highlight the important role of "the primary information release platform of the government", building "one website and one station" in the whole region, deepening the achievements of intensive construction, and further improving the quality of government services. In 2019, the district government successfully completed the construction of an intensive government website platform and incorporated various information resources and user spaces into the information resource library of the city for unified management. In 2020, the district government completed the intensive construction of three main categories of government website functions, namely information release, interactive communication and government service, and became the first among the 16 district governments in Beijing to launch the interactive communication function of English-language government website, thereby improving the foreign-related service on its portal website; it improved the construction of interactive channels such as intelligent questions and answers, consultation, live streaming interaction, and public opinion solicitation, thereby realizing the reply to consultation letters on the same day of their reception and timely disclosure of consultation letter-related data; it had set up on its portal website a "consultation" column, integrated the "consultation" website column, 66,007,070 consultation platform and 12,345 compliant acceptance platform, conducted hot spot search and big data analysis on all issues involved in the consultation work, sorted out high-frequency questions and answers, and complete the special column of "echoes of government affairs" on its website. It established a "echoes of government affairs" column on its portal website to broaden the effective channels for the interaction between the government and the public, providing better interactive channels such as intelligent Q&A, consultation, complaint, live broadcast interaction and public opinion collection that basically cover the online interactive needs of the public and enterprises. The replies to consultations were given by professional consultants of the District Administrative Service Bureau of the district government on the same day of their reception, with standardized and complete content.

3. Promoting law-based performance of duties and law-based governance of the district and taking multiple measures to solve the problems in the disclosure of government information upon application

The district government, as one of the first pilot units of openness of government affairs in China, took the lead in breaking through the old mechanism, and adopted various effective means of openness in accordance with the revised Regulations, thereby achieving "losing zero lawsuit" in information disclosure-related administrative litigations in the whole district for two consecutive years, and further improving the people's satisfaction with the performance of duty by administrative organs.

Firstly, laying a solid systemic foundation through institution building. The district government organically combined the openness of government affairs with government service, retained the government information disclosure division to be responsible for the work of disclosure of government information upon the application, formulated institutional documents such as Work Rules for the Disclosure of Government Information upon Application, Work Manual for Disclosure of Government Information upon Application and Measures for Standardizing Subjects of Obligation, and adhered to the normalized mechanism whereby "whoever adopts or keeps a document shall be responsible for its disclosure, whoever performs a duty shall appear in court to respond to the lawsuit against the performance of the duty, and whoever violates regulations shall be held responsible for the violation" in the whole region.

Secondly, broadening the thinking of openness through business training. By relying on the government expert database and a team of legal advisers, the district government explored various forms of business training and obtained the greatest common denominator among preventing and controlling legal risks, promoting the standardized performance of government duties, and meeting the needs of the public, and "invigorated" the training on the disclosure of government information upon application. It provided general training programs throughout the district, mainly providing all-round instructions on such aspects of the work as the application of laws and regulations, reply procedures and typical cases, and point-to-point training programs by entering into government departments and conducts targeted training in light of each department's responsibilities and prominent problems, and salon-style training by building salon interactive platforms, carrying out in-depth discussions on key issues and difficult cases, and sharing experiences.

Thirdly, improving people's satisfaction through "one-to-one" services. Through the analysis and judgment of the contents of applications for information disclosure, the district government further grasped the focus of attention of the public with respect to government information, regularly reviewed the contents of applications, and provided relevant information to the corresponding government organs for their reference through such channels as business departments, the live-broadcast room for interaction between the government and the people and the reporting of work by the government to the public, so as to enable them to accurately respond to public demands. Through symposiums jointly organized by information disclosure departments, business departments and legal departments, it provided "one-to-one" accurate services to the public on the spot. For example, since many applicants had applied for the disclosure of government information related to the renewal of house demolition permits, the district government, after communication and coordination with the District Housing Management Bureau, which was the competent department of housing demolition, turned the information about renewal of house demolition permits into the information to be voluntarily disclosed by the government. In view of the more than 300 applications for the disclosure of information about the reconstruction project of dilapidated houses in Sanlihe South Area, the district government organized a meeting of representatives of local residents of the area by relying on the project headquarters and relevant business departments and invited relevant professionals to answer the questions raised by the applicants on the spot. And in view of the fact that a citizen had applied for the disclosure of information about the resettlement housing under an unfinished project eight times without success and brought an administrative lawsuit each time, the district government invited the business department and the legal department to have a discussion with the applicant to win his understanding and support. As a result of this effort, the applicant has not applied for administrative reconsideration or brought an administrative lawsuit on this issue since then.

Fourthly, promoting the standardized and law-based performance of duties through the identification of demands. In the review of the work of government information disclosure upon application in the district, the district government found that some administrative organs still did not strictly follow the relevant legal norms when exercising their functions and powers and performing their administrative duties. It took this problem seriously and carried out active explorations, discussed and evaluated potential legal risks, and regularly provided reasonable suggestions on administration by law to relevant administrative organs. Up to now, it has put forward a number of suggestions on the rationalization of the work of administration by law, including the suggestions that "the name of the government should be used cautiously in legally prescribed non-governmental duties", that "the content of government information released externally should be standardized", that "the source management system of official document attributes should be strictly implemented" and that "the information management work of permanent and temporary institutions should be strengthened".

4. Exploring innovative service models and comprehensively improving the effectiveness of openness of government affairs

Firstly, promoting the whole-scenario application of blockchain and the implementation of policies on the optimization of the business environment. In 2020, the district government took the lead in the whole city in introducing blockchain technology into the field of government service, covering nine scenarios, including deregistration of enterprises, cancellation of enterprise social security accounts, establishment and change of micro-credit companies, social medical assistance, marriage registration, identification of urban and rural residents eligible for subsistence allowances, construction garbage landfill permit, joint completion acceptance of construction projects, and the opening of supermarkets and one scenario application, namely on-site verification of electronic licenses. It realized the sharing of data and materials, reduced costs by handling affairs through blockchain, and allowed users who forgot to bring their ID cards with them to handle their affairs through facial recognition. Through the "9 + 1" blockchain application scenario, the Administrative Service Center of Xicheng District reduced the number of required application materials by 15, the required number of visits by applicants to the Center by 13, and the time for the handling of applications by 20 working days, thus raising the work efficiency through scientific and technological empowerment and improving the convenience of services through collaborative work. By April 3, 2021, the district government had handled 74 cases of government service, including four cases of deregistration of enterprises, one case of social medical assistance, one case of construction garbage landfill permit, and one case of identification of urban and rural residents eligible for subsistence allowances, through "9 + 1" application scenario, and 67 cases, including the change of registration of practicing doctors and allocation of the quota of passenger cars, through the application of electronic licenses. The Xicheng Branch of the Beijing Municipal Commission on Planning and Natural Resources actively promoted the application of scenarios, and launched seven application scenarios of "blockchain plus real estate registration", providing such services as online inquiry, online reservation, online payment, and EMS delivery, allowed citizens and enterprises to log in to the online service platform of real estate registration to handle their affairs, formally implemented the system of electronic licenses of real estate registration with all electronic licenses of real estate registration deposited for anti-counterfeiting through blockchain technology, allowing them to be previewed and downloaded by users.

Secondly, building the function of government new media and giving full play to its role as the bridge connecting the government and the public. The district government has developed a communication matrix that combines traditional media with new media and opened its official accounts on Weibo, WeChat, Douyin and Toutiao. Take the government Weibo as an example. In July 2011, the account "Beijing Xicheng" was officially opened first on Sina.com, and then on Tencent.com and people.com.cn, forming a pattern of simultaneous release on the three major platforms. By 2019, it had more than 885,000 fans and extensive social influence; the account "Xicheng Home", a brand created by the district government with "district-neighborhood-residence" as its construction structure, "community-housing estate-building" as its governance area, and "residents" as the center of its services, had become a unified channel for the district Party committee and district government to connect with the public. By May 27, Xicheng Home had a total of 440,000 registered users, of which 165,000 had completed certification, and released more than 1,700 notices. In addition, government WeChat accounts have also developed rapidly. Focusing on the official WeChat account of "Beijing Xicheng", the district government gathered official WeChat official accounts of various commissions, departments, bureaus and sub-district offices in the district to form a systematic government WeChat account matrix. The district government has also created the WeChat official account "Xicheng e-Service", which has an interactive consultation function, publishes a monthly list of frequently asked questions accumulated in the interactive consultation, and responds to hot issues of public concern through such forms of policy interpretation as cartoons, pictures, questions and answers and small videos, thus making the contents of important documents and major decisions "understandable" to the public, and providing practical and accurate government information and government services in light of the people's actual needs. Now the district government has realized the synchronized release of information on the "Echoes of Government Affairs" column of its websites and on its WeChat official account, video accounts, Xicheng Daily, Douyin Short Video, Aauto Quicker, Xinhuanet, Beijing Daily and other platforms, with the highest number of hits per article reaching 600,000.

Thirdly, relying on the innovative mechanism of community service centers to realize the accurate push of policies at the community level. The 15 community government service centers in Xicheng District have realized the accurate policy delivery service, changed their service mode from that of "people looking for policies" to that of "policies looking for people", actively studied the objects of policy implementation, accurately pushed policies aimed at benefiting the people and enterprises, provided personalized guidance services, developed an accurate portrait of government services, and enhanced the applicability of policies. The district government implemented precise management with the support of government data and in light of the actual needs of different groups such as retirees, unemployed people and students, providing "customized" one-on-one guidance to archived personnel in the handling of retirement, unemployment registration, employment services and other businesses, improved the release channels and enhanced the arrival rate of policy information and realized the all-round and whole-chain quick access to policy information by such means as paper materials, SMS notification, WeChat official account interpretation, video communication, and in-home coaching, achieved 100% coverage of the corresponding population by the push of such service policy information as concentrated participation in elderly care and childcare insurance and "unemployment payment", accurately identified the needs of enterprises and citizens to ensure the full implementation of policies, and realized the "intelligent matching" of policies, enterprises and the unemployed when pushing policies for the unemployed, and enabled the enterprises that provide jobs to the unemployed to get policy dividends, thus realizing the "mutual benefit and win–win" in policy implementation.

3 Existing Problems in the Work of Openness of Government Affairs

1. The consciousness of openness still needs to be enhanced

Currently, some government departments do not attach enough importance to the openness of government affairs and are satisfied with only completing the tasks given to them by their superiors. As a result, those responsible for the openness of government affairs and government information disclosure do not have a high consciousness of voluntary disclosure and enthusiasm for work and can get their work done only after repeated urging. The relevant work posts in some government departments have poor stability, with frequent changes of personnel and incomplete and irregular handover of work.

2. The openness mechanism needs to be improved

In recent years, the district government has carried out a lot of fruitful work in promoting and ensuring the whole-life-cycle openness and whole-chain management of government policies. Nevertheless, there are still some problems in the work, such as insufficient interpretation of policy documents, lack of diversity in the form of interpretation and low quality of interpretation, tardy and incomplete disclosure of information about major decision-making and major issues, and incomplete disclosure of administrative law enforcement information.

3. Intelligent services need to be improved

The level of development of intelligence application technology and network interaction technology in the district is still far from meeting the standard of highly automated and intelligent open government work in the core areas of the national capital. The automatic replies to questions raised by users given by the "intelligent robot" in the "interaction between government and people" column of the website of the district government are still not accurate enough, and there is still a certain gap between the content and result of the replies and the actual demands, and the matching between the standardization of website background data and the intelligence of front desk "robot" needs to be further strengthened.

4 Direction and Prospect of Future Development

1. Enhancing the consciousness of the efficient application of the revised Regulations

Firstly, improving the quality of open government work through meetings and training. The district government should regularly hold special meetings on the open government work attended by the main leaders of all government organs in the district and meetings of the leading group on government information and openness of government affairs of the district government. The main leaders of the district should personally summarize, assess, and promote the work at such meetings. Secondly, using the revised Regulations to guide and promote open government work. The district government should strengthen the awareness of the revised Regulations among staff members by carrying out an article-by-article study, so as to ensure that every one of them is able to publicize the revised Regulations, analyze relevant cases, and accurately apply the revised Regulations and relevant cases in the work. Thirdly, firmly establishing the awareness of taking the full list as the standard of voluntary disclosure. The district government should strengthen the inspection of the source production, reform and adjustment, and dynamic updating of the whole list of each government organ, and include such acts as changing or deleting the whole list without authorization in the score deduction items of the performance evaluation system, so as to ensure that the whole list disclosed by each government organ is complete in content, high in quality, supported by statements of accounts, and corresponds to the actual powers.

2. Strengthening the whole-life-cycle policy disclosure mechanism

Firstly, establishing a trace mechanism. The district government should disclose on its website the "whole life cycle" of policies, which includes five links: solicitation of suggestions on policy-making, deliberation in policy formulation, public release of policies, interpretation and application of policies, and evaluation of the effect of policies, leaving traces on the website in the whole process. Secondly, implementing the whole-process disclosure mechanism. With the exception of those that should be kept confidential according to law, major issues involving public interests and the rights and interests of the public should be disclosed in the whole process. The time period for solicitation of opinions on policy documents should not be less than five days and the whole process should be recorded in detail. Thirdly, strengthening the supervision and cooperation mechanisms. The district government should standardize the administrative law enforcement behavior, implement the responsibility system of subjects of supervision, ensure effective supervision over the law enforcement departments supervisory departments, disclose in a concentrated way information about the whole process of administrative law enforcement activities in the form of "inspection reports", and uphold the seriousness and authority of the supervision mechanism with the attitude of "calling a spade a spade".

3. Strengthening the smart and accurate service function of the website

Firstly, enhancing the pertinence of policy interpretation. The district government should continuously raise the scientific and technological services and application level of its portal website, make full use of big data technology to analyze, collect and summarize information about the users of the website, and provide the public with effective services and policy interpretation. Secondly, improving the accuracy of the search function. The district government should enhance its awareness of "search as a service" and further optimize and upgrade the search engine of the portal website by relying on new technologies, so as to achieve a high match between the search results and public needs and realize accurate information search and accurate policy push. Thirdly, improving the level of intelligence of interaction between government and people. The district government should collect all the questions raised by users through the "consultation" column of its portal website, the 66,007,070 consultation platform and the 12,345 complaint acceptance platform as well as the valid answers to them, strengthen data classification and integration, update the content of Q&A knowledge base in a timely manner, carry out technical research, deepen and expand the scope of intelligent Q&A services, and gradually realize active, intelligent and effective response to public concerns.

The Tax Practice of Promoting Implementation, Standardization and Service Through Openness of Government Affairs

Research Team of Tax Publicity Center of the State Taxation Administration of the People's Republic of China

Taxation plays a basic, supporting and safeguarding role in state governance and the field of taxation has always been one of the key fields of openness of government affairs. The state attaches great importance to the openness of government affairs, and the main leaders have made many arrangements for and demands on this work. In 2020, tax authorities throughout the country thoroughly implemented the decisions and arrangements made by the CPC Central Committee and the State Council on the openness of government affairs. In accordance with the spirit of the third meeting of the National Leading Group for Openness of Government Affairs, they adhered to the principle of "taking openness as the norm and non-openness as the exception", ran the openness of government affairs through the whole process of tax work, made new progress and new achievements in the openness of government affairs, and played a positive role in promoting the modernization of taxation.

1 Adhering to the Openness of Decision-Making and Promoting the Targeted Implementation of Tax and Fee Policies

In 2020, the State Taxation Administration (hereinafter referred to as the Administration) vigorously promoted the openness of major tax decisions, disclosed tax and fee policy documents in a timely and active manner, strengthened policy interpretation, further guaranteed the public's right to know, right of participation and right of

Research Team of Tax Publicity Center of the State Taxation Administration of the People's Republic of China (✉)
The State Taxation Administration of the People's Republic of China, Beijing, China
e-mail: 13693186775@163.com

H. Tian and Y. Lv (eds.), *Assessing Government Transparency in China (2021)*,
https://doi.org/10.1007/978-981-99-9734-3_6

supervision, raised the level of the openness of government affairs and the level of government services of tax authorities, and created sunshine taxation.

1. Strengthening the pre-disclosure of major decisions

The Administration conscientiously implemented the system of pre-disclosure of major decisions, clarified the decision-making subjects and the scope of major administrative decisions, further improved such working mechanisms as mass participation, expert consultation, risk assessment and public release, increased the transparency of and public participation in major decisions, and extensively solicited the opinions of representatives of tax administrative counterparts, chambers of commerce, trade associations, and the general public on all important reform programs and major policies and measures that involve the vital interests of the people and need to be widely known by society, especially the formulation of tax regulations and normative documents that affect the vital interests of tax and fee payers, except for those that should be kept confidential according to law. In 2020, it successively solicited public opinions on the *Consumption Tax Law of the People's Republic of China (Exposure Draft)*, the *Announcement of the State Administration of Taxation on Several Issues Concerning Resource Tax Collection and Management (Exposure Draft)*, and the *Decision of the State Administration of Taxation on Amending the Measures for the Trial of Major Tax Cases (Exposure Draft)*. Before soliciting public opinions, it adhered to the practice of simultaneous research, simultaneous drafting and simultaneous submission for approval and simultaneous publication of the policy and measure documents and their explanations, so as to enable the public to better understand the policies and measures. Local tax authorities carried out the work of pre-disclosure of decisions in accordance with unified arrangements. For example, the Shanghai Municipal Tax Service formulated and published the annual list of key tasks and major decisions, held symposiums to listen to the opinions and suggestions of enterprises, experts and other stakeholders, invited the media to attend major meetings as observers, and publicly solicited opinions and suggestions on the Announcement of the List of Minor Tax Violations Subject to "No Tax Administrative Punishment for First-time Violation" in the Yangtze River Delta Region (Exposure Draft) and the Announcement on the Discretion Benchmark of Administrative Penalty for Declaration- and Invoice-related Tax Violations in the Yangtze River Delta Region (Exposure Draft), and adopted reasonable opinions and suggestions solicited through various channels.

2. Strengthening the openness of tax and fee policies

The Administration actively disclosed laws, administrative regulations, rules and normative documents related to the performance of duties by tax authorities and tax policies and measures aimed at promoting reforms, economic development, and improvement of people's livelihood through online channels such as the Internet, WeChat and client-side, gave full play to the role of tax websites as the primary platforms of the openness of government affairs, set up a "tax policy database" on tax websites to disclose policy documents and related interpretation materials in a concentrated and unified manner, and took full advantages of tax websites of being able to learn and to provide support and guarantee at any time to effectively disclose information about tax and fee policies related to epidemic prevention and control and social and economic development and their implementation. In 2020, it focused its efforts on such matters as supporting the protection, rescue, and material supply, encouraging public welfare donations, supporting the resumption of work and production, stabilizing foreign trade and expanding domestic demand, timely formulated operational documents for the implementation of preferential tax and fee policies adopted by the state in support of epidemic prevention and control and economic and social development, which were published on websites on the same day of their issuance, followed by key interpretations by the media and experts to ensure that state policies and regulations are fully and timely known by grassroots tax officials as well as market entities. It also confirmed the validity label of each normative document issued since 2013, so as to facilitate access and consultation by the public, and updated and issued 58 country (region)-specific investment tax guides (thus increasing the total of tax guides issued by the Administration to 104) to help enterprises "go global".

3. Optimizing policy interpretation and response to public concerns

To ensure the implementation of various policies, enable tax and fee-payers to understand and make good use of various tax and fee policies and fully enjoy policy dividends, the Administration took multiple measures, focused on major decisions and arrangements, continuously improved the interpretation capacity, broadened interpretation channels, diversified interpretation forms, and actively responded to public concerns, so as to ensure that the public truly know, understand, and easily obtain the information about the policies. It strengthened policy interpretation by focusing on the central work, interpreted major national strategies of tax service, released 308 principles of Q&A in four batches, and provided human–computer interaction services such as intelligent Q&A, thereby effectively solving the problem of different understandings of policy details by different local governments; issued and updated the Guidelines on Preferential Tax and Fee Policies in Support of Epidemic Prevention and Control and Economic and Social Development and strengthened the interpretation of preferential tax and fee policies and tax collection and management service measures focusing on the coordinated development of Beijing-Tianjin-Hebei Region, Guangdong-Hong Kong-Macau Greater Bay Area, Yangtze River Economic Belt, Hainan Free Trade Zone and other major national strategies; broadened channels and improved the effect of policy interpretation, promoted the transformation of the openness of government affairs function of tax authorities from one of social openness to one that attaches equal importance to social openness and openness to lower-level organs. In 2020, it carried out a series of "down to the grassroots" video training around the implementation of several batches of laws and policies issued by the state, including preferential tax and fee policies for epidemic prevention and control, individual income tax reform policies, the *Vehicle Acquisition Tax Law* and the *Resource Tax Law*, so as to ensure that the policies are not distorted or omitted in the process of implementation by tax authorities at all levels. In 2020, the Administration participated in the press conferences and policy briefings of the State Council Information Office more than ten times and held its own quarterly press conferences to introduce the situation of the implementation of tax policies and respond to social concerns by tax authorities. The persons in charge of relevant departments under the State Taxation Administration were interviewed by CCTV and other major central media, in which they timely interpreted major tax policies and measures, demonstrated the effect of policy implementation, and conveyed authoritative voices to society. In 2020, taking advantage of a broad audience, strong authority and great influence of online interviews, it held three online interviews with the theme of supporting preferential tax and fee policies and measures for epidemic prevention and control on its portal website, in which leaders of the Administration and persons in charge of relevant departments under it exchanged opinions and interacted with netizens. Local tax authorities, in conjunction with local government information offices, released information in an intensive manner on their platforms, and their leaders and heads of business departments under them attended "Online Interview with Directors" in local media and other website columns to interpret the tax and fee policies and tax collection and management service measures aimed at helping the resumption of work and production. It strengthened in-depth policy interpretation by innovating the forms of interpretation, accurately grasping the needs of tax and fee payers for preferential tax and fee policies during the epidemic period and interpreting the policies in a three-dimensional and multi-directional way through e-books, short videos, animation and long pictures, created the authoritative policy interpretation video program "Tax Lecture Hall", in which lectures were given by heads of relevant departments of the Administration, launched a total of 19 courses in three batches, namely, "Interpretations of Preferential Tax and Fee Policies", "Questions and Answers" and "Interpretations of Hot Policies", which received positive reports from authoritative media such as the portal website of the State Council, Xinhua News Agency and China News Service, with the number of views of the "Tax Lecture Hall" on the website of Xinhua News Agency reaching 1.01 million. In 2020, the Administration launched a series of short videos of illustrated policy interpretations, including "Understanding at a glance: taxes and fees that can be reduced or exempted during the epidemic" and "Teaching-by-doing: calculation of taxes", made a series of Vlog short films, including "Entrepreneurial college students take you to experience how convenient it is to start a new enterprise" and "Handling affairs at government departments: experiencing smart taxation", compiled the e-book Guidelines on Preferential Tax and Fee Policies in Support of Epidemic Prevention and Control and Economic and Social Development, created short video series brands such as Understanding Tax and Fee Policies in Seconds, Q&A about Taxes, Post-it Notes about Taxes and Small Classroom of Tax Law. A total of 256 short videos were released with a cumulative number of views of 50 million.

2 Adhering to the Openness of the Exercise of Powers and Promoting the Transparency and Standardization of Tax Law Enforcement

In 2020, the Administration adhered to law-based tax administration, highlighted optimization and coordination, attached equal importance to quality and efficiency, focused on the "three systems", published lists of powers and responsibilities, promoted the standardized exercise of tax law enforcement power, and run the openness of the exercise of power through all aspects and the whole process of the construction of the rule of law in the field of taxation.

1. Full disclosure of list of powers and responsibilities

In accordance with the principles of highlighting key points, carrying out the work in an orderly and law-based manner, and providing precise and convenient services for the people, the Administration advanced the compilation of lists of powers and responsibilities and the power operation charts. The List of Powers and Responsibilities of the State Administration of Taxation (for Trial Implementation), which covers 27 items and 61 sub-items in four fields, was compiled and made public on the website of the Administration, laying a foundation for further promoting the formation of a national operation system of lists of powers and responsibilities of tax authorities characterized by organic linkages between various parts from top to bottom, smooth operation, transparency and high efficiency. It made arrangements for tax authorities at or below the provincial level to prepare a list of powers and responsibilities to fully disclose their duties and competencies, law enforcement basis, law enforcement process, remedy channels, etc. of tax authorities, and establish and improve the mechanisms for dynamic adjustment and disclosure of lists and operation flowcharts. By July 2020, the taxation system had fully disclosed the lists of powers and responsibilities and the operation flowcharts and realized the full coverage of the lists of powers and responsibilities, thereby effectively promoting the fairness and justice of tax law enforcement and providing strong support for transforming government functions and deepening the simplification of administrative procedures and delegation of powers to lower levels.

2. Orderly disclosure of information about tax law enforcement situation

In recent years, tax authorities throughout the country have strengthened the *ex-ante*, interim and *ex-post* openness and enhanced their capacity for and level of tax law enforcement, constructed the administrative law enforcement publicity system, the system of whole-process recording of administrative enforcement actions and the system of legality review of major law enforcement decisions, and build the "1 + 3 + N" system covering one basic system, three management systems and 27 operational guidelines, clarified the list of items of legality review of major law enforcement decisions, improved the workflow of whole-process recording of law enforcement, and actively disclosed such law enforcement information as law enforcement documents and progress of handling of tax items, thereby making tax law enforcement more transparent, traceable and supervised, improved the mechanism for public release, cancellation and updating of tax law enforcement decision information, and timely disclosed tax law enforcement information to the public through law enforcement information publicity platforms, tax websites, new government media, tax service halls and other channels. In 2020, the taxation system disclosed more than 8.8 million pieces of information such as information about administrative licensing, equipped tax law enforcement personnel with nearly 70,000 law enforcement recorders, recorded more than 1.4 million pieces of law enforcement information, established nearly 6,000 interviews (inquiry) rooms, assigned nearly 25,000 legality reviewers, who reviewed the legality of more than 290,000 major law enforcement decisions.

3. Continuously advancing the "spot check mechanism featuring the random selection of both inspectors and inspection targets and the prompt release of results"

The Administration adopted and issued the measures for the management of databases of directories of random spot check objects and databases of directories of random spot check law enforcement inspectors, comprehensively integrated databases of directories of inspection objects, voluntarily disclosed the list of tax law enforcement inspectors, and improved the "spot-check mechanism featuring the random selection of both inspectors and inspection targets and the prompt release of results" or "double random" spot check mechanism. Spot-check objects and law enforcement inspectors were all selected by the "double random platform", the scheme, process and results of spot-checks all left traces in the system, and the results of spot-checks were released to the public in a timely manner through its portal website, WeChat official account, tax service halls and unified platform for administrative law enforcement information publicity, so as to promote fair law enforcement and consciously accept social supervision. It cooperated with the General Administration of Market Supervision in issuing a list of joint spot-checks, promoted joint law enforcement by provincial tax services and market supervision departments at the same level, and integrated the "double random spot-check" of tax authorities into the overall plan of joint law enforcement of the two departments.

3 Adhering to the Openness of Services and Promoting Convenient and Efficient Tax and Fee Payment

The Administration has always adhered to the concept of taking taxpayers and feepayers as the center, closely focusing on optimizing the tax business environment and deepening the reforms aimed at "simplification of administrative procedures, decentralization of powers, combination of decentralization with appropriate control, and optimization of services", optimized the tax and fee payment process, innovated "non-contact" tax and fee payment methods, increased the convenience, efficiency and transparency of tax payment, and continuously enhanced the sense of gain and satisfaction of tax and fee payers.

1. Comprehensively disclosing new measures for facilitating citizens' handling of tax affairs

In 2020, the Administration conducted the "Spring Breeze Action to Facilitate Citizens' Handling of Tax Affairs" for the seventh consecutive year with "Fighting against Covid-19, Promoting Development and Serving the Building of a Moderately Prosperous Society in All Respects" as its theme, and launched and made public 76 tax service measures in 24 categories focusing on four aspects of work, namely "supporting the prevention and control of Covid-19 and helping enterprises solve their problems, actively supporting enterprises to re-open for work and production, sparing no effort in serving the national development strategy, and effectively optimizing the tax business environment". For example, it further expanded the scope of items subject to online handling of tax affairs and payment of fees and realize the online handling of more than 90% of taxpayers' major tax-related services; and expanded the scope of paperless declaration of export tax refunds, and shortened the average time for processing normal export tax refunds nationwide by 20% on the basis of ten working days in 2019. In accordance with the arrangements made by the State Administration of Taxation, local tax authorities refined service measures for effectively supporting epidemic prevention and control and helping enterprises to re-open for work and production. For example, Jiangsu Provincial Taxation Administration fully incorporated tax affairs and payment of fees into the "integrated network" of local government services, promoted notification of all tax affairs at one time, realized progress tracking, node inquiry and interactive consultation of tax-related matters by tax and fee payers, and promoted online application and online inquiry of tax service matters.

2. Continuously facilitating the handling of tax affairs and payment of fees

In 2020, tax authorities throughout the country vigorously promoted "non-contact" handling of tax affairs, simplified related procedures and materials, and continuously improved the efficiency of taxation. The Administration, in conjunction with the National Development and Reform Commission, the Ministry of Finance and other departments, issued the Notice by Thirteen Departments, Including the State Taxation Administration of Several Measures for Facilitating the Reform of Tax and Fee Payment and Optimizing the Taxation Business Environment to steadily expand the scope of items subject to online handling of tax affairs and payment of fees, and actively guide tax and fee payers to pay taxes through "non-contact" channels such as e-tax agencies, self-service tax terminals and mobile phone clients, and released the List of "Non-contact" Online Tax Payment Items and the List of Key Tax-related Service Items Including Resumption of Work and Production, made 214 tax and fee payment items available for online handling, of which 203 items can be handled online in the whole process, so that the people can learn about policies by scanning QR codes, consult tax affairs online, handle tax affairs on the Internet and via cell phone. The World Bank's Business Environment Report in 2020 shows that the ranking of China's tax indicators has been further improved.

3. Improving the channels of public participation

In 2020, the Administration strengthened the collection of information about taxpayers' demands. Local tax authorities had set up opinion and suggestion boxes in tax service halls to collect, process and give feedback on the information, extensively collect information about taxpayers' demands through questionnaire investigation, taxpayers' forums, and door-to-door visits, among others, relied on the 12,366 tax service platform of the Administration to investigate taxpayers' demands by means of "non-contact" online questionnaires, give timely responses to commonly asked questions, actively promoted the rating of government services, and brought the tax service halls, e-tax agencies, 12,366 tax service hotline and self-service tax terminals into the scope of the evaluation. During the period from February to June 2020, the Administration, in view of the fact that some enterprises had encountered such problems as difficulties in production and operation and the tight capital chain and that some financial personnel of enterprises was unable to return to their work posts and make tax returns, extended the tax declaration period five times, and tax authorities throughout the country handled the applications for extension of declaration for 216,000 taxpayers to help enterprises in difficulty relieve their financial pressure.

4 Optimizing Platform Construction and Creating Multiple Channels of Openness of Government Affairs

In 2022, the Administration steadily advanced the "Internet Plus Taxation" Action Plan, promoted the data integration, service integration and application integration of tax websites, administrative law enforcement publicity platforms, 12,366 tax service platforms and new government media, and continuously raised the level the informatization construction of platforms of openness of government affairs.

1. Building the tax website into the primary platform of the openness of government affairs

In accordance with the Guide to the Development of Government Websites, the Administration endeavored to build the tax website into a platform for more comprehensive openness of government affairs, more authoritative policy release and interpretation and public opinion guidance, and more timely response to public concerns and provision of convenience services, continuously upgraded its portal website, optimized service functions such as the government information disclosure directory system, intelligent search, policy inquiry database and "Internet plus Tax Supervision", and deepened the construction of service functions such as tax consultation, interactive communication and data download. In 2020, the State Taxation Administration set up new columns such as "Services for Small and Micro Enterprises and Individual Industrial and Commercial Households", "Tax and Fee Reduction" and

"Epidemic Prevention and Control" on its portal website to promote the disclosure of information about key issues in key areas such as tax and fee reduction; while optimizing its own services, it connected e-taxation agencies, natural person e-taxation agencies and 12,366 Tax Service Platform, promoted the front-end integration of tax service functions, innovated and provided human–computer interaction functions such as intelligent Q&A, and strived to create an integrated network of tax service that enables people to handle their tax affairs without leaving home; established a special webpage for the "Belt and Road Initiative" on its portal website to disclose in a concentrated way policies and administrative regulations on the "Belt and Road Initiative" tax collection administration cooperation mechanism, and opened the English real-time online consultation function on its English webpage to provide convenient tax-related consultation services for foreign-funded enterprises and foreign individuals by relying on the 12,366 bilingual knowledge base. Various provincial-level tax administrations fully implemented the website construction management standards, standardized management of the opening of websites, content page, platform construction, security management, management mechanism, etc., comprehensively optimized the access and service experience, relied on their portal websites to create a brand-new column of openness of government affairs, and took "five-openness" as the main line to disclose information about the openness of decision-making, the openness of implementation, the openness of management, the openness of service and the openness of results in prominent positions of the special column, and displayed by category government information disclosed on their own initiatives, so as to facilitate the inquire and access by the public and better serve tax and fee payers and grassroots tax officers.

2. Standardizing the construction of administrative law enforcement information disclosure platforms

In 2022, the Administration made overall arrangements for provincial tax services to set up administrative law enforcement publicity platforms on their tax portal websites, and uniformly collect and disclose information about major cases of tax violations and dishonesty, administrative expropriation, administrative licensing, administrative inspection, administrative penalty, law enforcement services and other law enforcement information, so as to facilitate public inquiry.

3. Deepening the construction of the "12,366" Tax Service Platform

In 2022, the Administration expanded "12,366" from a single manual service hotline to a comprehensive service platform integrating such functions as tax consultation, tax-related inquiry, taxpayer school, tax affairs handling service, online interaction and tax-related professional services, so as to further meet the needs of tax and fee and payers, improved the informatization level of the "12,366" Tax Service Platform, introduced online consultation, artificial intelligence and cloud technology, gave full play to the role of big data, and launched the "intelligent consultation" module, set up a column on preferential tax policies for supporting epidemic prevention and control on the "12,366" Tax Service Platform, made a QR code of "Knowing Everything Through a QR Code", and published various and easy-to-understand publicity products through the column with the number of hits in the column reaching 3.931 million, the number of scans of the QR code reaching 1.68 million, and the number of hits of various epidemic prevention and control products, such as animation videos and long pictures, exceeding 122 million in 2020.

4. Expanding the openness platforms of new media

In 2022, the Administration actively expanded its new media communication platforms, opened accounts of such new media as WeChat, Weibo, Baijiahao, Toutiao, People's Daily and Zhihu (Quora) and two short video accounts, namely a Tencent Microvision account and CCTV Video account, and developed and built the mobile client of the State Taxation Administration. At present, the total number of fans of the new media platforms of the Administration exceeds 17 million. In 2020, more than 5,000 pieces of information were released on these platforms, with a total of 237 million page views. The WeChat account of the State Taxation Administration was awarded the title of Excellent Government WeChat Account in the 19th Performance Evaluation of Digital Government Service Capability of Government Websites in China in 2020. At the same time, the Administration made overall plans to build a new tax media matrix with itself as the leader, provincial tax services as the main body, city and county tax services as supplements and characterized by overall coordination, the linkage between upper and lower levels, interactive communication and quick response. Based on the needs of tax and fee payers and the social and economic development of Guangdong Province, the Guangdong Provincial Tax Service established and improved the new media product incubation chain of "demand generation-subcontracting-creative proposal-demonstration and guidance-implementation", opened the information sharing channels between the three major platforms of portal website, WeChat account and Weibo account, realized the release from the same source, clustered development, and giving voice through the matrix, constructed the publicity matrix of "One City, One Brand", and successively won the "The Most Influential Government WeChat Account Award", "Annual Openness of Government Affairs Award" and "Government Affairs Communication Award" at Guangdong Internet Government Affairs Forum. With a total of over 11.6 million fans, its official WeChat official account "Guangdong Taxation" became the first government WeChat official account in Guangdong Province with over 10 million fans, and had been awarded the "Most Influential Government WeChat Account" at Guangdong Internet Government Forum for four consecutive years.

5 Optimizing Supervision and Management and Improving the Quality of the Openness of the Taxation System

In 2020, the Administration strictly implemented the *Regulations on the Disclosure of Government Information*, closely focused on the key tasks of openness of government affairs, continuously strengthened overall coordination, improved working mechanisms, enhanced the quality of the team, reinforced supervision and evaluation, and improved the quality and efficiency of the openness of the taxation system.

1. Strengthening organization and leadership

In 2020, the leaders of the Administration attached great importance to the openness of government affairs. The main leaders gave instructions on document release, policy interpretation, response to public concerns, and the "down to the grassroots" direct policy enjoyment mechanism. The responsible persons of the relevant business departments of the Administration served as the leaders of the Leading Group for the Openness of Government Affairs and presided over the Leading Group meetings to study and coordinate major issues. In accordance with the Key Tasks of Openness of Government Affairs in 2020, it carried out studies and formulated the List of Key Tasks of Openness of Government Affairs in the Taxation System, which specified 23 key tasks of the openness of government affairs in the following five aspects: promoting the openness of the exercise of powers by focusing on law-based administration of taxation, promoting the interpretation and giving guidance in the study of tax and fee policies by focusing on ensuring the "stability on the six key fronts and security in the six key areas", promoting the openness of tax and fee services by focusing on the optimization of tax business environment, promoting the institutionalization and standardization of openness of government affairs by focusing on the implementation of the *Regulations on the Disclosure of Government Information*, and promoting the improvement of the quality and efficiency the openness of government affairs by focusing on the implementation of the responsibility system. In accordance with the requirements of the Administration, local tax services strengthened leadership, increased manpower, and effectively carried out the work of openness of government affairs.

2. Improving working mechanisms

In 2020, the Administration paid special attention to the implementation of the *Regulations on the Disclosure of Government Information*, the construction of supporting institutions and the optimization of platforms, strengthened the supervision over the implementation, and improved the quality and efficiency of the openness of government affairs, standardized the workflow of government information disclosure, improved the dynamic adjustment mechanism for disclosure of government information, strengthened the whole chain management of government information, combined the openness of government affairs and official document management, standardized the management of the disclosure options relating to the adoption and release of documents and the document disclosure work, improved the review mechanism for information release, and maintained strict standards on the "text, policy and disclosure" of government information. It adopted and issued the *Standards for Handling Applications for Government Information Disclosure by Tax Authorities* so as to make uniform statements, adopt uniform standards and disclose uniform documents in replying the same type of applications, and standardize the handling of government information disclosure applications in the taxation system and strengthened the management of government information disclosure ledgers of various departments under the Administration. In 2020, a total of 1,904 applications for information disclosure by the taxation system and the satisfaction rate of the handling work was further improved. In accordance with the work requirements issued by the General Office of the State Council, the Administration unified the content, data and statistics and filling format of the annual reports of tax authorities at various levels, strengthened the review and assessment of the contents of the annual reports of local tax authorities, and gave timely guidance for the correction of non-compliance with requirements, errors and omissions in content, etc. in the reports, thereby further improving the quality of annual reports.

3. Promoting the standardization of the openness of grassroots government affairs

In recent years, the Administration has thoroughly implemented the requirements of the *Guiding Opinions of the General Office of the State Council on Comprehensively Promoting the Standardization of Openness of Grass-roots Government Affairs,* promoted the further implementation of the *Standard Guidelines on the Standards for Openness of Grass-roots Government Affairs in the Field of Tax Administration,* carried out the pilot work of constructing a special area for the openness of government affairs in tax service halls, and made overall plans for promoting the standardization of the openness of grass-roots government affairs in the taxation system. In 2020, Guangdong Provincial Tax Service piloted the establishment of the first special area on the openness of grass-roots government affairs in the national taxation system in Guicheng Tax Service Hall of the Tax Service of Nanhai District of Foshan City, which organically integrates such services as government information inquiry, policy interpretation, hot spot inquiry, tax guidance, information disclosure application, and feedback on opinions and suggestions, thereby promoting the implementation of the openness of government affairs by grass-roots tax authorities.

4. Improving the work quality of the team on the openness of government affairs

The Administration took the *Regulations on the Disclosure of Government Information* as an important content of the implementation of the legal study system of leading cadres, continuously strengthened the training of tax cadres, especially leading cadres, and included the *Regulations on the Disclosure of Government Information* in the compulsory courses of the initial training of civil servants to enhance their awareness of openness, relied on the platform of "Promoting the Development of Taxation through Learning" to release relevant courses on the openness of government affairs for cadres in the tax system throughout the country, and set up a national talent pool for the openness of government affairs in the taxation system and held training on special topics.

5. Strengthening the evaluation and accountability system of the openness of government affairs

In order to give play to the guiding role of performance management, the Administration has set up a performance index of "openness of government affairs" with its score accounting for 4% of the total score of performance evaluation, and carried out quantitative evaluations of various aspects of the work of openness of government affairs, such as information disclosure, policy interpretation and response to public concerns, thereby not only giving extra encouragement to advanced units through the awarding of points and publicity but also spurring backward units on through deduction of points and supervising them to make rectification in time.

The Suzhou Practice of Boosting Openness of Government Affairs by Servicing Enterprises with the Policy Calculator

Project Team of the Office of Suzhou Municipal People's Government

In the information age, government information, as a public resource, has become an increasingly important factor of production that can produce great economic value and social benefits. It is one of the legislative purposes of the *Regulations on the Disclosure of Government Information* to give full play to the service role of government information in people's production, life and economic and social activities. Since 2020, local governments at various levels and departments under them have adopted many enterprise-benefiting policies in the process of promoting pandemic prevention and control and economic and social development as a whole and released them to the public by relying on government information disclosure platforms such as government websites and government affairs new media, providing strong support for winning "double victories" in pandemic prevention and control and economic and social development. Due to a large number of policy-making organs and their scattered release platforms, the arrival rate and landing rate of some enterprise-benefiting policies were not satisfactory and this prevents the policies from playing their full role. To meet the needs of enterprises, Suzhou Municipal Government has strengthened the management, development and utilization of enterprise-benefiting policies by utilizing new Internet technologies, and innovatively launched the Policy Calculator, which helps enterprises find information about enterprise-benefiting policies, and provided high-quality policy consultation services for enterprises free of charge, with good results. The Policy Calculator is an application developed by the Suzhou Municipal Bureau of Industry and Information Technology to provide enterprises with free consultation services relating to enterprise-benefiting policies. By breaking down and classifying a massive amount of enterprise-benefiting policies collected, it creates a database of conditions of the application for the enjoyment of enterprise-benefiting policies and uses big data algorithms and artificial intelligence technology to match the conditions of application for enterprises-benefiting policies

Project Team of the Office of Suzhou Municipal People's Government (✉)
Suzhou Municipal People's Government, Suzhou, China
e-mail: 13693186775@163.com

H. Tian and Y. Lv (eds.), *Assessing Government Transparency in China (2021)*,
https://doi.org/10.1007/978-981-99-9734-3_7

with enterprise data and "enterprise resume" information submitted by enterprises themselves, so as to "calculate" in one second which enterprises-benefiting policies an enterprise can enjoy. To find the Policy Calculator, an enterprise just needs to log in to the website https://www.qyfw.suzhou.com.cn/, or subscribe to the WeChat official account "General Entrance to Enterprise Service in Suzhou". Taking the Policy Calculator of Suzhou City as an example and in light of the practice of serving enterprises, this report observes, discusses and summarizes the ways of strengthening the management, development and utilization of government information resources with a view to better promoting the development of enterprises.

1 The Policy Calculator is Based on the Practical Need for Developing and Utilizing Government Information Resources

Premier Li Keqiang pointed out in 2016, that more than 80% of information and data resources in China are in the hands of government departments at various levels, and it would be a great waste to "put it aside without utilization".[1] Therefore, it is of great significance to strengthen the management, development and utilization of massive government information resources, awaken the "sleeping" government information resources, and enable them to create greater value in servicing the development of enterprises.

1. The need to build a service-oriented government

The task of accelerating the transformation of government functions and building a service-oriented government that people are satisfied with requires further optimizing government services. As far as government information disclosure is concerned, "the task of building a service-oriented government that people are satisfied with means that, with the gradual transformation of government function, the open government work should also be transformed from one that is supervision-oriented to one that attaches equal importance to supervision, governance and service".[2] With the development of government information disclosure in breadth and depth, the improvement of the relevant institutions, and the rise of its level of informatization, administrative organs have basically disclosed all the information that should be disclosed on their own initiatives as required by law, but there is still much room for improvement in the integration and utilization of government information resources. Apart from demanding access to relevant government information, enterprises also expect more convenient inquiry methods and more accurate inquiry results, so that government information can better serve their development. The government should take measures to meet these demands and expectations of the enterprises.

[1] Di Zhang (2016).

[2] Jie Xiao (2019).

In light of the demand of enterprises for information about enterprise-benefiting policies, the government should provide relevant public services by strengthening the management, development and utilization of government information resources in a targeted manner, so as to facilitate and support business startup and innovation.

2. The need to promote the implementation of policies

The *Decision of the CPC Central Committee on Major Issues Pertaining to Comprehensively Promoting the Rule of Law* puts forward the specific requirements of whole-process openness of decision-making, implementation, management, service and results. Apart from the openness of decision-making, the other four kinds of openness all involve the implementation of institutions and policies. The *Opinions of the General Office of the CPC Central Committee and the General Office of the State Council on Promoting the Openness of Government Affairs in an All-round Way* also emphasize the need to promote implementation, standardization and service through openness. To promote implementation through openness means to better promote the implementation of major decisions, important policies and reform measures by effectively carrying out the open government work. The life of policies lies in their effective implementation. In recent years, many policies have been issued by governments at various levels and departments under them to benefit enterprises. To get through the "last mile" of the implementation of these policies, it is necessary to effectively manage, develop and utilize the information about the policies. On the one hand, the comprehensive collection of enterprise-benefiting policies enables enterprises to have more convenient access to information about the policies, thereby raising the arrival rate of the policies. On the other hand, providing enterprises with free policy consultation services is also conducive to optimizing government services, raising the landing rate of enterprise-benefiting policies, fully releasing policy dividends, and benefiting more enterprises.

3. The need to build a digital government

The deep integration of new Internet technologies such as big data, cloud computing and artificial intelligence with government services provides a technological guarantee for the construction of digital government as well as an important support for the comprehensive deepening of government information disclosure. In recent years, local governments have made active exploration and positive progress in realizing the inquiry of policy information, interactive consultation, handling of affairs and management of data resources "all on one network", thereby promoting the innovation of the means, models and concepts of state governance. Strengthening the management, development and utilization of government information resources, promoting the integrated utilization of such resources, and giving full play to their economic value and social benefits are important contents of the construction of a digital government. The increase of information resources at the disposal of the government and the scenarios of their application have created new tasks in the management, development and utilization of government information resources and made it more difficult for the existing core metadata processing and classification methods of government information to effectively meet the actual needs of enterprises. Therefore, it is necessary for relevant government departments to be guided by the needs of enterprises, actively use new Internet technologies to improve government information management, development and utilization, and continuously reduce the cost and raise the efficiency of information management, so as to better gather government information resources and meet the information needs of enterprises.

4. The need to deepen information disclosure

Article 8 of the *Regulations on the Disclosure of Government Information* provides that people's governments at all levels shall strengthen the well-regulated, standardized and information technology-enabled management of government information resources and the construction of Internet-based open government information platforms. The *Notice of the Information Disclosure Office of the General Office of the State Council on Standardizing Government Information Disclosure Platforms* clearly states that government information disclosure platforms are platforms for strengthening the management of key government information. At present, the requirements for government information management are mainly directed at key government information such as administrative regulations, rules and normative documents, and aim to solve such problems as the lack of understanding of the basic situation and imperfect systems. For example, the Ministry of Justice launched on its website the "Administrative Regulations Database", which discloses the current effective administrative regulations in a centralized and uniform manner. In addition, Article 18 of the *Regulations on the Disclosure of Government Information* requires that an administrative agency shall establish and improve a dynamic adjustment mechanism for government information management, regularly assess and review government information it withholds, and disclose to the public such government information the public disclosure of which is permitted due to changes in circumstances. Therefore, strengthening the management of government information resources and carrying out the whole life cycle management of government information will become a basic work of government information disclosure in the future. As a scholar points out, "We must take information management as the starting point of adapting government information disclosure to the requirements of the Internet age. High-quality information disclosure can be realized only with high-quality information management".[3]

5. The need for local governments to optimize the business environment

The business environment is the soil on which enterprises survive and develop. Suzhou, a city with a rate of dependence on foreign trade of about 120%, passed multiple tests such as the impact of the Covid-19 pandemic on its economic operation and realized a regional GDP of two trillion yuan and a total output value of industrial enterprises above designated size 3.48 trillion yuan in 2020. One of the contributing

[3] Yanbin Lv (2016).

factors to this achievement is its innovative action to optimize the business environment and build "the Most Comfortable City" business service brand. According to the Report on the Evaluation of Business Environment by 10,000 Private Enterprises in 2020, released by the All-China Federation of Industry and Commerce, Suzhou ranked third in the whole country in the evaluation of business environment. "At the local empirical level, a good business environment mainly includes an accurate and effective policy environment, a transparent and efficient government affairs environment, a fair and standardized law enforcement environment, a pro-business and safe social environment, etc."[4] The *Regulations on Optimizing the Business Environment*, which came into effect on January 1, 2020, require that people's governments at all levels and their departments should adhere to openness and transparency of government affairs. Enterprise-related policies, as the government information on which the attention of enterprises is focused, have a special position in building a market-oriented, law-based and internationalized business environment. Strengthening the management, development and utilization of enterprise-benefiting policies not only responds to the concerns of enterprises but also helps to reduce the institutional transaction costs of enterprises and create a development environment of fair competition for various market players.

2 The Problems in the Implementation of Enterprise-Benefiting Policies that Policy Calculator is Designed to Solve

No matter how good a policy is, its effect will be greatly reduced if it is not implemented effectively. The implementation of enterprise-benefiting policies has a direct impact on the development of enterprises, especially private enterprises and small and medium-sized enterprises. Therefore, in developing the Policy Calculator, Suzhou Municipal Government took the increase of the arrival rate and landing rate of enterprise-benefiting policies as its objective and carefully examined factors affecting the implementation of the policies, which included the following.

1. Too many policy-making organs

On the one hand, enterprise-benefiting policies involve governments at many different levels. Due to the great differences between different regions in economic and social development, the practical problems encountered by different local governments are also different. The policies formulated by higher-level government organs are often more general in nature and some of them require lower-level government organs to issue more operable implementation rules in light of local conditions. Government organs at the national, provincial, municipal and county levels have formulated a large number of enterprise-benefiting policies. On the other hand, these policies involve many different government organs, mainly those that are closely related to

[4] Meiying Luo (2020).

economic development or provide services to enterprises, such as those in charge of development and reform, science and technology, industrial information, finance, human resources and social security, commerce, culture and tourism, intellectual property rights, and taxation. As a result, a large number of enterprise-benefiting policies have been formulated by governments at all levels and departments under them. For example, the Ministry of Industry and Information Technology and the portal website of the State Council (https://www.gov.cn/) jointly launched the SME Policy Database, which contains policy documents on the fight against the Covid-19 pandemic promulgated since January 26, 2020. By June 28, 2021, the database contained 403 national policies and 1,422 local policies and the databases relied on by the Policy Calculator of Suzhou also contained more than 6,900 enterprise-benefiting policies promulgated by governments at various levels and departments under them.

2. Scattered policy release platforms

Corresponding to large numbers of enterprise-benefiting policies and policy-making organs, the platforms for releasing enterprise-benefiting policies are scattered, with local governments at all levels and departments under them mainly relying on their own portal websites and government new media to release enterprise-benefiting policies. At present, there is no platform for the unified and comprehensive release of enterprise-benefiting policies nationwide, and it is not convenient for enterprises to find such policies. The enterprise-benefiting policies released by local governments at various levels and departments under them vary in terms of the specific methods of support for enterprises, and the conditions, materials and channels of application for the enjoyment of the policies. The enterprise-benefiting policies released by governments at different levels have different geographical scopes of application. The lower the level of a policy, the smaller its geographical scope of application and the stronger its local characteristics. For example, the enterprise-benefiting policies formulated by a county government are usually only applicable to enterprises registered in the county. The ability of a national-level policy database to collect local policies weakens with the lowering of the administrative level of policy-making organs from the provincial level to the municipal level and to the county level. For example, the SME policy database launched by the Ministry of Industry and Information Technology in conjunction with the portal website of the State Council mainly contains local policies at the provincial level, with few municipal-level policies and even fewer county-level policies.

3. The lack of professional teams in small and medium-sized enterprises

For enterprises, especially small and medium-sized enterprises, enterprise-benefiting policies are closely related to their development and therefore are the government information that they pay special attention to. Because of human resource costs, enterprises, especially small and medium-sized enterprises, are often unable to assign special personnel to collect information about such policies. Even if some enterprises are able to assign special personnel to collect information about such policies, due to the limitations in knowledge, experience, technology and other conditions of such personnel, their collection of policy information is like "looking for a needle in a haystack", which makes it difficult for them to fully grasp the information. On top of that, enterprise-benefiting policies are diverse in type and highly professional, which makes it more difficult for enterprises to identify and utilize them. Although many enterprise-benefiting policies have been issued by governments at all levels and departments under them, due to the lack of authoritative, comprehensive and convenient access channels, the realization rate of some enterprise-benefiting policies is not high, and enterprises in urgent need of policy support, especially small and medium-sized enterprises and start-up technology enterprises, have failed to complete the precision connection with the policies benefiting them.

4. The low efficiency of manual review of policies

Matching enterprise situations with policy requirements is a task that requires skill. Even if enterprises obtain relevant policy documents, it is sometimes difficult for them to understand and use these policies well. In the face of massive information about enterprise-benefiting policies, it is difficult for even the staff of administrative organs, let alone the employees of enterprises, to complete in a short time the task of manually matching policies with applicable enterprises. Applying new Internet technologies such as big data, cloud computing and artificial intelligence to the collection, process and comparison of enterprise-benefiting policies can not only raise work efficiency and the accuracy of analysis results but also make the database and analysis results more convenient for daily management and for utilization at any time.

5. The blocking points in the application for the enjoyment of enterprise-benefiting policies

On the one hand, the application for the enjoyment of enterprise-benefiting policies has a strong time-demanding characteristic. If enterprises miss the application period for the enjoyment of a policy, they will not be able to enjoy the dividends brought by the policy. The main reasons why enterprises miss enterprise-benefiting policies are as follows: in the face of massive enterprise-benefiting policies, it is difficult for enterprises to identify the preferential policies that "belong" to themselves; some enterprises do not have an accurate understanding of the policies and do not think themselves eligible for enjoying the policies and therefore give up the application for the enjoyment of the policies; some do not have a clear idea about their "short boards", especially those that can be made up, and fail to carry out targeted rectification and improvement, resulting in the low success rate of application. On the other hand, the application for the enjoyment of policies needs to be made more convenient for enterprises. According to media reports, the main factors that affect the application for the enjoyment of enterprise-benefiting policies by enterprises are as follows: some enterprise-benefiting policies lack operability, their application requirements and procedures are not clear enough, and no consultation telephone is provided; some administrative organs lack the awareness of active service and wait for enterprises to come to them for supporting policies; some online service platforms are not sufficiently publicized or properly maintained after their establishment, resulting in their low penetration rate and utilization rate; and the commitments made in some enterprise-benefiting policies have not been met or not fully met.

6. Varying quality of social consultation services

Third-party service entities entrusted by enterprises to apply for the enjoyment of enterprise-benefiting policies play an active role in improving the efficiency of policy application. However, some third-party service entities charge enterprises high service fees by taking advantage of their special relationship with relevant functional government departments, thus increasing the burden on enterprises. A small number of third-party service entities have interest relations with relevant government functional departments, and apply support policies by illegal means, thus easily leading to such problems as abuse of power, tunneling, and fraudulent obtainment of fiscal funds. Enterprises not only have to pay fees but also are easily swindled by such entities as a result of their lack of knowledge about policies. In view of these problems, it is necessary for the government to respond to the actual needs of enterprises, take effective measures to help them find information on enterprise-benefiting policies, and provide them with related free consultation services. As long as government information is made public and necessary guidance is provided for enterprises, many enterprise-benefiting policies can be applied by enterprises themselves.

In view of the above problems that affect the implementation of enterprise-benefiting policies, the Government of Suzhou City has given full play to the positive role of government information disclosure in serving enterprises and developed a Policy Calculator from the perspective of strengthening the management, development and utilization of government information resources, thereby providing a solution to the problems strongly complained about by enterprises such as difficulty in finding, distinguishing and enjoying enterprise-benefiting policies.

3 Launching the Policy Calculator to Change the Policy Management Mode from "Enterprises Looking for Policies" to "Policies Looking for Enterprises"

On July 28, 2020, the Suzhou Municipal Government officially launched the Policy Calculator to innovate the management, development and utilization of enterprise-benefiting policies, thereby realizing the change of policy management mode from "enterprises looking for policies" to "policies looking for enterprises" and greatly reducing the difficulties faced by enterprises in searching for enterprise-benefiting policies. The Policy Calculator enables enterprises to get an intelligent policy matching report in one second and provides free consultation services to all enterprises in the city, thus promoting the effective implementation of enterprise-benefiting policies.

1. Comprehensively collecting enterprise-benefiting policies

The scope of the collection of enterprise-benefiting policies is not limited to the policies issued by Suzhou Municipal Government but covers enterprise-benefiting policies issued by governments at all levels and departments under them, as long as they are applicable to enterprises in Suzhou, so as to include all the enterprise-benefiting policies that enterprises in Suzhou can enjoy. At present, a database of enterprise-benefiting policies with complete policies and convenient retrieval has been initially established. It contains more than 6,900 enterprise-benefiting policies publicly released by the departments of development and reform, science and technology, industry and information technology, commerce and finance at the national, provincial, municipal and county levels, providing enterprises with an integrated authoritative inquiry platform for enterprise-benefiting policies. The daily maintenance of the database has been strengthened, updating every six hours to ensure that the enterprise-benefiting policies in the database are the latest and most comprehensive. Considering that Suzhou, as a big city open to the outside world, has many foreign-funded enterprises and frequent international economic and trade exchanges, the database includes 96 English versions of enterprise-related policies. In order to help enterprise users to understand policies in one picture, a column of "Policy Illustrations" is set up on the platform to provide policy illustration products related to enterprise-benefiting policies.

2. Effectively processing policy information

The platform first reviews and verifies collected enterprise-benefiting policies, eliminating invalid policy information. Then, it breaks down and classifies the verified enterprise-benefiting policies by industry type, level of issuance, issuing department, the direction of support and other dimensions, refines the substantial policy information, and establishes a database that can match conditions of application with the conditions of enterprises. In light of the actual situation in Suzhou, it divides the enterprise-benefiting policies into 28 industrial types such as big data, blockchain, medicine and intelligent manufacturing, and eight support directions, namely preferential subsidy, honorary qualification, industrial support, talent incentive, loan insurance, intellectual property rights, comprehensive planning and scientific and technological cooperation. To help enterprises accurately find the enterprise-benefiting policies they can enjoy, it provides multiple retrieval options such as retrieval by policy title, policy level, issuing department, starting date of application and date of issuance.

3. Innovatively applying data

According to the conditions of application for the enjoyment of enterprise-benefiting policies, the platform scientifically set up "enterprise resumes" for enterprises to fill in. By collecting publicly disclosed enterprise data and combining them with the "enterprise resumes" information submitted by the enterprises themselves, it creates a profile for each enterprise and uses big data algorithms and artificial intelligence technology to carry out matching calculations between enterprise profiles and massive policy information. In this way, an intelligent matching report can be produced in only one second. A report includes such information as all policies that meet the application conditions of an enterprise, the estimated amount of the fund that the enterprise can apply, the degree of matching between a specific policy and the enterprise, the time period of application, application channels, and the method of support. With concise and clear content, the report helps enterprises to apply for the enjoyment of policies in an accurate manner. After registering as a user, an enterprise can enjoy the above policy consultation services free of charge. In addition, for the frequently applied national, provincial, and municipal level enterprise-benefiting policies, the platform provides application guides and application entrances in the column of "Application Navigation". It has also set up a column of "Today's Applications" in a prominent position on its homepage to display in a concentrated way the enterprise-benefiting policies currently available for application, reminding enterprises of the deadlines for application and remaining days before the expiration of the application periods, so that they can apply in time.

4. Accurately pushing policy information

For registered enterprises, the policies in the Policy Calculator can be searched by enterprises themselves or "pushed directionally" to them by the platform. The platform has launched the function of subscription to enterprise-benefiting policies. An enterprise can select such subscription options as the type, keywords and industry category of the enterprise-benefiting policies it is looking for and the platform will automatically push the relevant policies to it. For the enterprise-benefiting policies newly issued by governments at various levels and departments under them, the platform will collect them in a timely manner and push them and the matching results to enterprises, thereby changing the policy management mode from "enterprises looking for policies" to "policies looking for enterprises", and from "enterprises seeking consultation from the government" to "the government providing policy consultation reports to enterprises on its own initiative". Through the accurate pushing of enterprise-benefiting policies, the platform enables enterprises to get the information about these policies at the earliest time possible, improves the arrival rate of the enterprise-benefiting policies adopted by governments at various levels and departments under them, and prevents enterprises from missing the deadline for the application for the enjoyment of the policies, thus effectively removing the final obstacles to the implementation of enterprise-benefiting policies.

5. Focusing on creating a good ecology

While providing enterprises with enterprise-benefiting consultation services, Suzhou Municipal Government innovatively provides more peripheral services, so as to improve the user viscosity of the Policy Calculator. The website of "General Entrance to Enterprise Service in Suzhou", which is relied on by Policy Calculator, has launched such service modules as "collection of affairs handling platforms" "collection of policies" "collection of requests" "collection of services" "collection of activities" and "collection of tools" to help enterprises to "find policies, services and activities" online and "enjoy policies, services and activities" offline. Among them, the "collection of affairs handling platforms" module includes 24 municipal-level online affairs handling platforms and nine county-level and district-level affairs handling platforms; the "collection of requests" module includes the municipal-level platforms that provide government feedback on requests of enterprise, which support the rapid response to the requests and consultations submitted by enterprises; the "collection of services" module provides information about municipal-level professional enterprise service institutions and service resources, including service supermarkets, heat maps of cooperation on opening-up and innovation, and the intermediary service supermarket platform of Suzhou City; the "collection of activities" module provides information about free enterprise-related public welfare activities carried out by various municipal-level government departments; the "collection of tools" module provides common tools such as self-testing tools for the scale and type of small and medium-sized enterprises, identification of high and new tech enterprises, rating of enterprise cloudification, calculation of weighted deduction, evaluation of small and medium-sized science and technology enterprises, etc., and their number is increasing along with the increase of the demands of enterprises. The above service modules have further optimized enterprise services and created a good ecology for the management, development and utilization of enterprise-benefiting policies.

By June 28, 2021, the Policy Calculator has nearly 39,000 registered enterprise users, covering many industries such as software and information services, research and experimental development, and special equipment manufacturing. The website has received more than 630,000 hits, made 52,000 matches, and achieved phased results in servicing enterprises: firstly, it reduces the application cost of enterprises. In the past, to get policy support, enterprises needed to assign special personnel to closely follow, collect and analyze enterprise-benefiting policies. Now, these tasks can be completed by using the Policy Calculator, which saves labor costs, reduces workload, and makes the preparation of application materials in a more targeted way, thus greatly improving the efficiency of the application. Secondly, it expands the scope of application of the policies. The Policy Calculator enables more enterprises to find preferential policies that "belong to them" and helps more enterprises successfully apply for the enjoyment of these policies. According to a sample survey conducted by Suzhou Industry and Information Technology Bureau, the success rate of enterprises applying for relevant policies through the Policy Calculator reached 92%, and 57% of them received RMB 100,000–500,000 yuan of government subsidy funds. Thirdly, it guides enterprises to focus on tackling key problems. The intelligent matching reports generated by the Policy Calculator provide guidance to enterprises on the application for the enjoyment of enterprise-benefiting policies that have a high match with them, but not yet reach 100% match. For example, an enterprise wanted to apply for a provincial-level project but did not know whether it met the conditions for the application of the project. By using the Policy Calculator, it found out that the degree of matching between itself and the project was 80%, with only one or two conditions not met. So, the enterprise increased its investment in research and development, and succeeded in the application for the project after making up its "short boards". The Policy Calculator gives full play to the guiding role of policies and guides enterprises to actively transform, upgrade, innovate, and develop themselves, ultimately achieving a win–win situation for the government and enterprises.

4 Implication of the Policy Calculator for Managing Government Information and Servicing the Development of Enterprises

The Suzhou Municipal Government, by launching the Policy Calculator to change the policy management mode from that of "enterprises looking for policies" to that of "policies looking for enterprises", has made some preliminary explorations and achieved good results in managing, developing and utilizing enterprise-benefiting policies, thus providing useful experiences for the management, development and utilization of government information resources in other fields. The experiences gained by the Suzhou Municipal Government in the exploration and practice of Policy Calculator mainly include the following.

1. Always focusing on the demands of enterprises

The key to promoting the disclosure of government information, optimizing the business environment and servicing the development of enterprises is to accurately identify the "worries" and "urgencies" of enterprises and to think and act from the perspective of enterprises. This is also true for the management, development and utilization of government information resources. In the process of policy implementation, what preferential policies enterprises can enjoy, whether they meet the conditions of application, what application processes they have, and what application materials they need to submit are the issues that enterprises are most concerned about. Relevant government organs should unblock the communication channels between government and enterprises, establish an evaluation and feedback mechanism for the use of government information disclosure platforms, actively understand the actual needs of enterprises for government information, strive to solve the problems encountered by enterprises in obtaining government information and enjoying policy dividends, strengthen government information management in a targeted manner, promote the implementation of the enterprise-benefiting policies, and enable enterprises to have a greater sense of gain.

2. Actively utilizing new Internet technologies

Both the "keeping" and "effective use" of government information resources depend on new Internet technologies such as big data, cloud computing and artificial intelligence. In collecting government information, it is necessary to promote the integration and sharing of government information by governments at all levels and departments under them, so as to ensure that massive and relatively accurate government information can be collected. In processing government information, they should use new Internet technologies to break down and classify collected government information, and unify the standards on and improve the quality of government information resources, so as to facilitate their further development and utilization by other administrative organs and social institutions. In the past, there existed the problem of emphasizing management and neglecting service in the management of government information resources, which was prominently manifested in the insufficient development of application scenarios of government information resources. Therefore, in the future utilization of government information, administrative organs should innovatively launch more application scenarios in light of their respective responsibilities and the needs of enterprises.

3. Improving the quality of policy documents

The quality of policy documents is the basic condition for their management, development and utilization. Some good policies are difficult to implement because of the lack of operability. Fundamentally speaking, it is necessary to improve the quality of administrative decision-making by fully demonstrating the necessity, feasibility and scientificity of policies, so as to prevent arbitrariness in decision-making. From the content point of view, the provisions of a policy should be specific, clear and practical, with less empty talk and more substance, so that it can be implemented without the need of formulating separate implementation rules, and its content can be easily managed and utilized technically. Policies don't have to be all-inclusive. They are effective as long as they can grasp the "pain points" of problems and solve them in a down-to-earth manner. Support policies for enterprises should be precise, simple and effective. The quality problems of policy documents found in the process of managing, developing and utilizing government information resources can be fed back to policy-making organs in an appropriate way, to be used as a reference for improving the scientificity of decision-making and the quality of policy documents in the future.

4. Innovatively providing policy consultation services

The preliminary goals of government information management include comprehensively collecting government information resources, facilitating access to policy information and understanding of information content by enterprises, and improving the arrival rate of government information. The higher goals of government information resource management include exploiting, developing and utilizing government information resources and giving full play to their economic value and social benefits in servicing the development of enterprises. Administrative organs should be encouraged to innovate in the management, development and utilization of government information in specific fields in light of their respective functions and the needs of enterprises, so as to help enterprises find government information and provide them with better policy consultation services. They should promote the transparency and standardization of government management and services by strengthening the management, development and utilization of enterprise-benefiting policies, treat all qualified enterprises equally, urge relevant government organs to earnestly fulfill their commitment to benefiting enterprises, reduce the space of power rent-seeking, and continuously improve the arrival rate and landing rate of enterprise-benefiting policies.

5. Choosing key areas to carry out pilot programs

Government information is not limited to policy documents. It involves a wide range of fields. In the management, development and utilization of government information resources, pursuing grandiose projects will hardly lead to any breakthrough. The purpose of government information management is not to manage the information for the sake of management, but to better serve economic and social development. Therefore, government organs responsible for the management of government information resources can start their work with authoritative, normative and stable policy documents in the fields most relevant to enterprises, and then gradually expand the scope of the work after accumulating certain experience. It should be noted that, in practice, the subjects of management, development and utilization of government information resources are not limited to departments responsible for government information disclosure or big data management, but become more and more multi-centered or de-centered. Some administrative organs have strengthened government information management in light of their own responsibilities and the needs of enterprises and, by doing so, achieved good results in servicing the development of enterprises.

References

Di Zhang, "What the government 'says' is what it 'does' on the issue of information disclosure", *Beijing Daily*, May 13, 2016.

Jie Xiao, "Promoting the openness of government affairs in the new era by being people-oriented", *Study Times*, September 9, 2019.

Meiying Luo, "Reform Practice and Administrative Jurisprudence of Optimization of Business Environment", 5 (2020) *Administrative Law Review*.

Yanbin Lv, "Government Information Disclosure System in the Internet Age: Problems and Countermeasures", 6 (2016) *Journal of Chongqing University of Posts and Telecommunications (Social Science Edition)*.

Report on Indices of Government Transparency of Pilot Free Trade Zones (2020)–From the Perspective of Information Disclosure on Government Websites of Free Trade Zones

Innovation Project Team on Rule of Law Index, Institute of Law, Chinese Academy of Social Sciences

In 2021, to promote the openness of government affairs in pilot free trade zones and the optimization of the business environment, the Center for Studies of the National Rule of Law Index of the Chinese Academy of Social Sciences and the Innovation Project Team on the Rule of Law Index of the Institute of Law of Chinese Academy of Social Sciences (hereinafter referred to as "Project Team") carried out investigation and assessment of the disclosure of government information by all pilot free trade zones in China (hereinafter referred to as "free trade zones") and all pilot free trade areas (hereinafter referred to as "free trade areas") under them.

Leaders of the Project Team: He Tian, director of the Center for Studies of National Rule of Law Index of Chinese Academy of Social Sciences, a research fellow at the Institute of Law, and a distinguished professor at the Law School of the University of Chinese Academy of Social Sciences, and Yanbin Lv, a research fellow at and the head of the Department of Survey and Studies of National Situation of the Rule of Law, Institute of Law, Chinese Academy of Social Sciences, and head the Teaching and Research Section of Constitutional and Administrative Law of the Law School of the University of Chinese Academy of Social Sciences. Other members of the Project Team: Xiaomei Wang, Ming Wang, He Wang, Wenbo Che, Wanyun Niu, Yingying Feng, Yanpeng Liu, Yi Qi, Xiaomin Mi, Chuqiao Yu, Yue Zhang, Ruijun Zhang, Changming Hu, Jingtao Hu, Mei Hong, Tiantian Hong, Yanjie Li, Fenpeng Tao and Jihua Lei. The following persons participated in the preparation of this report: He Wang, Wanyun Niu, Yi Qi, Chuqiao Yu, Yue Zhang, Ruijun Zhang, Jingtao Hu, Tiantian Hong, Fenpeng Tao and Jihua Lei.

Innovation Project Team on Rule of Law Index, Institute of Law, Chinese Academy of Social Sciences (✉)
Institute of Law, Chinese Academy of Social Sciences, Beijing, China
e-mail: 13693186775@163.com

H. Tian and Y. Lv (eds.), *Assessing Government Transparency in China (2021)*,
https://doi.org/10.1007/978-981-99-9734-3_8

1 Background of the Assessment

Building free trade zones is an important measure for comprehensively expanding the opening-up, deepening the reform and optimizing the business environment. According to the *Opinions of the Ministry of Commerce on Supporting the Further Innovative Development of Pilot Free Trade Zones*, China will encourage pilot free trade zones to strengthen international trade and investment cooperation, actively participate in international economic and trade cooperation, build a scientific business environment assessment system, further optimize government services, and create a law-based, internationalized and facilitating business environment. The *Regulations on Optimizing the Business Environment*, promulgated in October 2019, provide that, in optimizing the business environment, China will adhere to the principles of marketization, rule of law and internationalization, continue to deepen the reforms aimed at simplifying procedures, decentralizing powers, combining decentralization with appropriate control, and optimizing services, and comprehensively advance the openness of decision-making, implementation, administration, services, and results, so as to enhance the rule-of-law level of the business environment and encourage foreign investment. The *Key Tasks in Promoting the Openness of Government Affairs in 2020*, issued by the General Office of the State Council in June 2020, state that China will strengthen the openness of government affairs around the optimization of the business environment by "improving the quality of openness of market regulatory rules and standards, improving the transparency and convenience of government services, and improving the pertinence and accuracy of the release and interpretation economic policies". The rule of law, stability and standardization are the keys to a good business environment, while fairness and transparency are the basis for optimizing the business environment. Therefore, improving government transparency is very important to strengthening the construction of pilot free trade zones.

2 An Overview of the Assessment

1. Assessment targets

By January 2021, China has established 21 free trade zones, namely: China (Shanghai) Pilot Free Trade Zone, established in September 2013; China (Guangdong) Pilot Free Trade Zone, China (Tianjin) Pilot Free Trade Zone and China (Fujian) Pilot Free Trade Zone, established in April 2015; China (Sichuan) Pilot Free Trade Zone, China (Liaoning) Pilot Free Trade Zone, China (Zhejiang) Pilot Free Trade Zone, China (Henan) Pilot Free Trade Zone, China (Hubei) Pilot Free Trade Zone, China (Chongqing) Pilot Free Trade Zone, and China (Shaanxi) Pilot Free Trade Zone, established in March 2017; China (Hainan) Pilot Free Trade Zone, established in September 2018 (later built as Hainan Free Trade Port, hereinafter referred to as "Hainan Free Trade Port"); China (Shandong) Pilot Free Trade Zone, China (Jiangsu) Pilot Free Trade Zone, China (Guangxi) Pilot Free Trade

Zone, China (Hebei) Pilot Free Trade Zone, China (Yunnan) Pilot Free Trade Zone, China (Heilongjiang) Pilot Free Trade Zone, established in August 2019; and China (Beijing) Pilot Free Trade Zone, China (Hunan) Pilot Free Trade Zone and China (Anhui) Pilot Free Trade Zone, established in August 2020.

During the data collection period (January 20, 2021 to August 11, 2021), China (Anhui) Pilot Free Trade Zone had no portal website and was not covered by the assessment. All the remaining 20 free trade zones were covered by the assessment.

With the exception of Hainan Free Trade Port, which covers no free trade area other than the whole of Hainan Island, the other 20 free trade zones cover 67 free trade areas. Lidao Islands Area, Northern Area, Southern Area, Ningbo Area and Hangzhou Area of China (Zhejiang) Pilot Free Trade Zone, Xiyong Area and Guoyuan Port Area of China (Chongqing) Pilot Free Trade Zone, Suzhou Area and Lianyungang Area of China (Jiangsu) Pilot Free Trade Zone, Harbin Area of China (Heilongjiang) Pilot Free Trade Zone, the Science and Technology Innovation Area, the International Business Service Area and the High-end Industry Area of China (Beijing) Pilot Free Trade Zone, Changsha Area, Yueyang Area and Chenzhou Area of China (Hunan) Pilot Free Trade Zone, and Hefei Area, Wuhu Area and Bengbu Area of China (Anhui) Pilot Free Trade Zone were not covered by the assessment because they had no portal website during the data collection period. All the remaining 48 free trade areas were covered by the assessment.

2. Assessment indices

Because of the different positioning and functions of different free trade zones and free trade areas, the Project Team designed two assessment index systems—one for free trade zones and the other for free trade areas—based on such documents as *Regulations on the Disclosure of Government Information*, the *Opinions of the General Office of the CPC Central Committee and the General Office of the State Council on Comprehensively Advancing Open Government Work*, the *Detailed Rules for the Implementation of the Opinions on Comprehensively Advancing Open Government Work* issued by the General Office of the State Council, the *Key Tasks in Promoting the Openness of Government Affairs in 2020*, and the *Regulations on Optimizing the Business Environment*.

(1) Assessment indices for free trade zones

The assessment indices for free trade zones include five level-one indices, namely, the openness of decision-making, the openness of administration, the openness of results, platform construction and information disclosure upon application. They cover 18 level-two indices (see Table 1). The openness of decision-making includes openness of planning and plans, pre-disclosure of major decision-making, disclosure of normative documents and policy interpretation; openness of administration includes an introduction to the free trade zone, institutional information and negative list; openness of results includes the annual report on information disclosure, disclosure of statistical data, the openness of the results of handling of suggestions from deputies to people's congresses and members of the Chinese People's Political

Consultative Conference (CPPCC), and institutional innovation; platform construction includes website construction, new media construction and interactive platform construction; and information disclosure upon application includes smoothness of application channels, timeliness of reply, standardization of the form of reply and standardization of the content of reply.

(2) Assessment indices for free trade areas

The assessment indices for free trade areas include five level-one indices, namely, the openness of decision-making, the openness of administration, the openness of results, platform construction and information disclosure upon application. They cover 28 level-two indices (see Table 2). Openness of decision-making includes openness of planning and plans, pre-disclosure of major decision-making, disclosure of normative documents and policy interpretation; openness of administration and service includes institutional information, list of powers and responsibilities, negative list, financial openness, list of intermediary service items, list of certification items, list of administrative charges, list of items subject to the notification and commitment system, and list of items of the "separating business licenses from permits" reform;

Table 1 Index system for the assessment of transparency of free trade zones in 2020

Level-one indices	Level-two indices
Openness of decision-making (40%)	Openness of planning and plans (20%)
	Pre-disclosure of major decision-making (25%)
	Disclosure of normative documents (30%)
	Policy interpretation (25%)
Openness of administration (25%)	Introduction to the free trade zone (10%)
	Institutional information (40%)
	Negative list (50%)
Openness of results (25%)	Annual report on information disclosure (20%)
	Disclosure of statistical data (60%)
	Openness of the results of handling of suggestions from deputies to people's congresses and members of CPPCC (20%)
	Institutional innovation (0)
Platform construction (10%)	Website construction (50%)
	New media construction (30%)
	Interactive platform construction (20%)
Disclosure upon application (0)	Smoothness of application channels (0)
	Timeliness of reply (0)
	Standardization of the form of reply (0)
	Standardization of the content of reply (0)

Note If the weight of an index is "0", it means that the result of the assessment of this index is used only for the purpose of statistical analysis, and not in the calculation of assessment scores

Table 2 Index system for the assessment of transparency of free trade areas in 2020

Level-one indices	Level-two indices
Openness of decision-making (20%)	Openness of planning and plans (20%)
	Pre-disclosure of major decision-making (25%)
	Disclosure of normative documents (30%)
	Policy interpretation (25%)
Openness of administration and services (35%)	Institutional information (10%)
	List of powers and responsibilities (15%)
	Negative list (15%)
	Financial openness (10%)
	List of intermediary services (10%)
	List of certification items (10%)
	List of administrative charges (10%)
	List of items subject to the notification and commitment system (10%)
	List of items of the "separating business licenses from permits" reform (10%)
Openness of implementation and results (35%)	Openness of administrative penalties (15%)
	Openness of administrative licensing (25%)
	"Double random inspection" (15%)
	Openness of major projects (15%)
	Annual report on information disclosure (10%)
	Openness of statistical data (15%)
	Openness of the results of handling of suggestions from deputies to people's congresses and CPPCC members (15%)
	Openness of the results of pilot programs (0)
Platform construction (10%)	Website construction (50%)
	New media construction (30%)
	Interactive platform construction (20%)
Disclosure upon application (0)	Smoothness of application channels (0)
	Timeliness of reply (0)
	Standardization of the form of reply (0)
	Standardization of the content of reply (0)

openness of implementation and results includes openness of administrative penalties, openness of administrative licensing, "double random inspection" (the regulatory mechanism featuring the random selection of both inspectors and inspection targets, the prompt release of results), openness of major projects, annual report on information disclosure work, openness of statistical data, openness of the results of handling of suggestions from deputies to people's congresses and CPPCC members, and openness of the results of pilot programs; platform construction includes website construction, new media construction and interactive platform construction; information disclosure upon application includes smoothness of application channels, timeliness of reply, standardization of the form of reply and standardization of the content of reply.

3. Assessment methods

In the assessment, the Project Team collected data on the disclosure of various kinds of information in the assessment index system from the website platforms, WeChat platforms and Weibo platforms of the free trade zones and free trade areas. The time period of data collection was from January 20, 2021 to August 11, 2021. Among them, website platforms were the main data source and assessment basis, while WeChat platforms and Weibo platforms were the sources of data only for the assessment platform construction.

3 Overall Assessment Results

1. Assessment results of free trade zones

The top ten in the ranking of assessment results of government transparency indices of free trade zones in 2020 are China (Fujian) Pilot Free Trade Zone, China (Guangxi) Pilot Free Trade Zone, China (Shanghai) Pilot Free Trade Zone, China (Guangdong) Pilot Free Trade Zone, China (Yunnan) Pilot Free Trade Zone, China (Tianjin) Pilot Free Trade Zone, Hainan Free Trade Port, China (Hunan) Pilot Free Trade Zone, China (Hebei) Pilot Free Trade Zone and China (Shaanxi) Pilot Free Trade Zone (see Table 3).

2. The assessment results of free trade areas

The top ten in the ranking of the assessment results of government transparency indices of free trade areas in 2020 are Wuhan Area of China (Hubei) Pilot Free Trade Zone, Shenzhen Qianhai Shekou Area of China (Guangdong) Pilot Free Trade Zone, Pingtan Area of China (Fujian) Pilot Free Trade Zone, Zhuhai Hengqin New District Area of China (Guangdong) Pilot Free Trade Zone, Xiamen Area of China (Fujian) Pilot Free Trade Zone, Nanjing Area of China (Jiangsu) Pilot Free Trade Zone, the Bonded Area of China (Shanghai) Pilot Free Trade Zone, Lin-gang Area of China (Shanghai) Pilot Free Trade Zone, Dalian Area of China (Liaoning) Pilot Free Trade Zone and Yingkou Area of China (Liaoning) Pilot Free Trade Zone (see Table 4).

Table 3 Assessment results of government transparency indices of free trade zones in 2020 (Unit: Points)

Ranking	Assessment targets	Openness of decision-making (40%)	Openness of administration (25%)	Openness of results (25%)	Platform construction (10%)	Total score (out of 100)
1	China (Fujian) pilot free trade zone	84.38	91.50	57.00	92.00	80.08
2	China (Guangxi) pilot free trade zone	89.50	78.00	18.00	84.00	68.20
3	China (Shanghai) pilot free trade zone	79.63	76.40	27.50	96.00	67.43
4	China (Guangdong) pilot free trade zone	77.73	98.00	6.00	100.00	67.09
5	China (Yunnan) pilot free trade zone	76.63	90.40	15.60	92.00	66.35
6	China (Tianjin) pilot free trade zone	65.00	81.40	40.00	92.00	65.55
7	Hainan free trade port	91.25	38.40	20.40	96.00	60.80
8	China (Hunan) pilot free trade zone	62.49	93.5	9.60	72.00	57.97
9	China (Hebei) pilot free trade zone	78.13	58.00	6.00	72.00	54.45
10	China (Shaanxi) pilot free trade zone	53.93	48.00	37.20	80.00	50.87
11	China (Zhejiang) pilot free trade zone	38.40	42.40	62.00	80.00	49.46

(continued)

Table 3 (continued)

Ranking	Assessment targets	Openness of decision-making (40%)	Openness of administration (25%)	Openness of results (25%)	Platform construction (10%)	Total score (out of 100)
12	China (Jiangsu) pilot free trade zone	45.63	66.00	18.00	88.00	48.05
13	China (Heilongjiang) pilot free trade zone	41.83	76.00	14.40	68.00	46.13
14	China (Liaoning) pilot free trade zone	41.50	72.00	15.60	62.00	44.70
15	China (Beijing) pilot free trade zone	80.16	8.00	14.40	50.00	42.66
16	China (Sichuan) pilot free trade zone	20.10	86.80	21.60	72.00	42.34
17	China (Shandong) pilot free trade zone	70.75	8.00	6.00	80.00	39.80
18	China (Henan) pilot free trade zone	33.65	18.80	6.00	92.00	28.86
19	China (Hubei) pilot free trade zone	42.00	4.00	6.00	84.00	27.70
20	China (Chongqing) pilot free trade zone	42.00	4.00	14.40	30.00	24.40
–	China (Anhui) pilot free trade zone	–	–	–	–	–

3. Weighted results of the assessment of free trade zones

Based on the assessment results of free trade zones and free trade areas, the Project Team calculated the final assessment results of various free trade zones by using the weighted average method, with the assessment result of a free trade zone and that of various free trade areas under it each accounting for 50% of the final weighted result. Among all the free trade zones in China, Hainan Free Trade Port had no free

Table 4 Assessment results of government transparency indices of free trade areas in 2020 (unit: points)

Ranking	Assessment targets	Openness of decision-making (20%)	Openness of administration and services (35%)	Openness of implementation and of results (35%)	Platform construction (10%)	Total score (out of 100)
1	Wuhan area of China (Hubei) pilot trade zone	94.00	74.55	81.93	78.00	81.37
2	Shenzhen Qianhai Shekou area of China (Guangdong) pilot free trade zone	96.75	64.70	80.03	100.00	80.00
3	Pingtan area of China (Fujian) pilot free trade zone	91.00	78.30	74.88	60.00	77.81
4	Zhuhai Hengqin new district area of China (Guangdong) pilot free trade zone	92.50	45.05	84.43	88.00	72.62
5	Xiamen area of China (Fujian) pilot free trade zone	88.25	84.55	41.60	100.00	71.80
6	Nanjing area of China (Jiangsu) pilot free trade zone	88.83	76.90	51.90	76.00	70.44
7	The bonded area of China (Shanghai) pilot free trade zone	46.50	74.75	69.58	100.00	69.81
8	Lin-gang special area of China (Shanghai) pilot free trade zone	74.00	62.20	62.88	100.00	68.58

(continued)

Table 4 (continued)

Ranking	Assessment targets	Openness of decision-making (20%)	Openness of administration and services (35%)	Openness of implementation and of results (35%)	Platform construction (10%)	Total score (out of 100)
9	Dalian area of China (Liaoning) pilot free trade zone	78.25	56.50	68.48	78.00	67.19
10	Yingkou area of China (Liaoning) pilot free trade zone	79.75	67.40	56.25	78.00	67.03
11	Central business district of Binhai new area of China (Tianjin) pilot free trade zone	90.05	47.40	60.78	90.00	64.87
12	Tianjin port area of China (Tianjin) pilot free trade zone	87.00	44.10	66.20	88.00	64.81
13	Guangzhou Nansha new district area of China (Guangdong) pilot free trade zone	15.60	74.60	71.85	100.00	64.38
14	Xi'an international port area of China (Shaanxi) pilot free trade zone	69.75	57.40	76.13	36.00	64.28
15	Kunming area of China (Yunnan) pilot free trade zone	81.00	50.90	55.88	78.00	61.37
16	Tianjin airport area of China (Tianjin) pilot free trade zone	59.75	50.60	62.58	82.00	59.76

(continued)

Table 4 (continued)

Ranking	Assessment targets	Openness of decision-making (20%)	Openness of administration and services (35%)	Openness of implementation and of results (35%)	Platform construction (10%)	Total score (out of 100)
17	Nanning area of China (Guangxi) pilot free trade zone	61.30	71.85	37.65	90.00	59.59
18	Zhangjiang high-tech area of China (Shanghai) pilot free trade zone	62.50	48.30	60.03	70.00	57.41
19	Zhengzhou area of China (Henan) pilot free trade zone	75.80	68.70	14.70	90.00	53.35
20	Luoyang area of China (Henan) pilot free trade zone	79.25	46.80	37.95	60.00	51.51
21	Lujiazui financial area of China (Shanghai) pilot free trade zone	16.40	49.70	61.53	88.00	51.01
22	World expo area of China (Shanghai) pilot free trade zone	22.40	46.20	58.43	60.00	47.10
23	Chengdu Tianfu new area of China (Sichuan) pilot free trade zone	81.00	59.70	6.00	74.00	46.60
24	Jinqiao development area of China (Shanghai) pilot free trade zone	17.20	49.00	55.03	58.00	45.65

(continued)

Table 4 (continued)

Ranking	Assessment targets	Openness of decision-making (20%)	Openness of administration and services (35%)	Openness of implementation and of results (35%)	Platform construction (10%)	Total score (out of 100)
25	Fuzhou area of China (Fujian) pilot free trade zone	67.75	33.70	42.30	50.00	45.15
26	South Sichuan port area of China (Sichuan) pilot free trade zone	79.25	50.20	11.50	66.00	44.05
27	Shenyang area of China (Liaoning) pilot free trade zone	51.50	59.00	16.35	72.00	43.87
28	Yangling demonstration area of China (Shaanxi) pilot free trade zone	68.50	55.80	11.50	60.00	43.26
29	Zhengding area of China (Hebei) pilot free trade zone	50.85	51.30	22.00	66.00	42.43
30	Qinzhou port area of China (Guangxi) pilot free trade zone	40.00	58.95	17.40	76.00	42.32
31	Central area of China (Shaanxi) pilot free trade zone	32.80	61.70	19.98	70.00	42.15
32	Chongzuo area of China (Guangxi) pilot free trade zone	38.60	41.10	31.53	78.00	40.94
33	Kaifeng area of China (Henan) pilot free trade zone	75.75	42.40	9.90	66.00	40.06

(continued)

Table 4 (continued)

Ranking	Assessment targets	Openness of decision-making (20%)	Openness of administration and services (35%)	Openness of implementation and of results (35%)	Platform construction (10%)	Total score (out of 100)
34	Daxing airport area of China (Hebei) pilot free trade zone	69.00	53.50	0.00	66.00	39.13
35	Jinyi area of China (Zhejiang) pilot free trade zone	54.02	52.90	9.83	61.00	38.86
36	Yichang area of China (Hubei) pilot free trade zone	20.10	73.20	6.00	61.00	37.84
36	Qingdao area of China (Shandong) pilot free trade zone	83.00	37.50	0.90	78.00	37.84
38	Caofeidian area of China (Hebei) pilot free trade zone	62.35	48.40	0.00	66.00	36.01
39	Heihe area of China (Heilongjiang) pilot free trade zone	61.15	45.20	3.00	60.00	35.10
40	Honghe area of China (Yunnan) pilot free trade zone	67.75	22.50	11.00	78.00	33.08
41	Liangjiang area of China (Chongqing) pilot free trade zone	44.15	31.70	23.05	36.00	31.59
42	Xiangyang area of China (Hubei) pilot free trade zone	67.00	15.30	6.90	56.00	26.77

(continued)

Table 4 (continued)

Ranking	Assessment targets	Openness of decision-making (20%)	Openness of administration and services (35%)	Openness of implementation and of results (35%)	Platform construction (10%)	Total score (out of 100)
43	Yantai area of China (Shandong) pilot free trade zone	46.10	10.50	3.00	100.00	23.95
44	Dehong area of China (Yunnan) pilot free trade zone	31.60	26.60	1.00	78.00	23.78
45	Jinan area of China (Shandong) pilot free trade zone	57.30	19.80	3.30	36.00	23.15
46	Xiong'an area of China (Hebei) pilot free trade zone	36.38	30.85	0.00	36.00	21.67
47	Chengdu Qingbaijiang railway port area of China (Sichuan) pilot free trade zone	42.30	2.00	0.00	60.00	15.16
48	Suifenhe area of China (Heilongjiang) pilot free trade zone	8.00	0.00	0.00	45.00	6.10
–	Lidao area of China (Zhejiang) pilot free trade zone	–	–	–	–	–
–	Northern area of China (Zhejiang) pilot free trade zone	–	–	–	–	–

(continued)

Table 4 (continued)

Ranking	Assessment targets	Openness of decision-making (20%)	Openness of administration and services (35%)	Openness of implementation and of results (35%)	Platform construction (10%)	Total score (out of 100)
–	Southern area of China (Zhejiang) pilot free trade zone	–	–	–	–	–
–	Ningbo area of China (Zhejiang) pilot free trade zone	–	–	–	–	–
–	Hangzhou area of China (Zhejiang) pilot free trade zone	–	–	–	–	–
–	Xiyong area of China (Chongqing) pilot free trade zone	–	–	–	–	–
–	Guoyuan port area of China (Chongqing) pilot free trade zone	–	–	–	–	–
–	Suzhou area of China (Jiangsu) pilot free trade zone	–	–	–	–	–
–	Lianyungang area of China (Jiangsu) pilot free trade zone	–	–	–	–	–
–	Harbin area of China (Heilongjiang) pilot free trade zone	–	–	–	–	–

(continued)

Table 4 (continued)

Ranking	Assessment targets	Openness of decision-making (20%)	Openness of administration and services (35%)	Openness of implementation and of results (35%)	Platform construction (10%)	Total score (out of 100)
–	Science and technology innovation area of China (Beijing) pilot free trade zone	–	–	–	–	–
–	International business service area of China (Beijing) pilot free trade zone	–	–	–	–	–
–	High-end industrial area of China (Beijing) pilot free trade zone	–	–	–	–	–
–	Changsha area of China (Hunan) pilot free trade zone	–	–	–	–	–
–	Yueyang area of China (Hunan) pilot free trade zone	–	–	–	–	–
–	Chenzhou area of China (Hunan) pilot free trade zone	–	–	–	–	–
–	Hefei area of China (Anhui) pilot free trade zone	–	–	–	–	–
–	Wuhu area of China (Anhui) pilot free trade zone	–	–	–	–	–
–	Bengbu area of China (Anhui) pilot free trade zone	–	–	–	–	–

trade area under it, so the assessment result of the free trade zone itself was taken as its final weighted result. The assessment score of the free trade areas under China (Hunan) Pilot Free Trade Zone and China (Beijing) Pilot Free Trade Zone that had no website was zero point. And China (Anhui) Pilot Free Trade Zone was not covered by the assessment because it had no website.

The top ten in the ranking of weighted results of the assessment of government transparency indices of free trade zones in 2020 are China (Fujian) Pilot Free Trade Zone, China (Guangdong) Pilot Free Trade Zone, China (Tianjin) Pilot Free Trade Zone, China (Shanghai) Pilot Free Trade Zone, Hainan Free Trade Port, China (Guangxi) Pilot Free Trade Zone, China (Yunnan) Pilot Free Trade Zone, China (Liaoning) Pilot Free Trade Zone, China (Shaanxi) Pilot Free Trade Zone and China (Hebei) Pilot Free Trade Zone (see Table 5).

4. The overall situation of openness of government affairs in free trade zones

(1) There were big differences and uneven distribution of assessment scores among various free trade zones

On the whole, there were big differences in the assessment results among various free trade zones. China (Fujian) Pilot Free Trade Zone ranked first with a score of 80.08 points. China (Guangxi) Pilot Free Trade Zone ranked second with a score of 68.20 points, which was 11.88 points lower than that of the first. China (Chongqing) Pilot Free Trade Zone ranked last with a score of 24.40 points, which was 55.88 points lower than the first. Moreover, among the 20 assessment targets, only seven scored above 60 points and only one scored above 80 points. Among the free trade areas, two scored above 80 points: Wuhan Area of China (Hubei) Pilot Free Trade Zone and Shekou Area of Shenzhen Qianhai of China (Guangdong) Pilot Free Trade Zone; four scored between 70 and 80 points: Pingtan Area of China (Fujian) Pilot Free Trade Zone, Hengqin New Area of Zhuhai of China (Guangdong) Pilot Free Trade Zone, Xiamen Area of China (Fujian) Pilot Free Trade Zone and Nanjing Area of China (Jiangsu) Pilot Free Trade Zone. Nine scored between 60 and 70 points: the Bonded Area of China (Shanghai) Pilot Free Trade Zone, Lin-gang Area of China (Shanghai) Pilot Free Trade Zone, Dalian Area of China (Liaoning) Pilot Free Trade Zone, Yingkou Area of China (Liaoning) Pilot Free Trade Zone, Central Business District of Binhai New Area of China (Tianjin) Pilot Free Trade Zone, Tianjin Port Area of China (Tianjin) Pilot Free Trade Zone, Guangzhou Nansha New District Area of China (Guangdong) Pilot Free Trade Zone, Xi'an International Port Area of China (Shaanxi) Pilot Free Trade Zone and Kunming Area of China (Yunnan) Pilot Free Trade Zone. Wuhan Area of China (Hubei) Pilot Free Trade Zone got the highest score of 81.37 points and Suifenhe Area of China (Heilongjiang) Pilot Free Trade Zone got the lowest score of 6.10, with a huge difference of 75.27 points between the two.

From the above, we can see that the situation of government information disclosure varied greatly from free trade zone to free trade zone and no unified standard had been formed.

Table 5 Weighted results of assessment of government transparency indices of various free trade zones in 2020 (unit: point)

Ranking	Assessment targets	Assessment result of the free trade zone[a]	Average assessment result of all free trade areas under the free trade zone[b]	Weighted assessment result[c]
1	China (Fujian) pilot free trade zone	80.08	64.92	72.50
2	China (Guangdong) pilot free trade zone	67.09	72.33	69.71
3	China (Tianjin) pilot free trade zone	65.55	63.15	64.35
4	China (Shanghai) pilot free trade zonc	67.43	56.59	62.01
5	Hainan free trade port	60.80	–	60.80
6	China (Guangxi) pilot free trade zone	68.20	47.62	57.91
7	China (Yunnan) pilot free trade zone	66.35	39.41	52.88
8	China (Liaoning) pilot free trade zone	44.70	59.36	52.03
9	China (Shaanxi) pilot free trade zone	50.87	49.90	50.38
10	China (Hebei) pilot free trade zone	54.45	34.81	41.92
11	China (Sichuan) pilot free trade zone	42.34	35.27	38.80
12	China (Henan) pilot free trade zone	28.86	48.31	38.58
13	China (Hubei) pilot free trade zone	27.70	48.66	38.18
14	China (Jiangsu) pilot free trade zone	48.05	23.48	35.77

(continued)

Table 5 (continued)

Ranking	Assessment targets	Assessment result of the free trade zone[a]	Average assessment result of all free trade areas under the free trade zone[b]	Weighted assessment result[c]
15	China (Shandong) pilot free trade zone	39.80	28.31	34.06
16	China (Heilongjiang) pilot free trade zone	46.13	13.73	29.33
17	China (Hunan) pilot free trade zone	57.97	0.00	28.99
18	China (Zhejiang) pilot free trade zone	49.46	6.48	27.97
19	China (Beijing) pilot free trade zone	42.66	0.00	21.33
20	China (Chongqing) pilot free trade zone	24.40	10.53	17.47
–	China (Anhui) pilot free trade zone	–	–	–

[a]The assessment result of a free trade zone is the total score of the assessment results of the free trade zone in Table 3
[b]The average assessment result of all free trade areas under a free trade zone is the average of the assessment scores of all the free trade areas under it
[c]The weighted assessment result of a free trade zone is the weighted result of the assessment score of the free trade zone itself and the average of the assessment scores of all the free trade areas under it, with both having a weight of 50%

(2) There were obvious regional differences in the assessment results of various trade zones

The weighted assessment results show obvious regional differences. The top five in the ranking of assessment results, namely China (Fujian) Pilot Free Trade Zone, China (Guangdong) Pilot Free Trade Zone, China (Tianjin) Pilot Free Trade Zone, China (Shanghai) Pilot Free Trade Zone and Hainan Free Trade Port, were all free trade zones in coastal regions, which generally had greater government transparency than those in inland regions. Moreover, free trade zones in the southern part of the country generally had greater government transparency than those in the northern part of the country. Four of the top five and six of the top ten in the ranking of assessment results were in the southern part of the country.

On the whole, there were obvious differences between coastal regions and inland areas as well as between southern regions and northern regions in the government transparency of free trade zones, with the situation in coastal and southern regions better than that in inland and northern areas regions.

(3) The construction of the open government platform in free trade zones remained weak

Since the establishment of China (Shanghai) Pilot Free Trade Zone in 2013, a total of 21 pilot free trade zones had been set up in China, covering 67 free trade zones. The latest ones were China (Beijing) Pilot Free Trade Zone, China (Hunan) Pilot Free Trade Zone and China (Anhui) Pilot Free Trade Zone, established in September 2020. Because of the different times of establishment, there were differences among free trade zones in the level of government information disclosure.

China (Anhui) Pilot Free Trade Zone had not yet established a portal website due to its late establishment. Among the 67 free trade areas, 19 had not established portal websites. Some free trade zones or free trade areas that had been established relatively late were also relatively weak in terms of website construction.

4 Assessment Results of Various Sections

1. Bright spots found in the assessment

(1) Openness of decision-making

i. The situation of disclosure of normative documents was satisfactory

Disclosure of normative documents is one of the important contents of websites of free trade zones and an important way for the public and enterprises to understand the policies of free trade zones. The assessment shows that among the free trade zones, 19, or 95.00% of the total, had set up a normative document column on their portal websites and the column was located in an obvious and easy-to-find position on most of the websites. The normative documents disclosed in the column include policies on cross-border business, investment, industrial promotion, regional innovation, and talent introduction. 15 free trade zones, or 75.00% of the total, published all the above-mentioned categories of documents in the column, thereby providing a convenient way for the public and enterprises to learn about the relevant documents of free trade zones. Among the free trade areas, 45, or 93.75% of the total, had set up a normative document column on their websites. Some free trade areas, such as Zhengzhou Area of China (Henan) Pilot Free Trade Zone, divided the normative documents column into two sub-columns, namely national policies and administrative regulations and local policies and local regulations, on their websites. Some others, including Dehong Area of China (Yunnan) Pilot Free Trade Zone, divided the normative documents column into such sub-columns as comprehensive documents, trade documents and investment documents. The column contained a wide variety of policy documents with local characteristics, including policies on cross-border business, investment, industrial promotion, regional innovation, and talent introduction. 15 free trade areas, or 45.83% of the total, published all the above-mentioned categories of documents in the column.

ii. Policy interpretation had been generally attached importance to and some free trade zones adopted diversified forms of interpretation

Policy interpretation is an important way for the public to understand the content of policies. The assessment shows that 15 free trade zones, or 75.00% of the total, had set up a policy interpretation column on their portal websites, and its location on most of the websites was adjacent to the normative documents column, so that it could be easily found and looked up. The number of policy interpretations issued by some free trade zones in 2019 and 2020 was quite large. For example, China (Guangdong) Pilot Free Trade Zone issued 22 policy interpretation documents in 2019 and ten in 2020, China (Shaanxi) Pilot Free Trade Zone issued 32 policy interpretations in 2019 and 14 in 2020, and China (Guangxi) Pilot Free Trade Zone issued 12 policy interpretations in 2019 and 20 in 2020. Some free trade zones, such as China (Tianjin) Pilot Free Trade Zone, Hainan Free Trade Port and China (Guangxi) Pilot Free Trade Zone, had adopted diversified forms of policy interpretation, including interpretation by text, long picture, questions and answers, and video.

Among the 48 free trade areas, 29, or 60.42% of the total, had set up a policy interpretation column on their portal websites. Some free trade areas had interpreted policies in a comprehensive way, issuing hundreds of policy interpretations. For example, Caofeidian District of China (Hebei) Pilot Free Trade Zone issued 357 policy interpretation documents in 2019 and 325 in 2020. In terms of the level of policy interpretation, 24 free trade areas, or 50.00% of the total, issued both interpretations of policies documents adopted by higher-level governments and interpretations of policy documents adopted by the governments at their corresponding level, with clear distinctions made between interpretations of policy documents at different levels. In terms of the form of policy interpretation, 24 free trade areas adopted two or more forms, such as interpretation by text, long picture, questions and answers, and video, to facilitate the understanding of the policies by the public.

iii. The overall development plans of free trade zones were clear

The overall development plan and annual plan of a free trade zone are the grand plans of the future development of the free trade zone, the starting point of the rational coordination of urban layout and urban construction projects, the guide to urban construction management and operation, and an effective way to help the public understand the prospect and direction of development of the free trade zone. It is very important to attach importance to the planning work and make it public. The assessment shows that 16 free trade zones, or 80.00% of the total, published their overall development plans on their portal websites.

Among all the free trade areas, 24, or 50.00% of the total, had set up a column of planning and plans on their websites; 28, or 58.33% of the total, published their overall plans, some of which were published as part of in the overall plans of the free trade zones to which they belonged; 37, or 77.08% of the total, disclosed the relevant policies such as those on special planning, regional planning and project plans, on their portal websites.

iv. The situation of pre-disclosure of major decision-making in free trade areas was relatively good

According to the *Opinions on Comprehensively Advancing Open Government Work*, government organs should implement the pre-disclosure system for major decision-making whereby before the adoption of important reform schemes, major policy measures and key engineering projects related to vital public interests and need to be widely known by the general public except for those that should be kept confidential according to law, their drafts and bases should be made public and public opinions extensively should be solicited through hearing, seminar, investigation and study, consultation, media communication and other means, and the situation of the solicitation and adoption of public opinions should be published by appropriate means. The assessment shows that there was still much room for improvement in the pre-disclosure of major decision-making in various free trade zones. Nine free trade zones published past draft decisions. Among them, Hainan Free Trade Port also published the interpretations of the drafts. With respect to the disclosure of information about the solicitation of public opinions, ten free trade zones, or 50.00% of the total, established clear channels for the solicitation of public opinions. Among the free trade areas, 28, or 58.33% of the total, published relevant drafts/exposure drafts of relevant decisions and five of them also published the interpretations of the drafts. In terms of the channels for solicitation of public opinions, 28 free trade areas, or 58.33% of the total, disclosed the relevant information, and three of them, or 6.25% of the total, disclosed the summaries and other information about the adoption of solicited opinions. The situation of pre-disclosure of major decision-making by free trade areas was better than that of their respective free trade zones.

(2) Openness of administration and services

i. The situation of publication of introductions to free trade zones was good

The main function of introductions to free trade zones is to help the public understand free trade zones. They are also one of the main channels for investors to learn about the free trade zones. The assessment shows that 17 free trade zones, or about 85.00% of the total, published an introduction to the overall situation of the zone and 16, or about 80.00% of the total, published introductions to the free trade areas under them. Among them, China (Fujian) Free Trade Zone and China (Guangxi) Free Trade Zone published comprehensive and complete introductions to themselves and the free trade areas under them, as well as their characteristic projects.

ii. The disclosure of leadership information was satisfactory

Disclosing the information about managerial leadership of free trade zones is a precondition for public supervision over the work of free trade zones. The assessment shows that most free trade zones disclosed their leadership information. Among the free trade zones covered by the assessment, 11 disclosed relatively complete information about their leaders on their websites. Among them, China (Guangdong) Free Trade Zone, China (Hunan) Free Trade Zone and China (Shaanxi) Free Trade Zone disclosed complete information about their leaders, including names, positions, experiences, and main responsibilities.

Among the free trade areas, 35, or 72.92% of the total, disclosed leadership information and 18, or 37.50% of the total, disclosed on their portal websites the complete information about all their leaders, including names, positions, work experiences and main responsibilities. Among various kinds of leadership information, the names, positions and experiences of the leaders were well disclosed: 35 free trade areas, or 72.92% of the total, disclosed names and positions of their leaders, 24, or 50.00% of the total, disclosed information about their leaders' experiences, and 31, or 64.58% of the total, disclosed information about each of their leaders' responsibilities.

iii. The disclosure of information about the institutional setup was generally good

The disclosure of information about institutional setup enables citizens and enterprises to choose the right government agencies or responsible persons for consultation and handling of their affairs in light of their actual needs and reduces their need to go to government agencies for information and service by sending government information or services to them instead. The assessment shows that most free trade zones disclosed information about their institutional setup, and 14, or 70.00% of the total, provided explanations of their institutional setup.

Of all the free trade areas covered by the assessment, 39, or 81.25% of the total, explained their institutional setup and 36, or 75.00% of the total, explained their institutional functions. Among them, seven disclosed the names of the heads of each institution, 17 disclosed the contact information of each institution, 13 explain the office hours and address information of each institution and three disclosed on their portal websites the complete basic information of each institution, including functions, contact information, office address, office hours, and information about the heads of institutions.

iv. The situation of disclosure of financial information was relatively good

Financial openness is an important part of the government's initiative to accept social supervision. The assessment shows that the situation of disclosure of financial information was relatively good. Among the free trade areas, 28, or 58.33% of the total, set up a special column on the financial budget and final accounts on their portal websites; 29, or 60.42% of the total, published their 2020 budget reports; 28, or 58.33% of the total, published the report on final accounts in 2019; and 28, or 58.33% of the total, disclosed information about "three official spendings" (spending on official overseas visits, official vehicles, and official hospitality). The situation of disclosure of information about the financial budget and final accounts and "three official spendings" was relatively good.

v. The disclosure of the list of intermediary service items was satisfactory

Disclosing the list of intermediary service items is conducive to the optimization of work procedures. The assessment shows that, among the 48 free trade areas, 40, or 83.33% of the total, published the list of intermediary services on their websites. In a special column on the website of Dalian Area of China (Liaoning) Pilot Free Trade Zone, various intermediary service items were classified into different categories. In terms of content, 14 free trade areas disclosed all the information on the list of intermediary service items, including project title, basis, time limit of intermediary service and charging standard, 40 disclosed the project titles and bases of intermediary services, 15 disclosed the time limit of intermediary services, and 18 disclosed the charging standards.

vi. The disclosure of the list of items subject to the notification and commitment system was relatively satisfactory

The assessment shows that 23 of the 48 free trade areas disclosed the catalog of items subject to the notification and commitment system, and 27, or 56.25% of the total, published the guide to the notification and commitment system. Among them, Kaifeng Area of China (Henan) Pilot Free Trade Zone published the catalog of items subject to the notification and commitment system and related service guide in the column "the system of separating business licenses from permits" on its website. Moreover, the Bonded Area of China (Shanghai) Pilot Free Trade Zone, Pingtan Area of China (Fujian) Pilot Free Trade Zone, Luoyang Area of China (Henan) Pilot Free Trade Zone, Nanjing Area of China (Jiangsu) Pilot Free Trade Zone and Kunming Area of China (Yunnan) Pilot Free Trade Zone published all the information about the results of notification and commitment, including decisions and letters of notification and commitment, on their respective portal websites. Although Xi'an International Port Area of China (Shaanxi) Pilot Free Trade Zone and Yichang Area of China (Hubei) Pilot Free Trade Zone did not disclose all the information, their decisions and letters of notification and commitment could be found on their websites.

vii. The disclosure of the list of items of "the reform of separating business licenses from permits" was relatively comprehensive

The assessment shows that 28 of the 48 free trade areas published the list of items of the local "reform of separating business licenses from permits" related to free trade areas, accounting for 58.33% of the total. Among them, 18 disclosed relatively complete contents of the list, including the titles and justification for the items, the levels and departments of examination and approval, reform methods, and measures for strengthening interim and *ex-post* regulation. Among them, the lists published by Xiamen Area of China (Fujian) Pilot Free Trade Zone, Dalian Area of China (Liaoning) Pilot Free Trade Zone, Yingkou Area of China (Liaoning) Pilot Free

Trade Zone and Dehong Area of China (Yunnan) Pilot Free Trade Zone not only were comprehensive in content elements but also had prominent local characteristics.

(3) Openness of implementation and results

i. The overall situation of disclosure of administrative licensing information was good

Administrative licensing is a powerful means for the state to regulate and control social, economic, political and cultural activities. The assessment shows that, among the free trade areas covered by the assessment, 11 had set up a special administrative licensing column on their websites, 22 published administrative licensing documents, 20 published decisions to grant administrative license and their document numbers, and 15 published the basis for granting licenses on their websites. Among them, 13 published administrative licensing decision documents with complete elements, including document number and basis, and two, namely Yingkou Area of China (Liaoning) Pilot Free Trade Zone and Fuzhou Area of China (Fujian) Pilot Free Trade Zone, published the contents of decisions not to grant the administrative license.

ii. The overall situation of the release of the annual report on government information disclosure in the free trade areas was good

The purpose of publishing the annual report on government information disclosure is to show the public the information disclosure work in free trade areas in the whole year, which is required by the Regulations on Government Information Disclosure. Among the 48 free trade areas covered by the assessment, 31, or 64.58% of the total, had set up a special annual report column on their websites, and 26, or 54.17% of the total, published the annual report, whereas, among the free trade zones, only China (Tianjin) Pilot Free Trade Zone published its annual report on information disclosure in 2020.

(4) Platform construction

i. The overall situation of website construction was good

Website is not only the main platform for a free trade zone to show itself to the public but also the main channel for it to carry out intensive information disclosure and a means to facilitate the access to information and handling of various affairs by the public. Therefore, website construction is an important part of information disclosure and service provision in free trade zones. The assessment shows that, with the exception of China (Anhui) Pilot Free Trade Zone, all free trade zones had contracted their own independent portal websites. Meanwhile, 15 free trade zones, or 75.00% of the total, provided on their own websites direct links to the websites of the free trade areas under them. Moreover, with the exception of the website of China (Sichuan) Pilot Free Trade Zone, the retrieval function of which was unusable during the period of assessment, the websites of all the other 19 free trade zones provided operable and convenient information retrieval functions.

Among the 48 free trade areas, 30 constructed their own independent websites, and the websites of another 16 free trade areas merged with the websites of relevant economic zones, bonded zones and other development zones to form integrated information disclosure platforms. Moreover, the website of Nansha New District Area of China (Guangdong) Pilot Free Trade Zone merged with the website of Nansha District People's Government; the Central Area of China (Shaanxi) Pilot Free Trade Zone did not have its own independent website, but set up a special column of "Trends of Free Trade" under the website of Xi'an Municipal Bureau of Commerce as its information disclosure channel. Meanwhile, among the 48 free trade areas that had their own websites, 46 provided retrieval functions on their websites, but the retrieval functions on the websites of two free trade areas, namely Fuzhou Area of China (Fujian) Pilot Free Trade Zone and Tianfu New District Area of Chengdu of China (Sichuan) Pilot Free Trade Zone, were unusable during the data collection period.

ii. The situation of the construction of new media was good

New media has many advantages in information disclosure, such as convenience, rapidity and easy access. The assessment shows that the overall situation of new media construction in various free trade zones was good. Of the 20 free trade zones, 17 provided links to or QR codes of their new media platforms on the homepages of their websites. 32 of the 48 free trade areas provided the links to or QR codes of their new media platforms on the homepages of their websites, and the information released by these new media platforms was updated in a timely manner.

iii. The situation of the construction of the communication platforms between the government and the people was good

Communication platforms between the government and the people are important bridges between the government, enterprises and the public as well as an important channel for government to get feedback on its decision-making. Meanwhile, the establishment of complaint platform is conducive to the rapid solution of problems and the better construction of a service-oriented government. Among the 20 free trade zones, 18, or 90.00% of the total, had set up communication channels between the government and the people or platforms for suggestions on their websites, and 17, or 85.00% of the total, opened service hotlines. Among the 48 free trade areas, 44, or 91.67% of the total, had built communication channels or platforms for suggestions on their websites.

2. Problems identified in the assessment

(1) Openness of decision-making

i. The openness of the short-term plans of free trade zones needed to be improved

Most free trade zones did not attach sufficient importance to the setup of the special column on planning and plans and the disclosure of their annual plans on their websites: only one free trade zone, namely China (Fujian) Pilot Free Trade Zone, had set up the column on the homepage of its website, but its contents were the planning documents of various trade zones issued by the State Council. Only three free trade zones, namely China (Fujian) Pilot Free Trade Zone, China (Hunan) Pilot Free Trade Zone and Hainan Free Trade Port, disclosed their development plans in 2021, and only two, namely China (Shaanxi) Pilot Free Trade Zone and Hainan Free Trade Port, disclosed their development plans in 2020.

Similarly, among the free trade areas, only four, or 8.33% of the total, published their annual development plans for 2021, and nine, or 18.75% of the total, published their annual development plans for 2020 on their websites, and the annual plans published by some free trade zones were actually three-year plans or five-year plans. Therefore, some free trade zones should improve their work of disclosure of short-term plans, annual plans and short-term development objectives, and all free trade zones needed to attach more importance to the disclosure of their planning and plans.

ii. The timeliness of publication of documents on the Internet needed to be improved

Official government websites are an important source for the public to obtain authoritative information. However, the assessment shows that the information disclosure by some assessment targets had become a mere formality, and the information in some special columns of their websites was not updated in a timely manner. For example, in the column of policies and regulations on the website of Lujiazui Financial Zone Free Trade Area of China (Shanghai) Pilot Free Trade Zone, only one piece of information was disclosed in 2020, and other pieces of information in the column were disclosed in 2011 and 2008. In a survey of the online publication of three randomly selected normative documents by free trade zones, the Project Team found that, among the free trade zones, six, or 30.00% of the total, were able to publish all three documents on the Internet within 20 working days after they were formulated, nine, or 45.00% of the total, failed to publish one of the three sampled documents on their websites in a timely manner, and two, or 10.00% of the total, failed to publish any of the sampled documents on their website in a timely manner. In the survey of the publication of interpretations of three randomly selected policy documents by the assessment targets, the Project Team found that only four free trade zones, or 20.00% of the total, published interpretations of all three policy documents online within three working days after the publication of the policy documents. The situation in trade areas was similar. With regard to the three randomly selected normative documents, among the free trade areas covered by the assessment, 17, or 35.42% of the total, published all three documents online within 20 working days after the documents were formulated; five, or 10.42% of the total, failed to publish any the documents in a timely manner; three, or 6.25%, failed to publish any of the documents, and only nine, or 18.75% of the total, published the interpretations of the three documents on their website within three working days after the publication of the documents.

(2) Openness of administration and services

i. The situation of disclosure of information about the personnel change in free trade zones was not satisfactory

Information about the change of government personnel reflects the work trends of free trade zones. Among the 20 free trade zones, only four, or 20.00% of the total, disclosed information about changes in government personnel, and the quality of disclosure was not high. For example, China (Shaanxi) Pilot Free Trade Zone disclosed only information about the employment of civil servants, but not information about other personnel changes. Among the 48 free trade areas, only 25 disclosed information about changes in government personnel. Therefore, free trade zones need to further improve the disclosure of information about changes in government personnel.

ii. The situation of the release of the negative list was not satisfactory

The negative list is an important factor in the optimization of the business environment, as well as one of the issues that investors are most concerned about. It directly sets the investment boundaries for investors. The assessment shows that the situation of the release of negative the list in pilot free trade zones was generally good, but there was still room for improvement. For example, only twelve free trade zones, or 60.00% of the total, published the Special Management Measures for the Access of Foreign Investment in Pilot Free Trade Zones (Negative List) (2020). Meanwhile, China (Shanghai) Pilot Free Trade Zone and China (Jiangsu) Pilot Free Trade Zone did not publish the list on their official websites until after 20 working days after its promulgation.

Among the 48 free trade areas covered by the assessment, only seven, or 14.58% of the total, published the negative list of market access in 2020 on their portal websites, and one of them failed to publish it within 20 working days after the document was promulgated; 24, or 50.00% of the total, published the negative list of foreign investment in 2020 on their portal websites, and five failed to publish the list within 20 working days after the document was promulgated.

iii. The publication of the lists of powers and responsibilities was unsatisfactory and the published lists were incomplete in content

Clear powers and responsibilities lead to clear tasks, which in turn lead to the effective implementation of the relevant systems. Implementing the system of power and responsibility lists of local government departments at various levels is an important reform task set by the CPC Central Committee and the State Council as well as an important measure for modernizing the state governance system and capacity and, as such, is of great significance for deepening the reform of the administrative system, optimizing the business environment, and building a law-based, innovative and clean government. The assessment shows that 23 free trade areas, or 47.92% of the total, published their list of powers and responsibilities. Among them, 23 disclosed the names of the powers and 22 disclosed the subjects of the powers in their lists. However, the disclosure of other contents of the lists was poor. For example, only 18 free trade areas disclosed the basis for the establishment of the lists. Among the free trade areas that published the list of powers and responsibilities, only six, or 12.5% of the total, disclosed the items of responsibility, and two, or 4.17% of the total, disclosed the forms of responsibility in their lists. The level of completeness of the disclosed lists was low.

iv. The information disclosure related to government procurement needed to be improved

The disclosure of government procurement information, especially government procurement contracts, was still a shortboard in free trade zones. The assessment shows that 21 free trade areas, or 43.75% of the total, disclosed information about government procurement programs and related invitations for bidding in 2020, and only three, or 6.25% of the total, disclosed information about procurement contracts. The level of information disclosure in this field urgently needed to be improved.

v. The disclosure of the list of certification items failed to meet the requirements

The disclosure of the list of certification items is an indispensable part of the optimization of the business environment. The assessment shows that 26 of the 48 free trade areas, or 54.17% of the total, disclosed the list of certification items. Among them, Nansha New District Area of China (Guangdong) Pilot Free Trade Zone, Luoyang Area of China (Henan) Pilot Free Trade Zone, Wuhan Area of China (Hubei) Pilot Free Trade Zone, Yichang Area of China (Hubei) Pilot Free Trade Zone, and Caofeidian Area of China (Hebei) Pilot Free Trade Zone published the list of certification items on their own websites, and all the other provided links to the government service websites on which the list was published. Among the 26 that published the list, only Nansha New District Area of China (Guangdong) Pilot Free Trade Zone, Shenyang Area of China (Liaoning) Pilot Free Trade Zone and Caofeidian Area of China (Hebei) Pilot Free Trade Zone disclosed all the information in the list of certification items, including the justifications for establishment, requesting entities, issuing entities, and application guide.

vi. The disclosure of administrative charges was not comprehensive

Publishing the list of administrative charges is conducive to further clarifying the charging standards and increasing the transparency of government affairs. The assessment shows that 29 of the 48 free trade areas, or 60.42% of the total, published the list of administrative charges. Among them, only 16 disclosed all the information in the list, including charging items, charging basis and charging standards, 29 disclosed the charging items and charging basis in the list, and 16 disclosed the charging standards.

(3) Openness of implementation and results

i. The openness of administrative penalty need to be improved

The setup of the administrative law enforcement column on the websites of free trade areas was not satisfactory. First of all, among the 48 free trade areas covered by the assessment, 13, or 27.08% of the total, had set up the administrative penalty column on their websites. Secondly, the information disclosed in the administrative penalty documents was incomplete. Of all the free trade areas covered by the assessment, 21, or 43.75% of all the total, published administrative penalty decision documents. Among them, some had not set up an administrative penalty column on their own websites but provided jump links to other websites on which the relevant information can be found. For example, the website of Lujiazui Area of China (Shanghai) Pilot Free Trade Zone did not have a column on administrative penalty, but provided a jump link to the website of Credit China (Shanghai), on which a user can find administrative penalty documents and administrative licensing documents of the free trade area with complete content elements through a search by document number. Except for these disclosed by nine assessment targets, the penalty decision documents disclosed by all other assessment targets were incomplete in content elements. Among the free trade areas that published administrative penalty decisions, 21 disclosed the document numbers, law enforcement bases and case names of administrative penalty decisions, but eight did not disclose the unified social credit codes of administrative counterparts. Meanwhile, the disclosure of channels of appeal against and remedies for administrative penalties was not satisfactory. Only nine free trade areas disclosed the channels of administrative reconsideration and administrative litigation on their websites, while 12 did not disclose any information about the channels of administrative reconsideration and administrative litigation.

ii. The disclosure of information about the "double random inspection" needed to be strengthened

As a brand-new means of supervision, "double random inspection" is a major reform and innovation of the concept and mode of government administrative regulation. By making regulation more standardized and law enforcement responsibilities traceable, it has become one of the statutory contents of government information disclosure and is of great significance for optimizing the business environment. The assessment shows that some assessment targets had set up a special column on their websites to disclose "double random inspection" information in a concentrated manner. For example, Dalian Area of China (Liaoning) Pilot Free Trade Zone and Yingkou Area of China (Liaoning) Pilot Free Trade Zone had set up a special column of "Regulation Lists" on their websites to disclose the lists of items of double random inspection by various departments. The lists were classified according to law enforcement subjects and contained such elements as the basis and content of random inspection and law enforcement subjects. They were updated in a timely manner, clearly classified and easy to consult. Generally speaking, however, the level of disclosure of lists of random inspection items was low. Among the 48 free trade areas, only 18, or 37.50% of the total, published lists of random inspection items. Of the free trade areas that had published their lists of random inspection items on their websites, only four published the lists with complete elements. They were: Guangzhou Nansha New District Area of China (Guangdong) Pilot Free Trade Zone, Tianjin Port Area of China (Tianjin) Pilot Free Trade Zone, Yingkou Area of China (Liaoning) Pilot Free Trade Zone and Zhengding Area of China (Hebei) Pilot Free Trade Zone. The lists published by other free trade areas had the problem of incomplete disclosure of information about double random inspection.

The disclosure of the results of double random inspections still needed to be improved: only 15 free trade areas, or 31.25% of the total, disclosed the results.

iii. The situation of publication of the annual report on government information disclosure by free trade zones was poor

The assessment shows that free trade zones did not attach importance to the preparation and publication of the annual report on government information disclosure. Among the 20 free trade zones, only three, namely China (Shanghai) Pilot Free Trade Zone, China (Tianjin) Pilot Free Trade Zone and China (Zhejiang) Pilot Free Trade Zone, accounting for 15.00% of the total, had set up a special column on the annual report on their websites, and only one, namely China (Tianjin) Pilot Free Trade Zone, published the annual report on government information disclosure in 2020. Moreover, what was published in the column of the Annual Report on Government Information Disclosure in China (Zhejiang) Pilot Free Trade Zone was not the annual report on government information disclosure, but the Department Budget of the Comprehensive Coordination Bureau of China (Zhejiang) Pilot Free Trade Zone in 2019. It can be seen from the above that the publication of the annual report on government information disclosure by free trade zones still urgently needed to be strengthened.

iv. The disclosure of statistical data needed to be improved

Statistical data is the most direct data to show the annual economic operation of free trade zones, as well as an important basis for market participants to understand the market situation of free trade zones. The assessment shows that, among the 20 free trade zones, only five, namely China (Shanghai) Pilot Free Trade Zone, China (Fujian) Pilot Free Trade Zone, China (Sichuan) Pilot Free Trade Zone, China (Zhejiang) Pilot Free Trade Zone and China (Shaanxi) Pilot Free Trade Zone, or 25.00% of the total, had set up a special column on statistical data on their websites. Only two of them published the economic operation data for 2019, 2020, and the recent time period in the column on their websites. Moreover, some free trade zones only mentioned their economic operation in news articles.

Among the 48 free trade areas, only 16, or 33.33% of the total, had set up the statistical data column on their websites. As far as the disclosure of economic operation data is concerned, only five free trade areas, namely Guangzhou Nansha New District Area of China (Guangdong) Pilot Free Trade Zone, Shenzhen Qianhai Shekou Area of China (Guangdong) Pilot Free Trade Zone, Zhuhai Hengqin New Area of China (Guangdong) Pilot Free Trade Zone, the Central Business District of Binhai New Area of China (Tianjin) Pilot Free Trade Zone and Pingtan Area of China (Fujian) Pilot Free Trade Zone, fully disclosed the data for 2019 and 2020. Moreover, some free trade zones only mentioned economic operation data in news articles, which were not official data released by relevant departments. In terms of disclosure of data on the number of new market entities, foreign trade and the use of foreign capital, only two free trade areas disclosed the data of newly established enterprises in 2019 and 2020 in a special column on their websites. Generally speaking, there was still room for improvement in the disclosure of economic operation data by free trade areas.

v. There was still room for improvement in the disclosure of the results of handling of suggestions of deputies to people's congresses and proposals of CPPCC members

According to the Circular of the General Office of the State Council on Effectively Disclosing the Results of Handling Suggestions of Deputies to the National People's Congress and Proposals of the Members of the National Committee of CPPCC, government organs should disclose on their own initiative suggestions of deputies to people's congresses and proposals of CPPCC members that can be made public after review. Especially they should give full play to the important role of information disclosure platforms of the government websites in disclosing in a concentrated way the results of handling of suggestions of deputies to people's congresses and proposals of CPPCC members, so as to facilitate public access. However, the assessment shows that none of the 21 free trade zones disclosed the summaries of, replies to, or results of the handling of suggestions of deputies to people's congresses and proposals of CPPCC members.

Among the 48 free trade areas, only two disclosed information about the overall situation of handling suggestions of deputies to people's congresses and proposals of CPPCC members in 2020, 13 published the full texts of replies to suggestions of deputies to people's congresses and 15 published the full texts of replies to proposals of CPPCC members.

(4) Platform construction

i. The release of information in special columns of websites needed to be rationalized

Classifying various kinds of information into different categories and disclosing them in special columns of websites helps the public quickly find the information they need. The classification of information by some assessment targets was unreasonable, resulting in the chaotic disclosure of information in columns on their websites, for example, disclosing planning documents, normative documents and policy interpretation documents all in the notice and announcement column. Moreover, the search bar on the websites of some assessment targets, such as Fuzhou Area of China (Fujian) Pilot Free Trade Zone and Kaifeng Area of China (Henan) Pilot Free Trade Zone, did not work. Releasing information in various columns of websites in a well-organized and reasonable manner is particularly important for easy access to information by the public.

ii. The construction of complaint and tip-off channels was not satisfactory

The situation of the construction of communication channels was generally good, but the construction of special complaint and tip-off channels was poor. Of the 20 free trade zones, only four, namely China (Shanghai) Pilot Free Trade Zone, China (Guangdong) Pilot Free Trade Zone, China (Guangxi) Pilot Free Trade Zone and

China (Hunan) Pilot Free Trade Zone, had set up clear complaint and tip-off channels. Among the 48 free trade areas, only 16, or 33.33% of the total, had set up the clear complaint and tip-off channels.

(5) Information disclosure upon application

i. The channels of information disclosure upon application in free trade zones were not smooth enough

Among the 20 free trade zones, only two, namely China (Tianjin) Pilot Free Trade Zone and China (Fujian) Pilot Free Trade Zone, provided online application channels. And of the 48 free trade areas, only 25 provided online application channels.

Moreover, the Information Disclosure Guide of the Administrative Committee of China (Shanghai) Pilot Free Trade Zone published on the website of China (Shanghai) Pilot Free Trade Zone provides three methods of application for information disclosure: first, online application through the government information disclosure column on the portal website of China (Shanghai) Pilot Free Trade Zone; second, application by letter, telegram or fax; and third, application in person. However, on the website provided by the Guide, members of the Project Team could not find "China (Shanghai) Pilot Free Trade Zone Administrative Committee" in the list of applications-accepting subjects. Zhangjiang High-tech Area of China (Shanghai) Pilot Free Trade Zone had the same problem: Zhangjiang High-tech Park Management Committee, which was designed as an applications-accepting subject in the Information Disclosure Guide of the Administrative Committee of Zhangjiang High-tech Area of China (Shanghai) Pilot Free Trade Zone, was not in the list of applications-accepting subjects on the online application platform provided by the Guide.

ii. The disclosure rate of replies to applications for information disclosure was not high and many replies were not standardized

The Project Team submitted information disclosure applications to China (Tianjin) Pilot Free Trade Zone on February 18, 2021, and to China (Fujian) Pilot Free Trade Zone on March 2, 2021, but received no reply from any of them by April 5, 2021 (after 30 and 23 working days, respectively).

The Project Team tested the information disclosure upon application of 21 free trade areas that provided the application link by submitting information disclosure applications. By April 5, 2021, it had received only 11 formal replies and three informal replies by telephone. Among them, one reply did not contain the notification of the applicant's rights to reconsideration and litigation, and three replies did not contain the document number and the notification of the applicant's rights to reconsideration and litigation.

5 Analysis of Assessment Results

1. The awareness of the openness of government affairs still needed to be enhanced

Building a transparent government is an important measure and guarantee for optimizing the business environment. The Regulations on Optimizing the Business Environment require that people's governments at all levels and their departments should adhere to the openness and transparency of government affairs, take openness as the normal and non-openness as the exception, and comprehensively promote the openness of decision-making, implementation, administration, service and results. As important windows of opening to the outside world, free trade zones undertake the important tasks of exploring, innovating and transforming government functions, so it is particularly important for them to promote the openness of government affairs.

The assessment shows that the level of openness of government affairs in some free trade zones was still low, the awareness of openness needed to be enhanced, and a large amount of information that the public and enterprises were concerned about had not yet been disclosed by the government on its own initiatives. The websites of some free trade zones were poorly constructed, with only some basic news reports on, but little substantive and effective information about, the free trade zones.

2. The legal status of the competent authorities was not clear

The organizational structure of free trade zones, constructed by the governments of provinces or municipalities directly under the Central Government to which they belong, varies from free trade zone to free trade zone, resulting in unclear legal status and organizational powers of the competent authorities of free trade zones.

Article 4 of the Measures for the Administration of China (Shanghai) Pilot Free Trade Zone provides that the Administrative Committee of China (Shanghai) Free Trade Zone is established as an external agency of the Municipal Government to undertake specific reform tasks of the free trade zone and plan, manage and coordinate administrative affairs related to the free trade zone. According to this article, the nature of the Administrative Committee of China (Shanghai) Free Trade Zone is an external agency of the Shanghai Municipal Government. However, the organization chart published on the website of China (Shanghai) Pilot Free Trade Zone shows that the Administrative Committee of China (Shanghai) Free Trade Zone shares the same office and staff with the People's Government of Pudong New District.

Some free trade zones, such as China (Fujian) Pilot Free Trade Zone, China (Guangdong) Pilot Free Trade Zone and China (Tianjin) Pilot Free Trade Zone, adopted another organizational structure in which the provincial Party committee and the provincial government set up a leading group for the work in the pilot free trade zone or a leading group for the promotion of the work in the pilot free trade zone, which sets up an office in the provincial department of or commission on commerce. The Measures for the Administration of China (Fujian) Pilot Free Trade Zone provide that a leading group for the work in China (Fujian) Pilot Free Trade Zone is established, which shall be responsible for making overall plans and coordinating the building and development of the free trade zone. The office of the leading group is located in the Commerce Department of Fujian Province, which shall undertake the daily work of the office of the leading group. The Regulations on China (Zhejiang) Pilot Free Trade Zone provide that the provincial people's government establishes a free trade zone advisory and coordinating body; an executive office of the free trade zone and a coordinating body shall be established at the provincial commerce department; China (Zhejiang) Pilot Free Trade Zone Administration Commission shall, as an external office of the provincial people's government, be responsible for the building, administration and other work of the free trade zone. This organizational structure combines the above two organizational methods. On the one hand, a coordinating body is set up in the provincial government, which set up an office in the provincial commerce department; on the other hand, an administrative committee of the free trade zone is set up as an external agency of the provincial people's government. Meanwhile, according to the website of China (Zhejiang) Pilot Free Trade Zone, the Administrative Committee of China (Zhejiang) Pilot Free Trade Zone shares office and staff with Zhoushan Municipal People's Government and the Administrative Committee of Zhoushan Islands New District in the form of "one body with three names".

The unclear legal status and different organizational structures of the competent authorities of various trade zones lead the chaos in information disclosure, and the lack of clarity in organizational competence and responsibility for information disclosure has a negative impact on the effectiveness of information disclosure.

3. The administrative bodies of different development zones shared the same office and staff, resulting in the mix-up of the information disclosed by different administrative bodies

The assessment shows that some free trade zones adopted the administrative mode of different administrative bodies sharing the same office and staff. Taking China (Tianjin) Pilot Free Trade Zone as an example. According to Article 8 of the Measures for the Administration of China (Tianjin) Pilot Free Trade Zone, the Administration Committee of China (Tianjin) Pilot Free Trade Zone (TJFTZ) has three local offices: Tianjin Port Office of TJFTZ, which shares office and staff with the Administrative Committee of Tianjin Dongjiang Port; Tianjin Airport Area Office of TJFTZ, which shares office and staff with the Administrative Committee of Tianjin Airport Economic Zone; and the CBD Office of Binhai New Area of TJFTZ, which shares office and staff with the Administrative Committee of the CBD of Tianjin Binhai New Area. As a result, the government information disclosed by the administrative bodies of free trade zones was mixed with and could not be distinguished from the government information disclosed by administrative bodies of the development zones. For example, in the 2020 Work Report of the Management Committee Tianjin Port Bonded Area on Government Information Disclosure, it is impossible to tell which information is disclosed by the Office of Tianjin Airport Area of China (Tianjin) Pilot Free Trade Zone. Another example is Guangzhou Nansha New District Area of China (Guangdong) Pilot Free Trade Zone. Its administrative committee shared the same office and staff with the Administrative Committee of Guangzhou Nansha Economic and Technological Development Zone, the Administrative Committee of

Guangzhou Nansha Bonded Port Area and the Nansha District Government. The link to Nansha Area of China (Guangdong) Free Trade Zone displayed on the website of China (Guangdong) Free Trade Zone jumps directly to the website of the People's Government of Nansha District, and it is difficult to tell whether a piece of information on the website was disclosed by the free trade area, the development zone or the district government.

4. The powers of different departments overlapped with each other and no measures were taken for their coordination

The operation of free trade zones will inevitably involve the overlapping of functions and powers of multiple departments, which in turn makes it difficult to disclose information in a coordinated way. Different information held by different departments could not be disclosed on the unified portal website of a free trade zone in a timely manner, leading to the dispersion, even blanks, in information disclosure. For example, the Measures for the Administration of China (Sichuan) Pilot Free Trade Zone provide that various areas of the free trade zone shall implement the system of relatively centralized administrative licensing power, and uniformly exercise their respective administrative licensing power in accordance with the law and that various areas of the free trade zone shall implement the system of relatively centralized administrative penalty power, and uniformly exercise their respective administrative penalty power in accordance with the law. However, no document on administrative licensing or administrative penalty was published on the websites of Chengdu Tianfu New District Area, Chengdu Qingbaijiang Railway Port Area, or South Sichuan Lingang Area of China (Sichuan) Pilot Free Trade Zone.

After a long period of construction, a relatively complete national system of government information disclosure has been basically established. However, currently there is still no unified national-level special document on the information disclosure work of free trade zones, which have different organizational structures and vague legal status. As a result, the information disclosure work of various free trade zones can only rely on the initiative and consciousness of the competent authorities of free trade zones and the unevenness of the level of information disclosure in various trade zones has been further aggravated.

6 Prospect

The construction of pilot free trade zones is of great significance for exploring new paths and models of opening to the outside world, accelerating the transformation of government functions and the reform of the administrative system, transforming the economic growth mode and optimizing economic structure, cultivating China's new competitive advantages in global competition, building new platforms of cooperation and development with other countries, and expanding the space for economic growth. The *Regulations on Optimizing the Business Environment* require people's governments at all levels and their departments to comprehensively advance the openness of decision-making, implementation, administration, services, and results, raise the rule-of-law level of the business environment, promote foreign investment, and improve the standardization of government administration and the predictability of business operations. In 2020, affected by the Covid-19 pandemic, all countries in the world suffered economic losses to varying degrees. Under the leadership of the CPC Central Committee, China took the lead in effectively controlling the spread of the pandemic nationwide and achieved positive economic growth. This has greatly improved the confidence of other countries in the Chinese market. Pilot free trade zones, as important windows to attract foreign investment and promote foreign trade, should further strengthen and improve their website construction and information disclosure to create a stable, fair and transparent business environment. We suggest that the Chinese government take the following measures to further promote information disclosure in free trade zones.

Firstly, formulating and improving special institutional documents on information disclosure in free trade zones. The Central Government can formulate unified standards for information disclosure in free trade zones by taking the relevant provisions of the State Council on government information disclosure as references, so as to provide free trade zones throughout the country with a clear basis to regulate their information disclosure work and improve their transparency and openness.

Secondly, clarifying the legal status of the competent authorities of free trade zones. The sharing of offices and staff by competent authorities of multiple administrative areas is intrinsically related to the vagueness of the legal functions and powers of the competent authorities. Reflected in the portal websites of free trade zones, this mixed administrative mode leads to unclear information search, chaotic webpage jump, difficulty in distinguishing the information disclosed by free trade zones from the information disclosed by other authorities, and information gap caused by unclear responsibilities. To avoid the mix-up of information caused by the sharing of offices and staff by competent authorities of multiple administrative areas, clear distinctions should be made between information disclosure by competent authorities of different administrative areas and levels.

Thirdly, exploring the reform of the mechanism for the openness of government affairs in light of the trend towards cross-departmental business collaboration. Efforts should be made to adapt to the direction of free trade zone construction and government service reform, break the traditional open government work mechanism with each department as a unit, and establish a mechanism adapted to inter-departmental administration and services in the new era, with matters, rather than departments, as the links.

Finally, improving the intelligent level of information disclosure and accelerating the platform construction in free trade zones. China should rely on the Internet and use new technologies to realize synchronous generation, automatic collection and directional intelligent push of information about free trade zones, improve the pertinence and arrival rate of information disclosure, and reduce delay in the updating of information. Meanwhile, the clarity of webpages and the rationalization of web columns are conducive to the display of the disclosed information and convenient for the browsing of and search for such information by the public.

Current Situation and Prospect of Government Press Releases in China

Innovation Project Team on Rule of Law Index, Institute of Law, Chinese Academy of Social Sciences

1 The Role of Press Release Work in Government Information Disclosure

Press release is an important channel of government information disclosure. Since China gradually established and improved the press release system, press release has become a normalized work and conscious behavior of state governance. As an important measure for promoting the democratic political process in China, an important way to enhance government transparency, and an important part of the news and public opinion work of the Party and the government, the press release work aims to achieve the overall goal of "promoting the modernization of the state governance system and capacity" in the process of comprehensively deepening the reform, and plays a vital role in the government information disclosure work.

Leaders of the Project Team: He Tian, Director of the Center for Studies of National Rule of Law Index of Chinese Academy of Social Sciences, a research fellow at the Institute of Law, and a distinguished professor at the Law School of the University of Chinese Academy of Social Sciences, and Yanbin Lv, a research fellow at and head of the Department of Survey and Studies of National Situation of the Rule of Law, Institute of Law, Chinese Academy of Social Sciences, and head the Teaching and Research Section of Administrative Law of the Law School of the University of Chinese Academy of Social Sciences. Other members of the project team: Xiaomei Wang, Ming Wang, Yafeng Wang, Wenbo Che, Yingying Feng, Yanpeng Liu, Zhiqun Liu, Yi Qi, Xiaomin Mi, Qiyuan Lu, Changming Hu, Mei Hong, Yanjie Li and Chenhan Gu. Authors of this report: Yafeng Wang, Zhiqun Liu, Yi Qi, Qiyuan Lu, Chenhan Gu, academic assistants of the Center for Studies of National Rule of Law Index of Chinese Academy of Social Sciences.

Innovation Project Team on Rule of Law Index, Institute of Law, Chinese Academy of Social Sciences (✉)
Institute of Law, Chinese Academy of Social Sciences, Beijing, China
e-mail: 13693186775@163.com

H. Tian and Y. Lv (eds.), *Assessing Government Transparency in China (2021)*,
https://doi.org/10.1007/978-981-99-9734-3_9

1. Releasing authoritative information

By holding a press conference to release authoritative information, the government can accurately convey information and interpret policies, so that the people can fully understand the government's guidelines, principles, policies and work trends. Currently, a systematic and professional press release system of governments at all levels in China has been formed. With a clear division of labor among governments at various levels, this multi-level press conference system is able to meet the people's demand for authoritative government information. Under the institutionalized and normalized press release system, press conferences are held at a certain frequency and the information release is maintained at a high density, so as to meet the public demand for information. In addition, press conferences are flexible in duration, can contain a large amount of information, and release authoritative information in multiple fields in an all-round way and, as such, is conducive to the accurate and rapid transmission of government policies and decisions to the people in the whole country, and helps to mobilize all available forces to promote the implementation of government policies, improve the level of government information disclosure, and further modernize the state governance capacity.

2. Responding to social concerns

Establishing a press release mechanism helps the government respond to public concerns in a timely manner and builds a bridge between the government and the public. The press release system is a platform for face-to-face communication, on which spokespersons and reporters can interact effectively and communicate fully. After some information is made public, people's understanding of it may be biased, so it is urgent to strengthen the interpretation of information and policies and the interaction between the government and the people. At a press conference, reporters can ask questions about ambiguous parts of the information disclosed by the government, and speakers can respond to the questions in a targeted way. The synchronicity and high efficiency of response to questions are also unique to the press release system. Especially at the critical moment of an emergency when information gathers instantly and the attention of the public is highly focused, the authority of the subjects of government press releases makes the content of press releases highly authoritative. Government organs, by responding to public concerns in a timely manner and showing the attitude of the government through a press conference, will be able to unite the people and enhance the credibility of the government.

3. Guiding public opinion

Because of the authority of the subjects and contents of press releases, the public trust in government press releases is unmatched by that in other news media. Therefore, the government press release system plays an important role in strengthening the role of mainstream media in guiding public opinion. Moreover, the government information disclosed in press releases often involves important issues that attract high public attention, and each press conference is given a clear value orientation. In addition, press releases have an extremely wide audience. Especially in the Internet age, their influence on public opinion is further enhanced through live broadcasting by various online platforms.

2 A Brief Review of the Press Release System in China

At present, with the all-round rise of social media, all members of the public are both recipients and releasers and disseminators of information. The formation time of public opinion has been greatly shortened, and the government press release system is facing a test. How to ensure the authority and accuracy of government press releases, innovate and improve the press release mechanism, and expand channels, enrich the content, and improve the communication power, influence and credibility of government press releases against the background of information explosion are the challenges faced by the press release system in the new era, as well as one of the keys to comprehensively deepening the openness of government affairs. During the period from the founding of the People's Republic of China to the early stage of reform and opening-up, China rarely released information in the form of a press conference, but mainly relied on traditional media such as newspapers and radio, and the press release system had not been established. In 1980, the Chinese government held an important press conference to release the results of the investigation and handling of the capsizing accident of the "Bohai No.2" offshore oil rig at home and abroad, which was the first time that the Chinese government held a press conference on an emergency.[1] Subsequently, China began to explore the establishment of a spokesperson system. In February 1983, the Publicity Department of the CPC Central Committee and the Central Leading Group for External Publicity jointly issued the *Opinions on Establishing the Spokesperson System and Strengthening the Work for Foreign Journalists*. In April 1983, the Chinese Journalists Association first introduced the spokespersons of various departments under the State Council and various people's organizations to Chinese and foreign journalists, thereby officially announcing the establishment of the spokesperson system in China.[2] In 1991, the Information Office of the State Council (SCIO) was established as the administrative organ responsible for government press release work.

Major emergencies are undoubtedly important boosters for government press release work. The year 2003 was an important node in the construction of the press release system in China. In order to disclose information about the SARS epidemic, SCIO intensified the holding of press conferences. By the end of the SARS epidemic, the State Council Office had held a total of eight press conferences, the importance of press releases and information disclosure was widely and profoundly recognized

[1] Manli Cheng, "The Construction of the Press Release System Along with Reform and Opening-up in China", 2 (2020) *Public Diplomacy Quarterly*.

[2] See "Construction of the Party Committee Spokesperson System", Information Office of the State Council of the People's Republic of China.

by all sectors of society for the first time, and the journey of institutionalizing the spokesperson began in China.

A review of the relevant documents on government information disclosure published in China in recent years shows that actively responding to social concerns and major public opinions, strengthening the interconnection with the media, and giving full play to the communication role of various media have always been emphasized by the government in the construction of the press release system. According to the *Opinions on Further Strengthening the Public Disclosure of Government Information, Responding to Public Concerns and Enhancing Public Confidence in the Government*, issued by the General Office of the State Council in 2013, China would further strengthen the development of the spokesperson system and the construction and management of government websites, and focus on building new media-based channels for government information release and interaction with the public, and respond to public opinion in a timely manner by releasing news online, organizing interpretations by experts, holding press conferences and accepting media interviews.

The *Key Points of the Work of Public Disclosure of Government Information in 2014*, issued by the General Office of the State Council in 2014, put forward higher requirements on the work: early detection and judgment of relevant public opinions and hot issues that need to be responded to, timely release of authoritative information, elimination of false rumors, and positive guidance of public opinion. They re-emphasized the need to strengthen the spokesperson system and the construction of information disclosure platforms such as government websites and government Weibo and WeChat accounts.

In the *Key Points of the Work of Public Disclosure of Government Information in 2015*, issued by the General Office of the State Council in 2015, it was stated that China would comprehensively strengthen the active disclosure work, including making better use of new technologies and means, paying attention to users' experience and information needs, and strengthening the connection and coordination between information released by different platforms and channels to ensure the accuracy and consistency of content of the information.

The *Opinions on Comprehensively Advancing the Open Government Work*, issued the General Office of the CPC Central Committee and the General Office of the State Council in February 2016, the *Notice on Further Improving the Response to Public Opinion in the Open Government Work*, issued by the General Office of the State Council in August 2016, and the *Detailed Rules for the Implementation of the Opinions on Comprehensively Advancing the Open Government Work*, issued by the General Office of the State Council in November 2016, all contained special provisions on actively responding to social concerns, including clarifying the responsibility for government response to public opinion, highlighting the emphases of public opinion collection, effectively carrying out the work of analyzing, distinguishing, classifying and handling of different situations, and responding to public opinion by releasing authoritative information, holding press conferences or briefings, and accepting media interviews, so as to achieve the objective of improving the effect of the response.

According to the *Key Points of Work of Public Disclosure of Government Information in 2016*, issued by the General Office of the State Council, in case of a major emergency, the local government and department responsible for handling the emergency are also the primary entities responsible for the release of the relevant information. The main responsible persons of the entities, as the "primary spokespersons" in the emergency, should react quickly, make their voice heard in time, and respond to public concerns in a timely manner; they should hold a press conference within 24 h after the occurrence of a particularly major or major emergency, make overall arrangements for the media release of major decision-making arrangements, actively provide materials to the media, hold briefings, and effectively carry out information release and interpretation work, so as to give full play to the role of the media.

The *Key Points of Open Government Work in 2017*, issued by the General Office of the State Council in 2017, required government organs to further improve the mechanism for policy interpretation and response to public concerns, strictly implement the time limits of releasing authoritative information within five hours at the latest and holding press conferences within 24 h for particularly major and major emergencies, and implement the system of circulation of a notice of criticism and the interview system to ensure that the responses to public concerns do not exceed the time limit and the contents of the responses are not perfunctory.

The *Key Points of Open Government Work in 2018* and *Key Points of Open Government Work in 2019* issued by the General Office of the State Council also require relevant government organs to actively respond to major social concerns, strengthen communication with news media, and improve the initiative, pertinence and effectiveness of the response to government affairs-related public opinion. In view of the Covid-19 epidemic, the *Key Points of Open Government Work in 2020* issued by the General Office of the State Council put forward the requirements of strengthening public health information disclosure around emergency response, including effectively utilizing various news media, timely and accurately releasing epidemic information, paying close attention to public opinion relating to the epidemic situation, and quick and positive responding to hot public opinion issues.

The *Key Points of Open Government Work in 2021* issued by the General Office of the State Council require relevant government organs to effectively disclose information about normalized work of epidemic prevention and control, improve the standardization level of the release of information about Covid-19 epidemic prevention and control, strengthen overall coordination before releasing major policies of social concern and important information with sensitive content, intensify information integration within the government system on the precondition of seeking truth from facts, and make unified statements.

In a word, after years of promotion, China's press release system has been gradually standardized and improved, and its role in the openness of government affairs and government administration has become increasingly prominent.

3 The Achievements Made by the Chinese Government in the Press Release Work

Government press release is not only an important way of disclosing government information and carrying out government publicity work but also a kind of dialogue and exchange between the government and the people, which is conducive to enhancing government transparency and safeguarding people's right to know and the right of supervision. In recent years, China has gradually increased the channels, diversified the forms, and realized the institutionalization, normalization and specialization of government press release. Government press release provides authoritative information to the people, meets the information needs of the people, and increasingly becomes a bridge of communication between the government and the people that can better win the people's support.

1. The channels have gradually increased

In recent years, the government has gradually increased the channels of press releases. First of all, government news can be released online through new media such as WeChat and Weibo, and offline through traditional media such as paper media, radio and television. As early as 2014, the General Office of the CPC Central Committee and the General Office of the State Council issued the *Guiding Opinions on Promoting the Integrated Development of Traditional Media and Emerging Media*. In September 2020, the General Office of the CPC Central Committee and the General Office of the State Council issued the Opinions on Accelerating the In-depth Integrated Development of Media. As a result, the integration of traditional media and emerging media has gradually accelerated and become a national strategy. It is precisely because the state attaches importance to the integration of traditional media and emerging media that the channels of government press releases have gradually increased. At the same time, the application of information technologies such as 5G, big data and artificial intelligence has increased the channels of government press releases on the one hand, and formed an intensive and efficient communication chain on the other hand. Nowadays, much government news is released and disseminated through TV, websites, WeChat, Weibo, Douyin and other channels, thus not only facilitating access to information by the public but also improving the coverage rate of government news. For example, during the Covid-19 epidemic, many local governments used various new media platforms to carry out live webcasts, while others, such as the Information Office State Council, used the 5G technology to hold remote video conferences. For another example, local governments had set up a government press release column on their official websites to announce government press conferences in advance, and release the video recordings or written records of press conferences after they were held, so as to facilitate access to official first-hand authoritative information by the public.

2. The forms have become increasingly diversified

In recent years, the forms of government press release have become gradually diversified. In practice, besides holding press conferences, the forms of government press release also include press briefing, briefing, press interview, press salon, media collective interview, exclusive interview, telephone questions and answers, news bulletin, statement, and news release. Each of these novel forms of press release has its own characteristics. Government press conference and press briefing have relatively high requirements, with grand form, complicated procedures and strong authority. As such, they attract high public attention and have a wide audience. Media collective interview, exclusive interview, discussion, etc. are highly interactive, with a relaxed atmosphere and many opportunities for journalists to ask questions. News bulletin, statement and news release are issued in light of specific situations, the needs of the media and materials available to the government, so they are highly authoritative and targeted.

Governments at all levels have been able to flexibly adopt different forms of press release, which have played a huge role in the fight against the Covid-19 epidemic. Adopting different forms of a press release in light of its theme and content can efficiently meets the information needs of the public on the one hand, and make government press release work more scientific and professional on the other hand. In addition, during the Covid-19 outbreak, some governments also innovated the forms of press release, for example, holding press conferences in various places outside the press conference hall according to their themes. During the Covid-19 epidemic, the Ministry of Foreign Affairs used the WeChat Group to hold the first regular online press conference in its history and Guangzhou Municipal Government carried out press activities in hospitals, parks, schools and other places.

3. The institution building has been strengthened

Up to now, China has gradually institutionalized and developed a mature working mechanism for government press release. Many departments under the State Council and local governments have formulated and promulgated relevant regulations. For example, the National Cultural Heritage Administration formulated the Measures of the National Cultural Heritage Administration for the Administration of the Press Release Work in 2017; the General Office of the Provincial Party Committee and the General Office of the Provincial Government of Jilin Province issued the *Notice on Further Strengthening the Government Affairs Press Release Work of in the Province in 2018*; and the Government of Changzhou City of Jiangsu Province established a press release day system in 2019, designating every Wednesday as the municipal press release day; the Government of Wenzhou City of Zhejiang Province started to implement the regular press conference mechanism in 2020, holding at least one regular press conference every month. Some local government departments and even township governments have established the government press release system and working mechanism. For example, the Jiangxi Provincial Department of Housing and Urban–Rural Development formulated the *Measures of Jiangxi Provincial Department of Housing and Urban–Rural Development for the Administration of Press Releases (for Trial Implementation)* in 2017; the Civil Affairs Bureau of Guiyang City of Guizhou Province formulated the *Regulations of Civil Affairs Bureau of Guiyang City on the Press Release System* in 2018; the Government of Tongling City of Anhui Province formulated the *Regulations of the Municipal Housing and Construction Bureau on the Press Release Administration System and Work Mechanism* in 2020; and the Government of Yongfeng Town of Tianchang City in Anhui Province formulated the *Regulations of the Government of Yongfeng Town on the Press Release Work* in 2020. Most of these institutional documents have provided for the content, form, process and news collection mechanism of government press releases. The institutionalized press release work has made government press releases more timely, authoritative and standardized.

4. The practice is becoming more and more normalized

In recent years, China's government press release has developed into an increasingly normalized multi-level system with wide coverage and become an important window for information disclosure. According to the *Assessment Report on the Implementation of the National Human Rights Action Plan of China (2012–2015)* issued by the State Council, the State Council Information Office (SCIO) organized 322 news conferences on the major meetings, major decisions and major work of the CPC and the State and the CPC Central Committee, the State Council and local CPC committees and governments organized more than 9,300 news conferences and news briefings between 2012 and 2015. In addition, according to the statistics of press releases published on the portal website of SCIO, in 2016, SCIO held 90 press conferences and 31 regular news policy briefings, various departments under the State Council held 843 press activities, and various provincial-level governments held 987 press activities; in 2017, SCIO held 88 press conferences and 22 regular policy briefings, various departments under the State Council held 1,204 press activities, and various provincial-level governments held 1,469 press activities; in 2018, SCIO held 109 press conferences and 48 regular policy briefings, various departments under the State Council held 1,049 press activities, and various provincial-level governments held 848 press activities; in 2019, SCIO held 166 press conferences and 74 regular policy briefings, various departments under the State Council held 972 press activities, and various provincial-level governments held 732 press activities; and in 2020, SCIO held 170 press conferences and 51 regular briefings on the State Council policies, various departments under the State Council held 1,126 press activities of the State Council and various provincial-level governments held 2,862 press activities (see Fig. 1).

Take Guangzhou and Beijing as examples. The Guangzhou Municipal Government held 241 press conferences in 2020, with an average of more than 20 per month; and the Beijing Municipal Government held 223 press conferences in 2020, with an average of nearly 19 per month. It can be seen from the above data that press release has become one of the common methods of government information disclosure, and the normalized press release system has greatly improved the information disclosure capacity of the government. In addition to high-frequency and normalized government press releases, local governments such as the Wuhu Municipal Government in Anhui Province also draw up their government press conference plans at the beginning of each year and regularly organized and carry out inspections on the government information disclosure and press releases work of various departments under them.

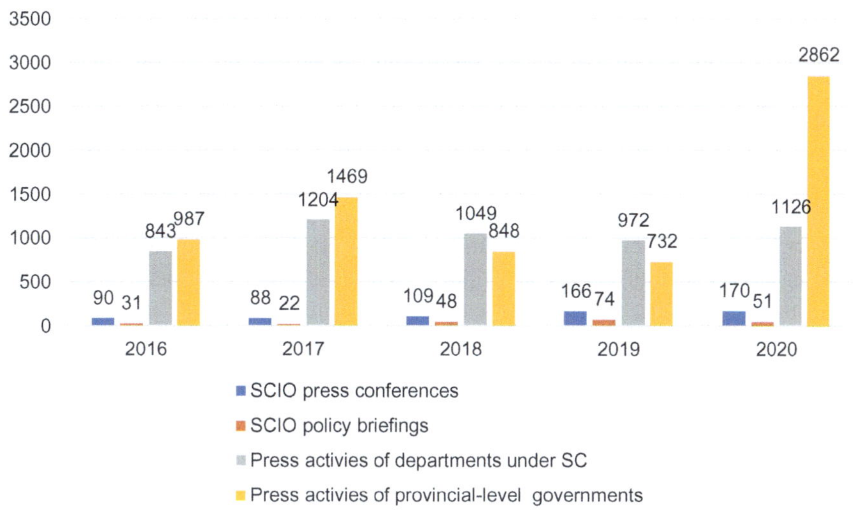

Fig. 1 Government press release data from 2016 to 2020

5. The timeliness of press releases has been continuously strengthened

Timeliness is of particular importance to the press release work, and the government needs to actively and timely release news and information on major issues to respond to social concerns and clear up confusion among the public. There is no doubt that timeliness has become one of the necessary principles of government press release work. Both the central and local governments have issued institutional documents to ensure the timeliness of government press release. For example, the *Notice of the General Office of the State Council on Effective Response to Public Opinions in Open Government Work* requires government organs to respond quickly to public opinions on government affairs involving particularly major and major emergencies, and hold a press conference within 24 h of the emergencies at the latest; the *Measures of the People's Government of Guizhou Province for the Press Release Work* stipulate that the first information release on a particularly major or major natural disaster, accident, or public health incident shall not exceed three hours after the occurrence of the incident. If the information cannot be released within three hours after the incident due to slow information submission or other reasons, it must be released within one hour after reception; the *Measures of Hainan Provincial Department of Commerce for News and Information Release on Major Events* stipulate that interpretations of important policies and regulations should be released within five working days after the introduction of the policies and regulations, and social hot spot information should be released within three days in light of public opinion and media interview demands. A press conference should be held within 24 h after the occurrence of major public opinions on government affairs or major emergencies; the *Provisions of the Agricultural Committee of Guizhou Province on Press Release Work* stipulate that regular government information should be released within five working days;

the first-time release of information about a serious agricultural emergency should not exceed three hours after the occurrence of the emergency. If the information cannot be released within three hours after the incident due to slow information submission or other reasons, it must be released within one hour after the reception; a press conference shall be held within 24 h after the occurrence of particularly major or major emergencies; the *Implementation Opinions of Zhenjiang Municipal People's Government on Further Strengthening and Improving Government Press Release Work* stipulate that announcements (bulletins) should be released within five working days of the date of their adoption. For a relatively large or general emergency, the initial information should be released within three hours after its occurrence, authoritative information should be released within five hours, and a press conference should be held within 24 h; the *Provisions of Beihai Municipal People's Government on the Routine Press Release System* stipulate that public opinions on government affairs involving particularly major or major emergencies should be responded to quickly, and a press conference should be held within 24 h at the latest. Other public opinions on government affairs should be responded to within 48 h.

The timely release of government news relies on not only the regulations on paper but also the implementation of the regulations in practice. In practice, many local governments in China are able to release information in a very timely manner. Especially after some emergencies and public events of public concern, they are able to make their voice heard at the earliest time possible, respond in time, guide public opinion, relieve public anxiety, firmly hold the power of speech, and prevent rumors from breeding. For example, an explosion occurred in Wucailong Gold Mine in Qixia City of Shandong Province at 14:00 on January 10, 2021; the Emergency Management Bureau of Qixia City received a report on the accident at 20:05 on January 11; and the on-site rescue headquarters held a press conference at 11:30 on January 12; the second press conference was held at 19:00 on January 12. For another example, an explosion occurred at Tianjiayi Chemical Co., Ltd., in Yancheng City, Jiangsu Province at about 14:48 on March 21, 2019 and the first press conference on the incident was held by the on-site command center at 9:00 on March 22. Since the outbreak of the Covid-19 epidemic, it has become the norm for local governments to regularly release epidemic information and to disclose epidemic information and cases of public concern through press releases in a timely manner.

6. The press release work has been significantly professionalized

Professionalized government press release work is conducive to the dissemination of the truth and explanation of the official positions of the government on the one hand, and to the transmission of values and the amassing of positive energy on the other hand. Meanwhile, in the face of emergencies, professionalized government press releases are also more effective in responding to social concerns, reassuring the public, and reducing the space for the spread of rumors. Government spokespersons are playing an increasingly indispensable role in more and more specialized government press releases. According to the list of spokespersons of central state organs and local governments in 2021 published by the SCIO, there are currently 28 spokespersons for relevant departments of the CPC Central Committee, one spokesperson for the Supreme People's Court, one spokesperson for the Supreme People's Procuratorate, 123 spokespersons for relevant departments of the State Council, 49 spokespersons for Party committees of provinces, autonomous regions, municipalities directly under the Central Government and Xinjiang Production and Construction Corps, and 52 spokespersons for people's governments of provinces, autonomous regions and municipalities directly under the Central Government and Xinjiang Production and Construction Corps. They are all full-time spokespersons and generally concurrently serve as leaders in charge of the press work in their respective organs. For example, the spokespersons of the Ministry of Foreign Affairs, the Ministry of National Defense and other ministries under the State Council are all heads of information departments (bureaus) of their respective ministries. Some of them have become the "online celebrity" of new media short videos because of their excellent professional ability and frequent witty remarks.

During the Covid-19 epidemic, the central and local governments have achieved excellent results in specialized government press releases, which contributed greatly to the prevention and control of the epidemic. For example, many local governments have taken Covid-19 epidemic prevention and control as the theme of press conferences, in which spokespersons or invited guests introduced local cases, epidemic prevention and control measures, medical treatment, resumption of production and of work, etc. in a well-organized way. At the end of each press conference, questions from reporters were answered to respond to social concerns. For another example, the Government of Beijing Municipality provided synchronous sign language interpretation at the press conferences held during the Covid-19 epidemic, which not only embodied the professionalism of press releases but also warmed people's hearts. For yet another example, during the Covid-19 epidemic, many local governments have invited medical and health experts, think tank scholars, enterprise representatives, community volunteers, police officers, medical staff, delivery men and other people from all walks of life to participate in press conferences and be interviewed by reporters, so as to enable the public to look at the epidemic situation from multiple perspectives and understand the real life of the people in the epidemic situation through different information sources.

4 Existing Problems in the Press Release Work in China

Currently, although the operation of the press conference system in China has become more and more standardized and efficient, there is still some room for improvement.

1. Problems with the online disclosure of the contents of press conferences

(1) The disclosure of information about press conferences is not timely

According to our investigation, except for a few exceptional cases, the governments of Beijing, Shanghai and Shenzhen are basically able to upload the information about a press conference to their portal websites on the day when the press conference is held, but the Government of Guangzhou has rarely been able to disclose the information about a press conference online on the same day of the press conference, but almost always disclose it a few days after. For example, its first press conference on the Covid-19 epidemic was held on January 28, 2020, but the content of the press conference was not uploaded onto its website until February 5. Its second press conference on the Covid-19 epidemic was held on February 7, 2020, but its content was not uploaded onto its website until February 9. Even recently, it sometimes still uploaded the content of a press conference one day after the press conference. For example, the content of the press conference on Guangzhou Night of "New Vitality of an Old City", held on February 26, 2021, was uploaded to its website on February 27, 2021.

In addition to the delay in uploading the contents of press conferences onto the Internet, some local governments also make mistakes about the dates on which the contents of the press conferences are uploaded on their websites. For example, on the portal website of Beijing Municipal Government, the dates on which the contents of the press conferences held on March 3, April 10, April 21 and November 17, 2020 were uploaded were indicated as March 2, April 9, April 20 and November 16, respectively, one day earlier than the press conferences were held.

Also, some local governments have the practice of uploading the contents of the same press conference in batches or uploading multiple press conferences at one time. For example, the Beijing Municipal Government uploaded the videos of a press conference held on November 14, 2020 on the same day as the conference, but the details of the spokesman's speech at the press conference on the next day. The Government of Guangzhou has the practice of uploading the contents of many press conferences onto its website at one time. For example, on June 15, 2020, it uploaded the contents of six press conferences, namely press conference no. 115 through no. 120, on the Covid-19 epidemic situation, all at one time.

(2) The contents of press conferences disclosed on the Internet are Incomplete

As far as the press conference work is concerned, it has become a self-evident rule to provide the live broadcast of a press conference when it is held and disclose the content of the press conference after it is held. However, our assessment shows that almost none of the assessment targets was able to disclose the contents of all its press conferences online. According to the statistics released by the SCIO, by December 31, 2020, 197 press conferences related to the Covid-19 epidemic situation were held in Beijing, 89 in Shanghai and 241 in Guangzhou. However, our assessment shows that, in 2020, the governments of Beijing, Shanghai and Guangzhou disclosed the contents of 192, 83 and 138 press conferences on the Covid-19 epidemic situation, respectively, on their websites. As far as Guangzhou Municipal Government is concerned, among the contents of press conferences it disclosed online, those of press conferences No.120 through No. 152 were missing, and these missing contents could not be found elsewhere on the Internet through search, indicating that they have never been disclosed online.

In addition, the assessment shows that the number of press conferences held in Shenzhen in 2020 shown in the "Press Releases" sub-column was different from that shown in the "Review of Past Press Conferences" sub-column under the "Press Conference" column of the website of Shenzhen Municipal Government: the former was 50 while the later was only 48. The two press conferences missing in the "Review of Past Press Conferences" sub-column were: the special press conference on the 10th anniversary of the establishment of the Qianhai Cooperation Zone, held by the Information Office of Shenzhen Municipal Government on August 21, 2020, and the special press conference on the prevention and control of Covid-19 epidemic, held by the Information Office of Shenzhen Municipal Government on August 28, 2020.

Furthermore, as part of a press conference, reporters' questions are as important as the spokespersons' speeches. They have the unique function of feeding back public opinions, and their contents can be regarded as reflections of recent public concerns. If the government communicates well with media reporters, it can respond to public concerns through the reporters' questioning session at the press conference, further interpret the released information, and prevent to a certain extent the fermentation of public opinions caused by unclear information release. However, text versions of press conferences published on the website of the Beijing Municipal Government rarely include reporters' questions, listing only the text versions of the answers to reporters' questions given at fewer than five press conferences. The Shanghai Municipal Government disclosed the spokespersons' speeches and reporters' questions at press conferences on two different pages of its website.

(3) The construction of online release platforms is not satisfactory

In recent years, China has achieved good results in releasing information about press conferences on new micro-platforms such as mobile phone clients of government service platforms and Weibo, with the external release platforms of press conferences becoming increasingly sound. However, the assessment shows that there are still many details that need to be optimized in the construction of information release platforms of government organs.

In terms of the convenience of information reading, unlike other assessment targets who integrate all information about a press conference on the Covid-19 epidemic situation into one webpage for release, the Beijing Municipal Government first releases the video recordings of the whole conference on one web page and then releases the speech of each spokesperson on one separate web page. For example, to disclose information about a press conference held in Beijing on May 5, 2020, which had four spokespersons, the Beijing Municipal Government created five web pages: one video webpage and one web page for each of the four spokespersons' speeches. This kind of disclosure leads to extremely massive and complicated contents of the press conference column on the website of the Beijing Municipal Government: nearly 700 web pages had been created to disclose information about the 221 press conferences on the Covid-19epidemic situation in Beijing, which brings unnecessary inconvenience for the public in reading and searching for the press conferences on specific dates. It is worth noting that the Beijing Municipal Government adopted a method similar to those adopted by other municipal governments for releasing information about press conferences on matters other than the Covid-19 epidemic situation, integrating all the information into one web page, but it adopted the above-mentioned completely different method in releasing information about press conferences on Covid-19 epidemic situation.

The assessment also shows that, except for the Beijing Municipal Government, most of the other assessment targets did not provide video recordings of press conferences, but only published the written record version of them on their websites. Although the Beijing Municipal Government has always provided written records of all government affairs-related press conferences except for those on the Covid-19 epidemic situation, it did not provide text records of press conferences on the Covid-19 epidemic situation until April 28, 2020. The public can get information about the previous 94 press conferences on the Covid-19 epidemic situation only by watching video playbacks. Moreover, some assessment targets also made mistakes in sorting, placing and linking press conferences on their websites. For example, on the website of the Beijing Municipal Government, two press conferences held in April 2020 were incorrectly placed between the press conferences held on September 2 and September 19, 2020. Similarly, on the website of the Guangzhou Municipal Government, press conferences No.94, No. 93 and No.92 were incorrectly placed between press conferences No. 80 and No. 82. In the "Press Releases" column on the website of the Shenzhen Municipal Government, there are two press conferences that were not held by Shenzhen Municipal Government one held by the Government of Guangdong Province and the other held by the Government of Nanshan District of Shenzhen City. Moreover, the links to the 121st and 129th press conferences on the Covid-19 epidemic situation in the press conference column of the website of the Guangzhou Municipal Government were incorrect, leading to the news reports of "The first live broadcast festival was launched in the whole city on June 6th" and "The Guangzhou Municipal Government actively plans to set up a lending service center and establish a risk compensation mechanism", respectively.

2. Problems with the content of press releases

(1) Press conferences cover too many and two complicated elements

Because of limited time, press conferences should be as concise as possible, releasing only the most important information. Putting all the information into a press conference will make it difficult for the audience to grasp the key information. Therefore, the organizers of a press conference should try to streamline its content and abandon the information that has little pertinence with the theme of the press conference or is not important, so as to make it easy for the audience to extract and grasp the key points.

The assessment shows that some government organs released unimportant information at press conferences. For example, at the press conference on the Covid-19 epidemic situation held on January 7, 2021, Beijing Municipal Government invited the deputy director of the Beijing Meteorological Bureau to introduce the recent weather situation and future weather trends, which were not closely related to the Covid-19 epidemic situation. At a press conference held on January 2, 2021, the spokesperson introduced the epidemic prevention measures taken by the Beijing

Institute of Technology, which, although related to the Covid-19 epidemic situation in Beijing, were not important enough to be released at the press conference. Similarly, the Guangzhou Municipal Government has repeatedly added information that had little pertinence to the Covid-19 epidemic situation to the press conferences on the Covid-19 epidemic situation, and sometimes even the theme of the whole press conference had little connection with the Covid-19 epidemic situation. For example, the theme of the 104th press conference on the Covid-19 epidemic situation in Guangzhou held on May 9, 2020 was the celebration of the 10th anniversary of the opening of the Guangzhou Grand Theatre, and the whole press conference had nothing to do with the Covid-19 epidemic situation. For another example, the 114th press conference on the Covid-19 epidemic situation in Guangzhou, held on May 28, 2020, took "Phoenix Flowers Bloom to Welcome the Opening of the 'Two Sessions'" as its theme, introducing the story of Phoenix Flowers, a special product of Guangzhou, which has nothing to do with the Covid-19 epidemic situation.

(2) The contents of some press conferences were too vague and general

The assessment shows that many government organs still use too much bureaucratic jargon and cliches and are obsessed with grand narratives at press conferences, mainly interpreting policies and explaining epidemic prevention measures from a macro perspective, and seldom giving specific examples. As a result, the contents of press conferences have increasingly become a set of fixed rhetoric, making it more difficult for the audience of press conferences to understand the specific measures taken by the government.

For example, with regard to the theme of school resumption in the spring of 2020, local governments held press conferences to announce to the public the school opening arrangements, the preparatory measures before the school opening, and the normalized epidemic prevention and control mechanism after the school opening. Generally speaking, the Guangzhou Municipal Government had done better than others in this respect. It paid special attention to reducing the use of bureaucratic jargon and using popular language and concrete examples at press conferences. For example, at the press conference held on April 23, 2020, leaders of the Guangzhou Municipal Government introduced various epidemic prevention and control measures taken by the municipal government for the reopening of schools from four perspectives and gave in-depth explanations or concrete examples for each measure. For example, it showed that the supply of epidemic prevention materials in schools could be adequately guaranteed by listing the daily production quantity of masks.

Compared with those in Guangzhou, some press conferences in Beijing, Shanghai and Shenzhen were vaguer and more general in content. For example, at the press conference held on April 12th, the Beijing Municipal Government only disclosed the macro institutional arrangements for school reopening, without explaining any concrete measure or providing any specific example. At the press conference held on April 22, 2020, the Shenzhen Municipal Government briefly introduced a series of prevention and control measures taken for school reopening but gave no practical example. In the press conference held in Shanghai on April 24, 2020, spokespersons of relevant departments did not take the initiative to introduce the situation of the reopening of schools but only answered relevant questions in the reporters' Q&A session. Furthermore, in answering the reporters' questions, the person in charge of the Shanghai Municipal Education Commission only briefly repeated the relevant provisions of the Guide to School Re-opening formulated by the Leading Group for the Prevention and Control of Covid-19 Epidemic in Shanghai Education System but did not mention any specific epidemic prevention measures other than these provisions.

Different from the official documents issued by the government, government press conferences take the public as their main audience. What they need to do is not repeat the provisions in official documents, but give vivid examples of concrete actions. Reading out a statement at a press conference will definitely have a negative effect on the release of information. Only by paying attention to the use of popular language and specific examples, can spokespersons of press conferences effectively narrow the distance between the government and the public and enable the public to understand the contents of press conferences.

5 Development and Prospect of the Press Release System in China

In the final analysis, the root cause of the problems existing in the operation of China's government press release system lies in the lack of understanding of its importance, the unclear standards of press releases, and the low level of professionalism of government press release work at various levels. Therefore, in the future, China should promote the further development of the press release system by enhancing awareness, raising the level of professionalism, clarifying the standards, and improving the quality of the press release work.

1. Enhancing ideological awareness and training professionals

China should further enhance the awareness of the importance of the press release system among government organs at all levels and their staff by means of publicity and training. At the same time, it should strengthen the targeted training for spokespersons, staff responsible for the openness of government affairs and other related staff, so as to familiarize them with the concepts, knowledge and skills of openness of government affairs and the press and publicity work.

2. Establishing an online release mechanism and clarifying and implementing relevant standards

Today, the Internet has become an important communication channel for the openness of government affairs. Even the press release work cannot be completely separated from the internet. Only by relying on the internet can we ensure that the content of press releases can be disseminated in the most efficient and extensive way. Therefore, special press release columns should be set up on the portal website and We Media of government organs at all levels to disclose the relevant contents of press releases in a centralized, timely and comprehensive manner, so as to enhance the effect of press releases.

3. Streamlining the contents and improving the quality of press releases

The press release work is different from general government information disclosure in that it requires government organs to pay attention to not only the authority and accuracy of the release of information but also its flexibility and acceptability by the audience. Therefore, the government should further increase the pertinence and popularity of the contents of press releases, improve its relationship with the audience through press releases, and enhance the public acceptance of the content of press releases.

Current Situation and Prospect of Disclosure of Information About Resumption of Operation and Production in Enterprises in the Process of Normalizing the Prevention and Control of the Covid-19 Pandemic

Innovation Project Team on Rule of Law Index, Institute of Law, Chinese Academy of Social Sciences

At the beginning of 2020, the production and operation in most enterprises in China were seriously affected by the outbreak of the Covid-19 pandemic. With the alleviation of the pandemic situation in China, repairing the damaged real economy has become the focus of work in various industries. From the beginning of February 2020, the government has accurately and steadily promoted the resumption of operation and production in enterprises, so as to enable the people to resume normal social life as soon as possible.

On December 16, 2020, "resumption of operation and production" was selected as one of the "Top Ten New Words in Chinese Media in 2020" issued by the National Language Resources Monitoring and Research Center. It refers to the matters and

---

Leaders of the Project Team: He Tian, the director of the Center for Studies of National Rule of Law Index of Chinese Academy of Social Sciences, a research fellow at the Institute of Law, Chinese Academy of Social Sciences and a distinguished professor at the Law School of the University of Chinese Academy of Social Sciences, and Yanbin Lv, a research fellow at and the head of the Department of Survey and Studies of National Situation of the Rule of Law, Institute of Law, Chinese Academy of Social Sciences and head the Teaching and Research Section of Administrative Law of the Law School of the University of Chinese Academy of Social Sciences. Other members of the Project Team: Xiaomei Wang, Yiming Wang, Wenbo Che, Yingying Feng, Yanpeng Liu, Xiaomin Mi, Zhang Lei, Qiyuan Lu, Changming Hu, Mei Hong, Yanjie Li, Suzhi Hou and Chuying Guo. Authors of this report: Lei Zhang, Qiyuan Lu, Suzhi Hou, Chuzhuan Guo, academic assistants the Center for Studies of National Rule of Law Index of Chinese Academy of Social Sciences.

Innovation Project Team on Rule of Law Index, Institute of Law, Chinese Academy of Social Sciences (✉)
Institute of Law, Chinese Academy of Social Sciences, Beijing, China
e-mail: 13693186775@163.com

H. Tian and Y. Lv (eds.), *Assessing Government Transparency in China (2021)*,
https://doi.org/10.1007/978-981-99-9734-3_10

a series of problems related to the gradual resumption of production and business operation in enterprises under the unified guidance of the state and local governments after a suspension of operation and production during a special period of time in which all or most of enterprises or institutions have been unable to carry out production or business activities due to some special reasons. On February 3, 2020, the Standing Committee of the Political Bureau of the CPC Central Committee held a meeting to hear the report on the pandemic prevention and control work and instructed governments at all levels to "spare no efforts in supporting and organizing various enterprises to resume operation and production on the precondition of effectively carrying out the pandemic prevention and control work". On March 4, 2020, the Central Government emphasized "promoting the resumption of operation and production according to the risk levels of the pandemic in different regions". On April 8, 2020, the Central Government set the task of "comprehensively promoting the resumption of operation and production" for the first time.

Promoting the resumption of operation and production in enterprises in a scientific and orderly manner not only tests the social governance ability of governments at all levels but also raised higher demands on the openness of government affairs. Disclosure of information about the resumption of operation and production is an activity of openness of government affairs in a special period and its effect reflects the actual situation of open government work in multiple dimensions. For this reason, the Innovation Project Team on the Rule of Law Index of the Institute of Law, Chinese Academy of Social Sciences (hereinafter referred to as the "Project Team") has carried out an investigation and evaluation of the situation of disclosure of information about the resumption of operation and production in various provinces, autonomous regions and municipalities directly under the Central Government.

1 The Necessity of the Disclosure of Information About the Resumption of Operation and Production

1. Disclosure of Information about the resumption of operation and production is an important part of government information disclosure

Government information disclosure is the main channel for citizens, legal persons and other organizations to obtain government information and participate in the making of public decisions concerning the vital interests of the people. The Regulations of the People's Republic of China on the Disclosure of Government Information clearly establish the principle of "taking disclosure as the norm and non-disclosure as the exception". As a result, actively disclosing government information and striving to improve the transparency of government work has become the new normal of open government work.

The Covid-19 pandemic has taken a heavy toll on the life and safety as well as the economic and property interests of the public. Resumption of operation and production is a measure for recovery and returning to normal social life after the success of pandemic prevention and control, which is as important as pandemic prevention and control itself. The information about the resumption of operation and production involves the adjustment of public interests, belongs to the category of public emergency response, and, as such, should be widely known by the public. Therefore, it should be disclosed by the government on its own initiative.

2. Information disclosure is the basic precondition for implementing the policy of the resumption of operation and production

In order to encourage enterprises to resume work and production, the government has issued a series of preferential policies for enterprises, such as financial support, training on pandemic prevention and tax incentives. On March 4, 2020, the General Office of the State Council issued the Notice on Further Streamlining the Approval Procedure, Optimizing Services and Promoting the Resumption of Operation and Production in Enterprises in an Accurate and Steady Way, which emphasizes the deepening of the reforms aimed at "simplifying administrative procedures, decentralizing powers, combining decentralization with appropriate control, and optimizing services", the streamlining of administrative approval and online services, and the promotion of the resumption of operation and production in enterprises in an accurate and steady way. The document requires governments at all levels to improve the convenience of services and simplify and optimize the approval procedure and conditions for the resumption of operation and production, vigorously promote the online handling of government services, accelerate the online handling of key matters such as resumption of operation and production, rely on online platforms to promote the implementation of preferential policies for enterprises, and promote the sharing of government data around the needs of resumption of operation and production, improve the mechanism for servicing enterprises in the resumption of operation and production, raise the efficiency of the approval of matters relating to the investment, production and operation of enterprises, provide service guarantee for coordinated resumption of operation and production in the whole industrial chain, and establish and improve the mechanism for responding to the demands of enterprises in the resumption of operation and production. This document points out the direction for the disclosure of information about the resumption of operation and production. Policy guidance is very important for pandemic prevention and control and the resumption of operation and production in enterprises. To encourage enterprises to resume operation and production, the government has issued a series of beneficial policies for enterprises, and increased support for enterprises in terms of human, material, financial, technical, information and knowledge resources to tide them over the difficulties. Disclosure of government information helps enterprises resume operation and production and is of great significance to the implementation of relevant policies.

2 The Results of Disclosure of Information About Resumption of Operation and Production

1. The information in the columns on the resumption of operation and production on government websites is clearly classified and released efficiently

"How to enable the public to get the government information concerning their vital interests in a more convenient way" is an important consideration in assessing the results of open government work. Taking the policy of the resumption of operation and production during the period of pandemic prevention and control as an example, in order to effectively cope with the pandemic and help micro, small and medium-sized enterprises resume operation and production, most local governments have set up a column on the resumption of operation and production in enterprises on their portal websites. Among them, the governments of Hebei Province, Jilin Province, Beijing Municipality, and Guangdong Province have also set up a special column on "response to the pandemic situation by micro, small and medium-sized enterprises", which contains all the relevant information helpful to micro, small and medium-sized enterprises in their normal operation and development during the period of pandemic prevention and control. The information in the column is classified by theme to enable users to find the information they need in an efficient and direct way, and the integration of information in the column also enables government organs to carry out open government work in a more organized way.

The effectiveness of information disclosure during the special period of the Covid-19 pandemic reflects the government's ability and level of emergency management and the question of what information local governments should disclose and how it should be disclosed in order to help enterprises resume production as soon as possible while effectively preventing and controlling the pandemic are worth reflecting on and studying. Some local governments have made great achievements in the disclosure of information on the resumption of operation and production and developed distinctive information release modes. Take Shanghai Municipal Government as an example. It has set up a special column "Supports and Services Given by Shanghai Municipal Government to Enterprises to Ensure Their Stable and Healthy Development" on its portal website. The column is independent of the special column on pandemic prevention and control and located in the "Responding to Concerns" sub-section of the "Openness Government Affairs" section of the website. The government documents on enterprises' response to the pandemic situation are disclosed in the "Municipal Government Documents" section of the website and classified by the issuing department and urban district. At the same time, a policy interpretation section has been set up on the website to help business operators search for the policies and measures relating to the orderly resumption of operation and production. The Government of Beijing Municipality has set up two special columns—"Supporting micro, small and medium-sized enterprises to cope with the impact of the Covid-19 pandemic and maintain steady development" and "Implementing policies benefiting enterprises in the resumption of operation and production"—on the center of the homepage of its portal website. The former is divided into the following sub-columns: "Latest news" which releases at the earliest time news related to enterprises since the outbreak of the Covid-19 pandemic, "Services", which contain information about various services related to the normal operation of enterprises, mainly including "Implementation of preferential policies for enterprises", "Services relating to the resumption of operation and production", "Financial services for micro, small and micro enterprise", "Services for small and micro enterprises" and "12,345 enterprise service hotline" to facilitate the search of relevant information by enterprises, "Supporting policies and Measures", which contains enterprise-related policies issued by Beijing Municipal Government and various district governments during the period of pandemic prevention and control involving rent reduction, stabilizing employment, financial support, tax reduction and exemption, etc., aimed at effectively helping business operators to resume operation and production in an orderly manner, "Hot questions", which brings together the questions about hot issues relating to the resumption of production in micro, small and medium-sized enterprises during the Covid-19 pandemic and provide answers to these questions in concentrated way, and "Videos of press conference", which brings together the video recordings and written records of all the press conferences related to enterprises' response to the Covid-19 pandemic held by Beijing Municipal Government since the outbreak of the pandemic. "Implementing policies benefiting enterprises in the resumption of operation and production" is a policy retrieval platform consisting of two parts: "Enterprise-benefiting policies and measures navigation system", which provides four retrieval options, namely search by service type, enterprise scale, industry field and main competent department. Enterprises can select the retrieval options according to their needs to search for corresponding policies and measures; and "Enterprise-benefiting items", which focuses on enterprise-related policies and measures issued by the government.

Some local governments have set up special platforms on "stabilizing employment and supporting enterprises" to release preferential policies for enterprises in a concentrated manner. For example, Beijing Municipal Government has set up a "Stabilizing Employment" section on its website to disclose employment policies issued by various departments under the municipal government and various district governments since the outbreak of the Covid-19 pandemic. The Government of Jilin Province has set up a sub-column on "Services for Small and Micro Enterprises and Individual Industrial and Commercial Households" in the "Fighting against Covid-19 Pandemic" column on its portal website, consisting of parts: "Policies" and "Services". The former collects the policies on and measures for the response to the pandemic by enterprises since the outbreak, which can be searched by department, district or subject matter. The matters involved in these policies and measures include the resumption of operation and production, stabilizing employment, finance and taxation, postponement of the payment of social security premiums, rent reduction and exemption, preferential policies on water and electricity, etc. The layout display of this sub-column is well organized, which is convenient for business operators to find relevant policies. The latter consists of four sections: "E-window for starting enterprises", Non-contact handling of tax affairs "Comprehensive services for the private economy (mass entrepreneurship and innovation)" and "Public services for small and medium-sized enterprises". By allowing users to handle related businesses online, they reduce close contact during the Covid-19 pandemic and help enterprises resume operation and production.

Local governments have given full support to enterprises in fighting the Covid-19 pandemic, released information in enterprise-related columns on their web portals in a timely manner, helped small and medium-sized enterprises fully understand the policies and measures introduced by the government and resume operation and production in an orderly manner, promoted pandemic prevention and control and economic and social development as a whole, and given full play to the substantial role of openness of government affairs at the stage of prevention and control of the Covid-19 pandemic.

2. The collections of policies are comprehensive and policy interpretations are detailed and rich in content

The outbreak of the Covid-19 pandemic has affected the pace of economic development. Under the condition of normalization of pandemic prevention and control, micro, small and medium-sized enterprises need government policy support in order to maintain their normal business operation, and one of the top priorities of the government is to convey the targeted measures taken by the central and local governments to society in a timely manner. The assessment shows that all provincial governments have set up a special column on micro, small and medium-sized enterprises-related policies on their portal websites to timely release relevant policy documents and guidelines on the prevention and control of the Covid-19 pandemic in the resumption of operation and production, and updated them synchronously on other official platforms such as Weibo and WeChat official accounts, so as to guide enterprises and public institutions to effectively carry out in employee health monitoring and risk identification, implement the pandemic prevention and control responsibilities system, and help the persons in charge of relevant entities to know the latest developments at the earliest time and adjust the corresponding measures for resuming operation and production in a timely manner.

The governments of Beijing Municipality, Jilin Province, Zhejiang Province and Shandong Province have classified the policy documents by multiple criteria to facilitate the retrieval of information by the public. Among them, the Government of Beijing Municipality has classified policy documents by four clear retrieval criteria: service type, enterprise scale, industry field and main competent department; the Government of Shanghai Municipality has also classified the policies adopted by various district governments to facilitate search by users. In the special period of prevention and control of the Covid-19 pandemic, it is particularly important for enterprises to accurately understand the targeted policy documents adopted by the government and take corresponding actions, which requires local governments to effectively carry out policy interpretation work and disclose the relevant information. Most local governments have provided interpretations of the policy documents relating to enterprises' response to the Covid-19 pandemic situation, so as to help micro, small and medium-sized enterprises understand the relevant policies and resume their normal production and operation. The Government of Beijing Municipality provides links to "relevant interpretations" and "related policies" for every policy document disclosed on its website, and all relevant contents can be seen on the same page, so as to enable users to have a comprehensive understanding of the document, and at the same time save their retrieval time. The contents of its policy interpretations involve the background of the adoption of the documents, the detailed explanation of the policies, and the specific operational procedures. By disclosing details of the government's considerations behind the adoption of the policies, these interpretations help the public understand the purposes of the government's policies and reduce the resistance to their implementation. The policies on the resumption of operation and production in Beijing are interpreted by relevant government departments. For example, the *Notice on Further Improving the Work of Stabilizing Employment and Resumption of Work through Unemployment Insurance* was interpreted by the Beijing Municipal Bureau of Human Resources and Social Security, and the *Urgent Notice on Strengthening Financial Support for Key Enterprises That Produce Pandemic Prevention and Control Supplies* was interpreted by Beijing Municipal Finance Bureau; and authoritative media with a large reading volume, such as *Beijing Daily* and *Xinhua News* Agency, also interpret the documents in detail to strengthen the publicity of policy measures. On this basis, the Beijing Municipal Government flexibly uses diversified media platforms to publicize relevant measures and their interpretations. For example, its official WeChat official account "Beijing Release" releases relevant information at the earliest time possible, opens up various channels to promote government measures, increases publicity efforts, and ensures that micro, small and medium-sized enterprises break the information barrier and make the best use of the circumstances in resuming operation and production.

The Shanghai Municipal Government has also set up the "Policy Interpretation" column on its portal website to release interpretations of policy measure documents, among which the *Guide for Shanghai Enterprises to Resume Operation and Production and Reopen the Market* has been updated to its sixth edition since the outbreak of the Covid-19 pandemic to provide guidance to the enterprises in Shanghai on implementing specific measures for coping with the pandemic.

It can be seen from the above that, in open government work, only when the policy information is not only conveyed to but also correctly understood by the public, can such government policies be truly known and used by the target audience, the value of the document information be realized, and the key role of openness government affairs in the pandemic prevention and control be given full play to.

3. Disclosing information about the latest developments and improving the quality of government affairs

The dynamic real-time follow-up on news reports about the resumption of operation and production allows people from all sectors of society to know the progress of implementation of local policies on resumption of operation and production, enables the government to timely find out the problems in the implementation of policies, and facilitates the supervision over the implementation of policies by the public. Since the outbreak of the Covid-19 pandemic, governments at various levels have disclosed information about the implementation of policies on the resumption of operation and production at the earliest possible time through their portal websites,

Weibo and WeChat official accounts and other news media, paid close attention to the effectiveness of policy implementation, and enhanced the transparency of government work, so as to keep all sectors of society informed about the latest developments in the restoration of local economic order and promote the quality of government service through social supervision and incentives.

Our assessment shows that the Beijing Municipal Government has achieved prominent results in the follow-up report on the resumption of operation and production, setting a good example for other local governments. It has set up the "Latest Information" section at the top of the column of "Micro, Small and Medium-sized Enterprises' Response to Covid-19 Pandemic Situation" which collects the latest information about the resumption of operation and production in enterprises and institutions in Beijing since the outbreak of the Covid-19 pandemic, tracks the implementation of government measures by enterprises in real time, and reports to the public the results of the implementation of a series of government policies in the fields of finance, taxation and human resources at different stages. Moreover, it has also set up a "press conference" sub-column under the column of "Micro, Small and Medium-sized Enterprises' Response to Covid-19 Pandemic Situation", which contains all the press conferences related to enterprises' response to the Covid-19 pandemic situation held by Beijing Municipal Government and enables people from all sectors of society to watch the video recordings of the press conferences at any time, browse the corresponding written records, and learn about relevant government measures and the latest developments in the resumption of operation and production and response to the pandemic situation by local enterprises. Publicity and real-time reporting of the progress of government work is a part of the openness of government affairs that should not be ignored. It enables people from all sectors of society to learn about the progress of government work, and develop an effective supervision mechanism and realize a qualitative leap forward in government work.

4. Responding to the concerns of enterprises and adjusting the direction of policies

The openness of government affairs should not be a one-way output of information. More importantly, the government should listen and respond to public opinion on policies. Information interaction can greatly improve the efficiency of policy implementation and incentivize the government to introduce more pragmatic policies and measures. To introduce targeted measures for the resumption of operation and production and implement them in an efficient way during the period of prevention and control of the Covid-19 pandemic, the government needs to understand the urgent needs of micro, small and medium-sized enterprises and respond to their concerns at the earliest time possible.

The practice of the Government of Qinghai Province of responding to social concerns is laudable. It has created a website on services for enterprises in the resumption of operation and production, which is independent of its official portal website, and at the center of the homepage of this website is the section of "Requests of Enterprises and the Public and Their Handling", in which an enterprise can submit the request for the resumption of operation and production together with its contact information. The progress of the handling of the requests is displayed in real time in this section. A sub-section of "completed cases" has been set up under this section to disclose the government's replies to the requests of enterprises for the resumption of operation and production, which can be used as references by other enterprises requesting the resumption of operation and production. The governments of Heilongjiang Province and Beijing Municipality have also set up channels of investigation on the resumption of operation and production, a column on suggestions and proposals and a section on unified answers to questions about hot issues on their portal websites, so as to keep abreast of the real situation of enterprises during the Covid-19 pandemic period. On the Service Network of the Government of Heilongjiang Province, a section on Covid-19 pandemic prevention service and industrial enterprises' requests for the resumption of operation and production was set up in the "Theme Services" column, which allows enterprises to submit requests for the resumption of operation and production online. Meanwhile, it has also set up a special column of "opinions and suggestions on coping with the Covid-19 pandemic situation and implementing the provincial government's policy of supporting the healthy development of small and medium-sized enterprises" in the "enterprise-benefiting services—services—services for small and medium-sized enterprises services" column of its portal website, so as to enable the public to put forward suggestions and proposals online. The Government of Hunan Province has set up a questionnaire on "the impact of the Covid-19 pandemic on enterprises in the province" in the interactive exchange section of its portal website. The questionnaire contains targeted key questions such as "What are the impacts of the Covid-19 pandemic on the production and operation of your enterprise?", "How long do you expect the funds in your enterprise's account will be able to support the operation of the enterprise?" and "What policies and measures do you want the government to introduce to help tide enterprises over the difficulties?" so that the government can improve its work in light of the feedback from the enterprises.

It can be seen from the above that the content of openness of government affairs includes not only the policies and measures adopted by the government but also the government's response to the demands and requests of the public. The openness of government affairs forces government departments to respond to social concerns as soon as possible, be problem-oriented, take into full consideration what the people are truly concerned about, and adjust the development direction of government work in time.

3 Problems in the Disclosure of Information on the Resumption of Operation and Production

1. Shortboards in the construction of platforms of openness

The assessment shows that, among provincial-level governments, 23, or 90.32% of the total, have set up a special platform column on the resumption of operation and production, 16, or 51.61% of the total, have set up a special platform column on the response to the Covid-19 pandemic by micro, small and medium-sized enterprises, and 10, or 32.26% of the total, have set up a special platform column on worker-related matters. Government portal websites are the primary platforms for government information disclosure, but eight provincial-level governments still have not set up a special column on the resumption of operation and production, which may lead to poor public access to relevant information. The release of information about the resumption of operation and production must cover the relevant policies on workers and enterprises. However, among the provincial-level governments, 21 have not set up a special platform for workers, and 15 have not set up a special column on the response to the Covid-19 pandemic by micro, small and medium-sized enterprises on their portal websites. It can be seen from the above that government departments need to strengthen the platform construction, give full play to the advantages of the authoritative official government portal websites, and further promote open government work.

2. Gaps and omissions in the disclosure of policy documents

In open government work, it is very important to disclose policy documents in time. Through the investigation of the disclosure of information on the resumption of operation and production, the Project Team found that among the provincial-level governments, 29, or 93.55% of the total, have disclosed policy documents on resuming operation and production, benefiting enterprises and stabilizing employment, and two, or 6.45% of the total, have not disclosed policies on the conditions for the resumption of operation and production. Although the objects of the survey are limited, they still reflect the problems in the openness of government affairs. In view of the inadequate disclosure of policy documents in open government work, the governments should make timely rectifications and fully disclose policy documents in accordance with the institutional requirements of openness of government affairs, so as to enable the public to obtain the information they need at the earliest possible time.

The investigation shows that, among the provincial-level governments, 11, or 35.48% of the total, classified policy documents by the adopting department, and four, or 12.90% of the total, classified policy documents by industry. Classification of policy documents helps the public find information they need and plays a positive role in raising the level of openness of government affairs. In addition, 18 provincial-level governments, or 58.10% of the total, interpreted the policy documents on resuming operation and production, benefiting enterprises and stabilizing employment. Interpretation of the documents enhances the public's understanding of government affairs and contributes to the implementation of government measures. There are still many provincial-level governments that have not classified or interpreted the documents. They need to further strengthen the interpretation of policy documents and optimize the methods of document disclosure in open government work.

3. The lack of details in disclosed information

Detailed disclosure of important information about government affairs plays an important role in the public's understanding of government affairs, supervision over administrative personnel, and participation in government affairs. Disclosing information about the resumption of operation and production helps the public to understand the overall situation of and the implementation of the policies on the resumption of operation and production during the Covid-19 pandemic period. It is also necessary for summarizing the work of governments at various levels relating to the resumption of operation and production and the latest progress they have made in the openness of government affairs. According to the survey data, there are still some shortcomings in the disclosure of information about the resumption of operation and production, especially in terms of the scope of information disclosure, and further improvement needs to be made by relevant government departments. According to the survey, among the provincial-level governments, ten, or 32.26% of the total, have disclosed information about the measures of risk identification and health monitoring after enterprises resumed operation and production, 14, or 45.16% of the total, have disclosed information about the protective measures they have adopted after enterprises resumed operation and production, and 21 have not disclosed information about risk identification and health monitoring measures for enterprises in the resumption of operation and production, and 17 have not disclosed of protective measures after the resumption of operation and production.

Among the provincial-level governments, six (including the governments of Hunan Province and Jilin Province), or 19.35% of the total, summarized the situation of resumption of operation and production in each city (district). Among the remaining 25 provincial-level governments, 12 failed to disclose the government's financial and tax policies for enterprises in response to the Covid-19 pandemic, and ten did not disclose information about the situation of resumption of operation and production. This situation is not conducive to keeping the public informed about the situation of the resumption of operation and production in enterprises and the implementation of relevant policies.

4. Limited channels of responding to social concerns and public opinion

The system of openness of government affairs plays an important role in guaranteeing people's democratic rights, promoting the construction of the democratic political system, and accelerating the process of socialist democracy and timely response to public concerns is conducive to upholding the interests of the broad masses of the people and promoting open government work. The survey shows that, among the provincial-level governments, only seven, or 22.58% of the total, have set up channels for investigating the resumption of operation and production on the relevant platforms, only two, or 26.45% of the total, have set up a special column on suggestions for the resumption of operation and production on their portal website, and only eight, or 25.81% of the total, have set up a special column of Q&A on hot issues relating to the resumption of operation and production on their portal websites. It can be seen from the above that the communication between the government and market entities such as enterprises and employees in the resumption of operation and production is still relatively limited. Many provincial-level governments have failed to provide a communication platform for enterprises and workers to report on the problems encountered in the implementation of the policy of resumption of operation and production, which makes it difficult for the public to convey their demands in a timely and accurate manner and for the government to identify and solve problems at the earliest time possible and adjust the policy direction in a targeted manner.

4 Prospect

The disclosure of information on the resumption of operation and production is of vital significance for the better and faster restoration of economic order and for comprehensively promoting the openness of government affairs during the period of prevention and control of the Covid-19 pandemic. Through information disclosure, government departments present the public policy measures closely related to the vital interest of people in all sectors of society and the situation of their implementation, thereby increasing the transparency of government affairs. On the one hand, quantifying the situation of promoting the resumption of operation and production in various areas and publicizing it with the help of the media can encourage the implementation of the policy of resumption of operation and production, expose the shortcomings "in the sunlight", and force government departments to solve the problems in a targeted manner, and accelerate the whole process. On the other hand, the disclosure of information about the resumption of operation and production during the Covid-19 pandemic prevention and control period is a portrayal of China as a country that responds in an orderly and calm way to public health emergencies as well as an important content of the open government work during the Covid-19 pandemic period. Digitizing the progress of resumption of operation and production will enable countries around the world to learn about the measures adopted by China for economic recovery during the pandemic period and provide them with some reference in the formulation of pandemic response policies and in coping with similar emergencies in the future. Public health emergencies are sometimes inevitable and the occurrence and disposal of every emergency need to be summarized and studied, so as to accumulate experience and lessons for future emergency response.

The survey shows that the disclosure of information about the resumption of operation and production in various provinces is still not satisfactory. The government should disclose information about the overall progress of resumption of operation and production to the public through official platforms, give full play to the positive publicity and incentive role of information disclosure, provide good guidance platforms for enterprises and workers, help them make scientific and rational judgments, and stabilize the market order during the pandemic. Therefore, the government should further improve the open government work, raise the efficiency and expand the scope of information disclosure, respond to social concerns in a timely manner, stabilize people's hearts, and improve the executive capability of the government.

1. Strengthening the construction of government websites and column setting

Establishing targeted special columns on official government websites is of great significance for promoting the openness of government affairs. Official platforms of governments are important channels for market players to learn about national policies and play an important role in building a service-oriented government and improving the level of government services. During the Covid-19 pandemic period, local governments at various levels should set up a column on the resumption of operation and production on their portal websites to provide a special platform for all people and entities to learn about related policy documents and solve their problems. Provinces also need to strengthen the construction of official government platforms and provide website platforms related to real-time hot spot policies. The investigation shows that the governments of Xizang Autonomous Region and Xinjiang Uygur Autonomous Region have done a good job in website construction: the retrieval functions of their platforms are very novel and the retrieval contents are relatively comprehensive, which can be taken as reference by other provinces.

2. Creating a multi-channel and three-dimensional disclosure mode

The openness of government affairs in the new era cannot be separated from the application of emerging technologies. Besides their official portal websites, governments at various levels should also make full use of new media and other official channels, such as Weibo and WeChat official accounts, to further expand the scope of information disclosure and raise the informatization level of openness of government affairs. On the one hand, they enable market players to keep themselves informed of the latest policy documents on the resumption of operation and production and related development trends through multiple channels and facilitate the implementation of the policies. On the other hand, they enable people in all sectors of society to see the practical actions taken by the government, thereby enhancing the credibility of the government.

3. Building interactive openness to better respond to public concerns

The public opinion solicitation column on government websites provides a channel for the public to participate in government work. According to the general requirements set out in the *Opinions on Advancing the Open Government Work in an All-round Way*, governments at various levels should pay attention to setting up a public opinion solicitation column in the construction of official websites. For example, in the process of the resumption of operation and production, the public opinion solicitation column on government websites provides a channel for the public to report the problems encountered in the process of restoring the order of production. After receiving relevant opinions, the government can respond to public concerns in a timely manner and solve problems closely related to the vital interests of the public, thus steadily promoting the overall process of resumption of operation and production. Responding to public concerns is an important step to promote the openness of government affairs. Only by listening to the opinions of various subjects and helping them solve problems in time can the government raise the level of openness of government affairs. In addition to the public opinion solicitation column, a special column should also be set up on government websites to disclose all the suggestions received by the government. On the one hand, it can improve the efficiency of government work, avoid the waste of government resources and enhance the executive capacity of the government; on the other hand, it can solve similar problems encountered by the public in a timely manner and improve the efficiency and quality of open government work.

4. Refining lists of openness of government affairs

Lists of openness of government affairs should be refined to provide a clear standard on what information can be disclosed and what information cannot be disclosed and avoid unnecessary confusion caused by vague standards. Detailed classification of information enables the government to make multidimensional integration of government affairs that need to be made public, form a unified understanding of "the extent to which information should be disclosed", and take the initiative to respond to emergencies without being thrown into confusion. At the same time, the progress of government work should be recorded and well documented, so as to facilitate access to the relevant information by the public, meet the social demand for government information, and effectively raise the level of government work.

5. Adjusting the scope and method of openness in a flexible way

The content of disclosure of government information should be updated in a timely manner, the scope of information disclosure should be constantly adjusted with the change of the situation of government work, and the method of information disclosure should be optimized in synchronization with the progress of implementation of government measures, so as to disclose government information in an all-round way and truly realize the openness and transparency of government work. During the period of Covid-19 pandemic prevention and control, the government should dynamically adjust the content and method of information disclosure in light of the process of the resumption of operation and production, provide the public with the information they need most at the earliest time possible, and make government affairs public in a way most convenient for the public to obtain the information. Through all-round information disclosure, the government keeps the public informed of the overall situation of the resumption of operation and production, provides enterprises with information necessary for making decisions on the future development strategy and handling of business affairs and enables them to adjust their business operation and production at any time in light of the progress of the resumption of operation and production, and ensure that the overall business development of enterprises is not affected by the Covid-19 pandemic situation. At the same time, the disclosure of information about the introduction and implementation of financial and tax policies can also to a certain extent boost the confidence of enterprises to resume their normal business operation.

Current Situation and Prospect of Disclosure of Health Knowledge Information

Innovation Project Team on Rule of Law Index, Institute of Law, Chinese Academy of Social Sciences

1 The Necessity of Popularizing Health Knowledge

The popularization of health knowledge is of great significance for improving the comprehensive quality of citizens. With continuous economic and social development, people are paying more and more attention to the quality of their life and to their own health. This naturally requires the continuous popularization of health knowledge, which helps people understand medical and health issues, effectively prevents health risks, saves medical and health resources, and improves people's quality of life. The popularization of health knowledge requires high professionalism. However, medical personnel with good health knowledge are relatively scarce and the channels for the broad masses of people to acquire health knowledge are limited in China. Moreover, with the rapid development of the Internet, the public can be easily misled by all kinds of erroneous and false health information. Therefore, it is particularly important to publicize and disseminate authoritative and accurate health knowledge information.

Leaders of the Project Team: He Tian, director of the Center for Studies of National Rule of Law Index of Chinese Academy of Social Sciences (CASS), a research fellow at CASS Institute of Law, and a distinguished professor at the Law School of the University of CASS, and Yanbin Lv, a research fellow at and head of the Department of Survey and Studies of National Situation of the Rule of Law of CASS Institute of Law, and head the Teaching and Research Section of Administrative Law of the Law School of the University of CASS. Other members of the project team: Xiaomei Wang, Yiming Wang, Wenbo Che, Yingying Feng, Yanpeng Liu, Xiaomin Mi, Shiju Li, Yana Lai, Qiyuan Lu, Wen Chen, Changming Hu, Mei Hong and Yanjie Li. Authors of this report: Shiju Li, Yana Lai, Qiyuan Lu, and Wen Chen, academic assistants of the Center for Studies of National Rule of Law Index of CASS.

Innovation Project Team on Rule of Law Index, Institute of Law, Chinese Academy of Social Sciences (✉)
Institute of Law, Chinese Academy of Social Sciences, Beijing, China
e-mail: 13693186775@163.com

H. Tian and Y. Lv (eds.), *Assessing Government Transparency in China (2021)*,
https://doi.org/10.1007/978-981-99-9734-3_11

Government organs should be the main force in health knowledge information disclosure. The popularization of health knowledge is a part of the performance of government duties as well as an important embodiment of the principle of exercising state power for the people and being people-centered. This requires government departments at all levels to take active measures to release authoritative and accurate popular science information, so as to meet the information needs of the people. Disclosing health knowledge information by government organs can ensure that the disclosed information is authoritative, timely and convenient for the people.

2 Current Requirements on the Disclosure of Health-Related Government Information

The disclosure of health information itself is an important part of the openness of government affairs of relevant government departments. Article 17 of the *Law on Popularization of Science and Technology*, promulgated in 2002, stipulates that state organs and public institutions of medical treatment and sanitation, family planning, etc. shall carry out activities to popularize science and technology in light of their own work. This shows that medical and health departments have the obligation of popularizing medical and health knowledge. The task of "Building a Healthy China" was first put forward at the Fifth Plenary Session of the 18th CPC Central Committee in October 2015. The *Outline of the "Healthy China 2030" Plan*, jointly issued by the CPC Central Committee and the State Council in October 2016, emphasizes in Section 4 of Chapter 21 the need for health-related departments to promote administration by law, the openness of government affairs and information disclosure and provides in Section 1 of Chapter 4 (Improving the Health Literacy of the Whole People) that China will establish and improve a health promotion and education system, build the health education service capacity, and popularize health knowledge among the whole people starting from an early age. The Healthy China Action Plan (2019–2030), issued by the Healthy China Action Plan Promotion Committee on July 9, 2019, stresses that people's health is an important indicator of national prosperity. China will popularize health knowledge, take improving health literacy as the precondition of improving the health of the whole people, and strengthen health education and promotion in light of the characteristics of different groups of people, so as to make health knowledge, behavior and skills a part of the overall qualities and abilities of the whole people and realize health literacy for all. The Healthy China Action Plan (2019–2030) also sets out the main indicators of the Action. Among them, the indicators of health knowledge popularization are as follows: among the major actions of Healthy China, health knowledge popularization is listed as the first item, which, at the individual and family levels, includes correctly understanding health, developing a healthy and civilized lifestyle, paying attention to health information, mastering necessary health skills, seeking medical treatment scientifically, using drugs rationally and creating a healthy family environment. At the government and social levels, the document set out the goals of raising the national health literacy rate to no less than 22% and 30% by 2022 and 2030, respectively, establishing and improving the "two databases and one mechanism" of health science popularization, building the national and provincial-level health science popularization expert databases, and carrying out health science popularization activities; it requires medical personnel to master the knowledge of health science popularization suitable for their posts and actively provide health guidance in the process of diagnosis and treatment, establishes an incentive and restraint mechanism to encourage medical and health institutions and medical personnel to carry out health promotion and education activities, encourages and supports the China Media Group and provincial-level radio and television stations to create high-quality health science popularization programs when conditions are ripe, mobilizes more social forces to participate in the popularization of health knowledge, develops and promotes health-appropriate technologies and support tools, carries out the construction of health promotion counties (districts), and strives to improve residents' health literacy.

The *Opinions of the State Council on Implementing Healthy China Action Plan*, issued in July 2019, emphasize popularizing health knowledge and improving health literacy in the part on basic principles and implementing the action plan for health knowledge popularization in the part on main tasks. The *Law on Basic Medical and Health Care and the Promotion of Health*, promulgated on December 28, 2019, emphasizes in Article 4 that the state and society respect and protect citizens' right to health, implement the 'Healthy China' strategy, promote a healthy lifestyle, optimize health services, improve health guarantees, create a healthy environment, develop the health industry and enhance citizens' full-life-cycle health conditions. At the same time, the state establishes a health education system, ensures citizens' access to health education and improves citizens' health literacy. Article 67 of the Law stipulates that people's governments at all levels shall strengthen health education and training of health professionals, establish a health knowledge and skill core information release system, popularize health science knowledge, and provide the public with scientific and accurate health information. Medical and healthcare, education, sports and publicity institutions, grassroots self-governing mass organizations and social organizations shall carry out publicity and popularization of health knowledge. When providing medical and healthcare services, medical and healthcare professionals shall carry out health education for patients. New media shall carry out public interest health knowledge publicity. The publicity of health knowledge shall be scientific and accurate. And Article 68 of the Law stipulates that the state incorporates health education into the national education system. Schools shall carry out health education in various forms, and popularize health knowledge, scientific fitness knowledge, and first-aid knowledge and skills. The *Key Tasks of Open Government Work in 2021*, promulgated by the General Office of the State Council, also require relevant government organs to vigorously carry out health science popularization activities.

The *Outline of the Action Plan to Increase the Population's Understanding of Science (2021–2035)*, issued by the State Council on June 25, 2021 (hereinafter referred to as the Outline), states in the part on principles that China will build a socialized pattern of popularization of scientific knowledge jointly promoted by the government, society and market, strengthen policy and legal safeguards, and promote the innovation and upgrading of the content, form and means and improve the knowledge content of popularization, so as to meet the needs of the whole society for high-quality popularization of science. The Outline puts forward five improvement actions to be implemented during the 14th Five-Year Plan period. In the part on actions for improving science literacy among young people, the Outline states that China will establish an effective mechanism for the linkage between science education resources inside schools and those outside schools, and encourage scientists, engineers, medical and health personnel and other scientific and technological workers to enter campuses to carry out education on science, physical hygiene, and self-protection and other safety and health education activities. In the part on actions for improving the science literacy of the elderly, the Outline points out that China will strengthen the health science popularization service for the elderly, rely on the health education system to promote the popularization of health science among the elderly in communities, villages, institutions and families, carry out activities such as health lecture hall and health publicity weeks for the elderly, and use such media as radio, television, newspapers and the Internet to popularize the knowledge of reasonable diet, food safety, mental health, physical exercise, rational drug use and emergency response, so as to improve the health literacy of the elderly, and make full use of community day care centers for the elderly, "popular science gardens", "Party building gardens" and other platforms to provide popular health science services for the elderly. According to the Outline, five key projects will be implemented during the "14th Five-Year Plan" period. The project on improving the informatization of popularization of scientific knowledge includes the funding plan for promoting popular science creation, the plan for improving the capacity for all-media dissemination of scientific knowledge and the intelligent popular science construction project. And the project on building the capacity for popularizing science knowledge at the grassroots level will establish an emergency science popularization education coordination mechanism, improve the grassroots science popularization service system, implement the grassroots science popularization service capacity building project, and strengthen the construction of a full-time science popularization team.

It can be seen from the above that, although the *Regulations on the Disclosure of Government Information* and other relevant administrative regulations do not clearly stipulate that relevant departments should disclose health-related Popular science information, relevant special laws and documents have clearly defined the duties and obligations of relevant government departments to disclose relevant Popular science information from the perspective of strengthening knowledge popularization.

3 Current Situation of Disclosure of Health Knowledge Information

This report selects three fields, namely disease prevention, disaster prevention and mitigation, and epidemic information, to carry out an investigation and analysis of the situation of disclosure of scientific knowledge information on the portal websites of health commissions under local governments during the period from February to the end of April 2021.

1. Construction of the special website column on popular science by health commissions

(1) Construction of the popular science column by health commissions on their portal websites

The investigation on the construction of the popular science column by health commissions on their portal websites mainly examines whether health commissions have set up a popular science column on their portal websites, how much information is disclosed in the column and how often is the content in the column updated. The objects of the investigation were the 49 governments of larger cities selected in the *Report of Government Transparency in China (2020).* The investigation shows that only 29 of the 49 governments of larger cities had set up a special popular science column on their portal websites, accounting for 59.18% of the total. They include the governments of Shijiazhuang City in Hebei Province, Shenyang City in Liaoning Province, Jinan City in Shandong Province, Jilin City in Jilin Province, Guangzhou City in Guangdong Province, Lanzhou City in Gansu Province, Luoyang City in Henan Province, Taiyuan City in Shanxi Province, Fushun City in Liaoning Province, Xuzhou City in Jiangsu Province, Zhuhai City in Guangzhou Province, Yinchuan City in Ningxia Hui Autonomous Region, Fuzhou City in Fujian Province, Benxi City in Liaoning Province, Xiamen City in Fujian Province, Tangshan City in Hebei Province, Shenzhen City in Guangdong Province, Wuhan City in Hubei Province, Xining City in Qinghai Province, Changsha City in Hunan Province, Chengdu City in Sichuan Province, Guiyang City in Guizhou Province, Handan City in Hebei Province, Hangzhou City in Zhejiang Province, Xi'an City in Shaanxi Province, Anshan City in Liaoning Province, Qingdao City in Shandong Province, Hohhot City in Inner Mongolia Autonomous Region and Zibo City in Shandong Province.

Popular science information has many different categories involving various aspects of life. Not many investigation objects have classified or labeled all the information in the column or further divided the column into sub-columns. A typical example is the website of the Health Commission of Shenyang City in Liaoning Province. The popular science column on the website is divided into two sub-columns: "Healthy Shenyang" and "Online and Offline Lecture Halls". The information in the former is classified and labeled by subject, such as "Pregnancy Classroom", "Daily Life Health Knowledge" "National Malaria Day" "National Eye Love Day" "World No Tobacco Day" and "Blood Donation Day". Generally speaking, "Healthy

Shenyang" tends to popularize general heath knowledge, while "Online and Offline Lecture Halls" popularizes more professional knowledge about caring for patients with specific diseases, and the two columns complement each other. The popular science column on the portal website of the Health Commission of Zhuhai City in Guangdong Province is set up in the "Business Management" section on the homepage of the website. The column is further divided into such sub-columns as "Science, Education and Publicity", "Disease Control" "Maternal and Child Health" "Elderly Health" and "Occupational Health", but the popular science content is concentrated in the "Science, Education and Publicity and Education" sub-column, while the contents of other sub-columns are relevant notices and policies. In addition, the health commissions that have classified the information in the popular science column on their websites include those of Jinan City in Shandong Province, Lanzhou City in Gansu Province, Yinchuan City in Ningxia Hui Autonomous Region, Shenzhen City in Guangdong Province, Wuhan City in Hubei Province, Xining City in Qinghai Province, Guiyang City in Guizhou Province, Handan City in Hebei Province and Chengdu City in Sichuan Province, accounting for 22.00% of the total. The timeliness of the updating of information in the popular science column varies greatly from city to city. Our observation shows that the health commissions of most cities are able to update the popular science column on their websites in a timely manner and have achieved good results. However, the health commissions of some cities have not been able to update the contents of the column on a regular basis. For example, there are only 10 pieces of popular science information in the Citizens' Health Information System on the website of the Health Commission of Xiamen City and all of them were released in 2013. The health service column on the homepage of the official website of the Health Commission of Lanzhou City in Gansu Province is divided into four sections: disease prevention, health maintenance and fitness, medication knowledge and introduction to specialized medical services. In the disease prevention section, a total of 193 pieces of information were released during the period from March 26, 2013 to April 16, 2020, but most of them were released in 2016 or earlier and only several pieces of information have been released since January 2020. In the health maintenance and fitness section, there are only five pieces of information and all of them were released on April 7, 2020. In the medication knowledge section, there are a total of 109 pieces of information. The latest one was released on July 28, 2015, and the earliest one was released on March 6, 2013. From the above, we can see that the column is not maintained on a regular basis and the release of information in the column has not been normalized: the frequency of updating the content in the column had been reduced from about once a week in 2013 to once a month in 2014 and to once in several months in 2015, and only a few pieces of information has been released since 2015. In contrast, the popular science column on the websites of health commissions of the following cities have been updated on a regular basis: Handan City in Hebei Province (updated once every three days on average), Hangzhou City in Zhejiang Province (updated once every two days on average), and Zibo City in Shandong Province (updated twice a week on average).

With the development of the economy, the progress of science and technology, and the enhancement of the consciousness of convenience for the people, government portal websites should be gradually upgraded, and their page design should also be more convenient for the public to browse and more pleasing to the eye. Our investigation shows that the design and construction of the portal website of the health commission of each of the 49 larger cities have their own advantages, but obviously, there is still much room for improvement. The Yellow Pages design of the website of the Health Commission of Shijiazhuang City in Hebei Province is old-fashioned with small font, crowded arrangements of various functions, and a suspended window on the left side that cannot be closed, and that of the Health Commission of Taiyuan City in Shanxi Province has the same problem. Although the health commissions of some cities have not set up a special popular science column on their websites, some popular science information can still be found on these websites through the internal retrieval function. Such information is disclosed in other columns, such as the information disclosure column, the news column, or the announcement column. For example, the Health Commission of Zhengzhou City in Henan Province has set up the sub-columns "134 questions public health personnel should be able to answer (I) and (II)" and "34 questions, 60 questions and 100 questions public health personnel should be able to answer" in the column of basic public health services, which contain collections of frequently asked health-related questions and answers to them. In addition, the portal websites of some health commissions provide links to other popular science websites. For example, although the Health Commission of Guangzhou City in Guangdong Province has a "Health Knowledge Popularization" column on its website, which contains 31 pieces of information disclosed during the period from April 26, 2019 to April 30, 2021, most of them are legal popularization information, and none of them is health knowledge information. However, there is a column entitled "Jointly Create and Share a Healthy Guangzhou" on the right side of the homepage of the website, which provides a link to the webpage of "Online Health Education Center", which is operated by the Health Publicity and Education Center of Guangzhou City and contains all kinds of popular science information. In the "Information Hall" section of the website, the information is divided into five categories, namely "Prevention and Treatment of Various Kinds of Diseases", "Life Health", "Traditional Chinese Medicine Treatment", "Population Health Care" and "Local Information". A total of 380 pieces of information were released in this section during the period from July 2013 to January 19, 2021. In addition, the website also has a knowledge base in the Online Heath Education Knowledge Library, which provides a keyword search function.

(2) Construction of the official WeChat account of health commissions

With the wide use of Weibo, WeChat and other platforms, there will be more and wider audiences for the popular science information disseminated by these platforms. Therefore, in addition to the popular science information provided on the portal website of health commissions, the Project Team has carried out a simple investigation on whether the health commissions of the 49 large cities have also opened official WeChat accounts and whether popular science information is regularly release on their official WeChat accounts.

The health commissions of Zibo City in Shandong Province, Hohhot City in Inner Mongolia Autonomous Region and some other cities provide clear information about their official WeChat accounts through their portal websites. Most of these that have not provided clear information about their official WeChat accounts through their portal websites have actually opened their official WeChat accounts, which can be easily found through a search. However, some health commissions do not provide information about their official WeChat accounts through their portal websites and it is difficult to determine which is their official WeChat account. For example, the Health Commission of Huainan City in Anhui Province does not provide information about its official WeChat account through its portal website. Through searching, we can find a number of possible official WeChat accounts of the Health Commission, such as "Healthy Huainan Online", "Healthy Huainan" and "Huainan Smart Medical Care". Only by comparing their contents can we determine which one is its official WeChat.

As far as the construction and development of official WeChat account is concerned, 29 investigation objects, or 59.18% of the total, have carried out health knowledge popularization on their official WeChat accounts. Among all the investigation objects that carried out the popularization of scientific knowledge, the timeliness of the updating of the health knowledge information varies from object to object. Those with high updating frequencies include the Health Commission of Guangzhou City in Guangdong Province, which updates the information on its official WeChat account "Guangzhou Health Link" once a week, adding eight pieces of information each time on average, the health commissions of Shenyang City in Liaoning Province and Jilin City in Jilin Province, which update the information on their official WeChat accounts almost every day, and the Health Commission of Ningbo City in Zhejiang Province, which adds five pieces of new information to its official WeChat account "Healthy Ningbo" every one or two weeks on average.

The setting of functional columns on the official WeChat accounts of some investigation objects needs to be further improved. For example, although the Health Commission of Datong City in Shanxi Province has set up a health science popularization module on its official WeChat account, when this module is clicked on, the system shows that it is still under construction. Although the Health Commission of Ningbo City in Zhejiang Province has set up the sub-columns on TCM conditioning, elderly health care, mental health and diet health under the health service column on its official WeChat account, no information has been released in any of these sub-columns. The contents of the official WeChat accounts of some investigation objects need to be further enriched and improved. For example, the information in the official WeChat account of the Health Commission of Wuxi City in Jiangsu Province does not have its own independent content but only provides links to the relevant content on its portal website.

2. The situation of the content construction of the popular science column on the websites of health commissions

A survey of the contents of popular science columns on the websites of the health commissions of 49 larger cities shows that there are still many problems in the

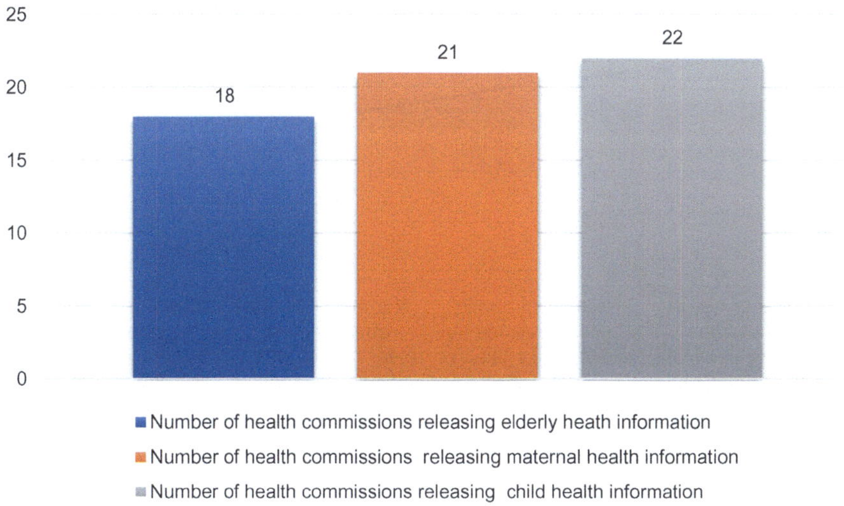

Fig. 1 Statistics on the number of investigation objects releasing health information about different vulnerable groups (the elderly, pregnant women and children)

popularization of health knowledge relating to vulnerable groups, some vaccines, prevention of infectious diseases, intestinal diseases and people's daily life.

(1) The popularization of health knowledge relating to vulnerable groups (the elderly, pregnant women, and children) is inadequate

Less than half of the 49 investigation objects have released information about the health knowledge relating to the elderly, pregnant women and children on their portal websites (see Fig. 1).

(2) The disclosure of information about scientific knowledge of some vaccines is insufficient

With respect to the popularization of vaccine information, the Project Team assessed the situation of disclosure of information about the scientific knowledge of cervical cancer vaccines, common influenza vaccines, hepatitis B vaccines and Covid-19 vaccines. The assessment shows that 30 local governments have released information about scientific knowledge of Covid-19 vaccines on their portal websites, which is higher than the number of governments that disclose information about the scientific knowledge of vaccines against cervical cancer, influenza and hepatitis B. This is probably the result of the actual need of epidemic prevention and control at the current stage (see Fig. 2). Among the other three kinds of vaccines, the information about cervical cancer vaccines has been released by the largest number of investigation objects on their portal websites. This is probably because the high price of cervical cancer vaccines and the imbalance between supply and demand have attracted social attention to this kind of vaccine. Cervical cancer vaccines are hard to get and have to

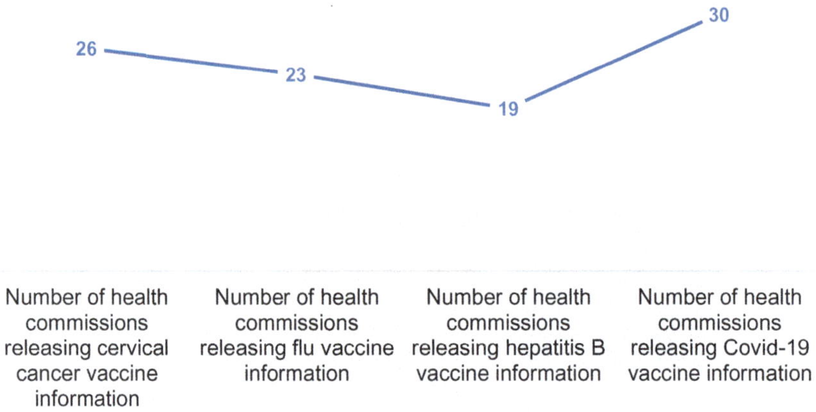

Fig. 2 Statistics on the numbers of investigation objects releasing information about some vaccines

be rationed in some areas and this situation has aroused public concern. As a result, the level of popularization of knowledge of cervical cancer vaccines is naturally higher than that of other vaccines. Nevertheless, there are still 23 local governments that have not released any information about the scientific knowledge of cervical cancer vaccines on their portal websites, and the levels of popularization of knowledge of other vaccines are even lower.

Therefore, on the whole, the situation of the release of information about scientific knowledge of vaccines on the portal websites of local health commissions is not optimistic. Local governments need to strengthen the popularization of vaccine knowledge and further promote the disclosure of relevant information.

(3) The popularization of knowledge of infectious diseases needs to be improved

The large-scale and cross-regional spread of infectious diseases poses a great threat to public health. Today, despite the advancement in medical science and technology, there are still some infectious diseases that cannot be cured once infected, such as AIDS, which is transmitted through blood, breast milk and other media. In the investigation, the Project Team observed the popularization of knowledge of prevention and control of such infectious diseases as AIDS, malaria, tuberculosis, measles and plague.

As can be seen from Fig. 3, among the health commissions of 49 cities, 8 have released information about plague prevention and control, 15 have released information about measles, 18 have released information about malaria, and 23 have released information about AIDS and tuberculosis. Obviously, there are great differences in the situations of the release of information about different kinds of infectious diseases. Compared with information about AIDS and tuberculosis, less information is released about plague in various cities throughout the country, which may be related to the current living and health conditions of the people in China. In 2020, China won the fight against poverty in an all-round way, greatly improved the living conditions

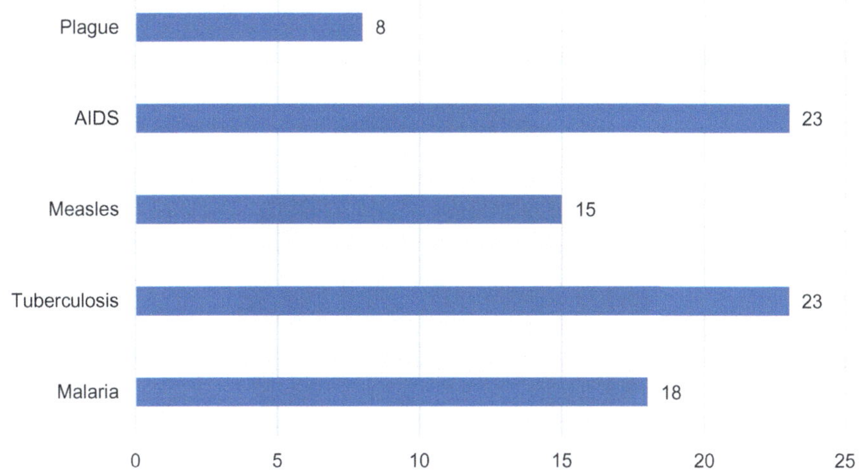

Fig. 3 The situation of popularization of knowledge of prevention of major infectious diseases (numbers of health commissions that have released the information about major infectious diseases)

of the people, and the medical technology and health conditions, and reduced the possibility and prevalence of plague infection. Therefore, the health commissions of some cities no longer took the popularization of knowledge of plague prevention and control as the focus of their work.

Intestinal infectious diseases are among the most common infectious diseases in the world with high incidence rates and wide epidemic ranges, especially in hot summer. The most common intestinal infectious diseases are acute bacterial infectious diseases, such as bacillary dysentery, typhoid fever, cholera and food poisoning. Most intestinal infectious diseases have gastrointestinal symptoms such as nausea, vomiting, abdominal pain, diarrhea and loss of appetite, and some are accompanied by fever, headache, limb pain, systemic poisoning and other symptoms. If not treated in time, they can cause serious complications and even lead to death. Therefore, once infected, they will cause great trouble to and have a serious impact on society and families. Better control and prevention of intestinal infectious diseases should be the focus of attention of society and relevant government departments.

Our survey shows that 18 of the 49 investigation objects have released information about the knowledge of prevention of intestinal infectious diseases, accounting for only 36.73% of the total, and nearly two-thirds of the investigation objects have not released relevant information (see Fig. 4).

(4) The popularization of the knowledge of daily life health science is inadequate

While paying attention to the prevention of various infectious diseases, people should develop good living habits in their daily life in order to stay healthy and avoid suffering from diseases. Therefore, the Project Team carried out an investigation on the situation of popularization of knowledge of prevention of myopia, National

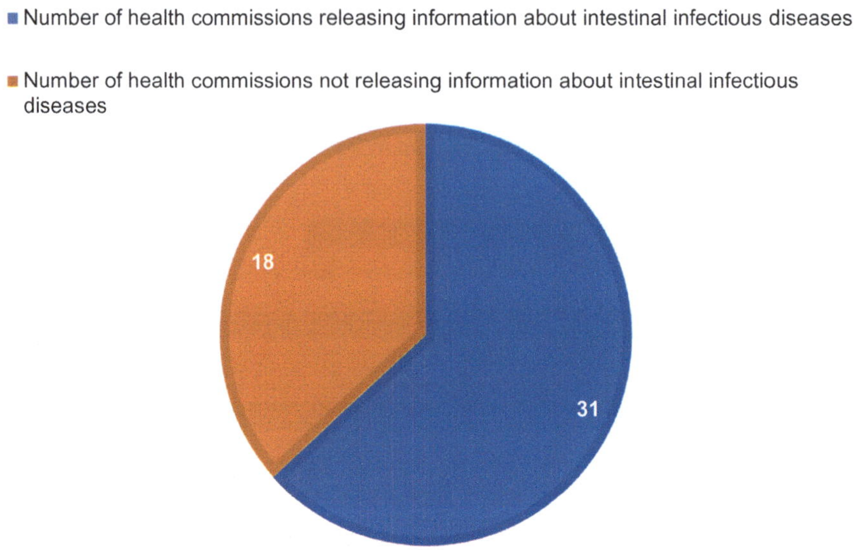

Fig. 4 Numbers of investigation objects that have released information about the prevention of intestinal infectious diseases

Love Teeth Day, the harms of staying up late, healthy diet, and "three highs" (hyperlipidemia, hypertension and hyperglycemia). The investigation shows that less than half of the investigation objects released information about daily life health knowledge. Among them, 23 released information about the knowledge of "three highs", while only eight, or less than one-sixth of the total, released information about the knowledge of the harm of staying up late (see Fig. 5). The release of information about other health knowledge also needs to be strengthened: among the investigation objects, only 20 released information about myopia prevention, 15 released information about the National Love Teeth Day, and 21 released information about daily healthy diet.

3. Popularization of knowledge of the Covid-19 pandemic

Take the popularization of the knowledge of the Covid-19 pandemic, which has ravaged the whole world since 2020, as an example. Since early 2020, various provincial-level and municipal-level governments and health commissions under them have released various information about the Covid-19 pandemic through such channels as government portal websites, health commission portal websites, press conferences and community grids. The scientific knowledge popularized has become increasingly rich in content with the change of actual needs, evolving from the understanding of the Covid-19 virus, the correct wearing of facial masks, and staying at home healthily at the initial stage to the updated points for attention in vaccination, the safety of imported frozen food, foreign mutated viruses, etc. at later stages, but the concrete situation of popularization and update of information vary from one investigation object to another. For example, the Hebei provincial government,

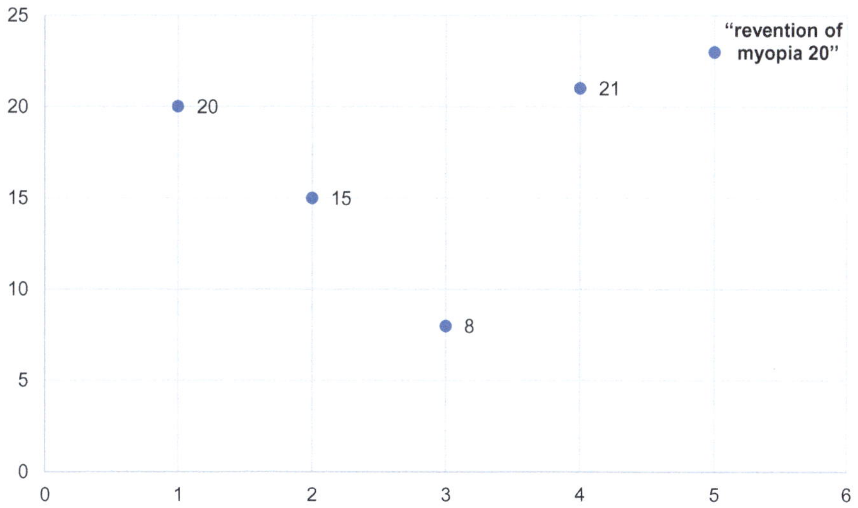

Fig. 5 Numbers of investigation objects that have released information about various kinds of daily life health knowledge

in addition to setting up a special platform on the prevention and control of the Covid-19 pandemic, has also set up a separate popular science section on its portal website, which released a total of 163 pieces of popular science information about the Covid-19 pandemic from January 25 to October 19, 2020, but only one in 2021. It is the only provincial government that provides information about the scientific knowledge of the Covid-19 pandemic on its own portal website; the Jilin Provincial government published 500 pieces of popular science information about the Covid-19 pandemic on its portal website from February 11, 2020 to January 25, 2021; the Health Commission of Tianjin Municipality released 322 pieces of popular science information about the Covid-19 pandemic in the special column on the prevention and control of the Covid-19 pandemic on its portal website from January 25, 2020 to November 24, 2020, but has not updated the content of the column since 2021; the Liaoning Provincial Government released 190 pieces of popular science information about the Covid-19 pandemic in a special column on its portal website from January 26 to April 26, 2020, but has not updated the content of the column since 2021, and the Liaoning Provincial Health Commission released a total of 310 pieces of popular science information on the Covid-19 pandemic platform from January 24, 2020 to January 27, 2021; the Fujian Provincial Health Commission released 247 pieces of popular science information on the Covid-19 pandemic prevention and control platform from January 20, 2020 to April 27, 2020 and 24 pieces of information about the Covid-19 pandemic-related laws and regulations since February 15, 2020, and the Fujian Provincial Government released 33 pieces of popular science information in a special column on the Covid-19 pandemic prevention and control on its portal website from January 23, 2020 to January 18, 2021, but only released two pieces of information in the column in 2021. In clear contrast, the Government of Heilongjiang

Province released a total of 355 pieces of popular science information on the Covid-19 pandemic prevention and control on its portal website from April 10, 2020 to April 30, 2021 and the Health Commission of Heilongjiang Province released 31 pieces of popular science information on its website from January 23, 2020 to January 29, 2021, but not all of them were about the Covid-19 pandemic situation. In addition, the Covid-19 pandemic prevention and control column of the website of the health commission contains 52 pages and 780 pieces of information, but only a small part is about the Covid-19 pandemic. The Beijing Municipal Health Commission has set up a special column "Overview of the Covid-19 Situation in Beijing" on the home page of its website, which is artistically designed and presents the relevant information in the form of charts, etc. The column consists of such sub-columns as "the latest information" "press conferences" "Beijing Health Kit" "related services", and "guide to Covid-19 prevention and control". It also has an English version.

In addition to the differences in quantity of information, there are also differences in the timeliness of information updating among various investigation objects. Taking the information about the latest points for attention on the vaccination against the Covid-19 virus as an example, the information was updated by the Government of Fujian Province on December 26, 2020, by the Government of Shaanxi Province on January 7, 2021, by the Government of Shanghai Municipality on January 19 and by the Government of Tianjin Municipality on March 21, 2021. In addition, the governments of Shanghai Municipality, Jilin Province, Tianjin Municipality and Liaoning Province have released no popular science information about the epidemiological investigation of the Covid-19 pandemic or centralized quarantine, and only a few pieces of obscure information about home quarantine and related health knowledge. With regard to the popular science information about foreign mutated viruses, only the Government of Jilin Province pushed an article entitled "What Should We Do When Mutated Viruses Come" on its WeChat platform in January. No relevant information has been released by other investigation objects.

The release of government information and popular science information is also a process of racing against rumors. Many local governments have released rumor-refuting information to timely clarify rumors and respond to social concerns. However, our investigation reveals that local governments generally have released some, but not much, rumor-refuting information. For example, the Government of Shanghai Municipality released a total of six pieces of rumor-refuting information in the news column of its portal website. The Government of Fujian Province released some pieces of rumor-refuting information, which are mixed with popular science information. There is one piece of rumor-refuting information on the portal website of the Government of Guangdong Province, which was released in January 2020. No rumor-refuting information is found on the portal websites of the Government of Shaanxi Province, the health commissions Tianjin Municipality, Liaoning Province and Guangdong Province, and the Government of Heilongjiang Province.

4 Analysis of the Causes of Problems

Generally speaking, the current situation of disclosure of health knowledge information by government organs is not satisfactory, which may be caused by the following factors.

1. Insufficient attention paid to the disclosure of popular science information

As China enters a new era, the Party and the government attach unprecedented importance to the disclosure of government information and take information disclosure as an important way to ensure the realization of democratic election, democratic decision-making, democratic administration and democratic supervision. However, the release of popular science information has not been paid enough attention to by government departments, which so far have taken the openness of administrative affairs as the focus of the open government work. The relevant government departments often focus on the popularization of the knowledge of prevention and control of an infectious disease only after the outbreak of an epidemic, which leads to a certain lag in the work of health science popularization.

2. The lack of unified standards and requirements of the disclosure of popular science information

There are no uniform standards and requirements of the disclosure of popular science knowledge. The staff responsible for website construction and information disclosure does not have a thorough understanding of the requirements of popular science work. There is no uniform standard, norm, or authoritative guidance regarding which popular science information needs to be disclosed and to what extent it is to be disclosed, which inhibits the development of popular science information disclosure work.

3. Inadequate construction of the professional team on the disclosure of popular science information

For a long period of time, government departments at all levels have generally faced such difficulties as the lack of specialized personnel and the low professionalism of such personnel in the work of openness of government affairs. The same problem also exists in popular science information disclosure work. Moreover, government departments at various levels often have no specialized institutions or full-time staff responsible for and targeted training on the disclosure of popular science information. They also lack the capacity for popular science information disclosure on online platforms as well as an accurate understanding of the key points of popular science work.

4. Unclear division of responsibilities for the popularization of science among different government departments

According to the relevant provisions of the Law on Popularization of Science and Technology, state organs, the military, societal organizations, corporate enterprises, public institutions, rural grassroots organizations and other associations shall carry out the work of promulgation of science and technology, and the National Health and Family Planning Commission (now the National Health Commission) is mainly responsible for the popularization of health science knowledge. To promote the popularization of health science, the former General Office of the National Health and Family Planning Commission issued a notice of issuing the Guidelines for the Generation and Dissemination of Health Science Popularization Information (for Trial Implementation) in 2015. The document contains the definition of health science popularization information, the principles and processes of generation of health science popularization information, and the principles and requirements of the dissemination of health science popularization information. However, it does not make a clear division of science popularization functions between higher and lower departments in the system. As a result, it is not clear whether the ministries and commissions under the State Council are responsible for defining the scope and content of health science popularization and their subordinate departments are only responsible for forwarding and conveying science popularization information, or both superior and subordinate departments have the obligation to generate and disseminate science popularization information. Meanwhile, there is no clear and specific standard for the evaluation of the effectiveness of science popularization work nor an incentive mechanism for science popularization workers. Under the condition of having only power but no responsibility, local government departments lack motivation and initiative in the science popularization work.

5 Prospect

Currently, there is still much room for improvement in the popular science information disclosure work of health commissions. The followings are some suggestions for further improvement of the work.

1. Enhancing the consciousness of popular science information disclosure

To do a good job in health science popularization, relevant departments must attach more importance to the work, take it as an important part of the openness of government affairs, and enhance their consciousness of popular science information disclosure. At the same time, they should strengthen the training of relevant staff on the basic understanding and the importance of the work, and improve the effectiveness of the training through the adjustment of its content, time, cycle, and method.

2. Clarify the standards and scope of popular science information disclosure

Government departments should formulate standards for the disclosure of popular science information. For example, standards should be adopted to clarify what kind of popular science information belongs to the scope of government information disclosure and what sub-columns should be set up under the popular science column on government websites and to ensure that common or important popular science information is disclosed and that the forms of popular science information disclosure are as diversified as possible. On this basis, they can further determine the requirements of popular science information disclosure and clarify the concrete work of the staff responsible for popular science information disclosure.

3. Strengthening the construction of popular science information disclosure platforms

Government websites are the primary platforms of government affairs disclosure. Therefore, popular science information disclosure should still take government websites as the main platforms. Government departments with relevant functions should set up special popular science columns on their portal websites, release and update popular science information in a timely manner, and enhance the pertinence, accuracy and interestingness of the information released. At the same time, they should give full play to the role of government We Media in the new era, and use various micro-platforms and We Media platforms operated by government agencies to disseminate authoritative popular science information released by government agencies, so as to increase public awareness.

4. Making good use of social media platforms to mobilize the whole society to participate in an orderly way

On the basis of ensuring the correctness of popular science information, efforts should be made to intensify and expand the scope of publicity to achieve the maximum result of popular science information disclosure, strengthen the regulation of various new media, and prevent clout-chasing and attention-grabbing health bloggers from wantonly distorting or over-interpreting information and turning correct popular science information into distorted "truth". In the investigation, only one new media channel, i.e. official WeChat account, was selected for the evaluation of popular science information disclosure work. In fact, WeChat, Weibo, Douyin, etc. have become important ways for Chinese netizens to express themselves and obtain information. Making good use of new media platforms is conducive to broadening the public's access to popular science information, realizing the sharing of health knowledge, and giving full play to the role of popular science knowledge.

5. Ensuring the timeliness and authority of the disclosure of popular science information

After the outbreak of the Covid-19 pandemic, the Chinese government, by rapidly popularizing relevant medical and health knowledge, has fully demonstrated its super-strong initiative, pressure resistance and ability to respond to emergencies. However, the ability acquired in times of crisis should not be abandoned after the crisis is alleviated. The relevant government departments should raise the efficiency of the operation of government portal websites and other information-releasing platforms, specify the updating frequency of popular science information, and dispose of outdated popular science information in a timely manner, so as to ensure that popular science information they released is timely and scientific. At the same time, they should establish a popular science information release mechanism, standardize the popularization of everyday science knowledge, improve the capacity for the popularization of scientific knowledge of coping with health emergencies, and ensure the timely, accurate and authoritative disclosure of popular science information.

SPRINGER NATURE

GPSR Compliance

The European Union's (EU) General Product Safety Regulation (GPSR) is a set of rules that requires consumer products to be safe and our obligations to ensure this.

If you have any concerns about our products, you can contact us on ProductSafety@springernature.com

In case Publisher is established outside the EU, the EU authorized representative is:

Springer Nature Customer Service Center GmbH
Europaplatz 3
69115 Heidelberg, Germany

The manufacturer's authorised representative in the EU is Springer Nature Customer Service Centre GmbH, Europaplatz 3, 69115 Heidelberg, Germany. If you have any concerns regarding our products, please contact ProductSafety@springernature.com

Printed and bound by CPI Group (UK) Ltd, Croydon, CR0 4YY
01/10/2026
02225896-0004